Collectio CCCC capitulorum

MONUMENTA IURIS CANONICI

CURAVIT

INSTITUTUM IURI CANONICO
MEDII AEVI PERQUIRENDO

SERIES B: CORPUS COLLECTIONUM
VOL. 11

MONUMENTA IURIS CANONICI
SERIES B: CORPUS COLLECTIONUM

VOL. 11

COLLECTIO CCCC CAPITULORUM

THE COLLECTION IN 400 CHAPTERS:
INTRODUCTION AND TEXT

Edited by
Sven Meeder

The Catholic University of America Press
Washington, D.C.

Copyright © 2025

The Catholic University of America Press

All rights reserved

The paper used in this publication meets the minimum
requirements of American National Standards for
Information Science—Permanence of Paper
for Printed Library materials, ANSI Z39.48-1992.

ISBN 978-0-8132-3847-0 (hardcover)
ISBN 978-0-8132-3848-7 (ebook)

∞

Cataloging-in-Publication Data is available from the Library of Congress

CONTENTS

Foreword vii

Preface ix

Abbreviations xi

Introduction xiii

    Manuscripts xvi

        Munich Clm 4592 (M) xvi

        Vienna 522 (I) xviii

        Paris BN MS lat. 2316 (L) xix

        Metz, BM MS 236 xxi

    The compiler's work xxii

    Sources xxvii

        Roman Law xxvii

        Synodus II S. Patricii xxix

        Collectio Sanblasiana xxxiii

        Statuta ecclesiae antiqua xxxvi

        Collectio canonum Hibernensis xxxviii

        Iudicia Theodori xxxix

    The Collectio CCCC in other texts xliii

        Poenitentiale Martenianum and the Paenitentiale

            ad Heribaldum xliii

        The Capitularies of Benedictus Levita l

    Text tradition, date, and provenance li

    Principles of this edition lvi

Collectio CCCC capitulorum

    Capitulatio 1

    Textus 15

v

vi Contents

Appendix 1: *Index titulorum*, Paris 2316, fols. 34v-35v 123

Primary sources 125

Secondary literature 129

Index fontium 135

FOREWORD

The title *Collectio CCCC capitulorum* ("*Collection in 400 Chapters*") may be both uninspiring and incorrect—the collection in fact contains 404 chapters—but with this fine edition Sven Meeder shows that this early medieval canonical work is both inspiring and interesting. Where its discoverer Friedrich Maassen only saw an uninteresting and poorly organized mixture of canons, Meeder now demonstrates that there is more to the collection than immediately meets the eye. It does, in fact, employ a thematic organization, in some sections innovating by juxtaposing passages from the Old and the New Testaments of the Bible. The collection is an early attempt at a systematic collection and is already, for this reason, worthy of our attention. It does not seem to have circulated very widely and is not today among the best known products of early medieval canon law. We are very happy to include it in the *Monumenta iuris canonici* as our earliest text so far, and we hope that it may inspire interest.

When this edition comes out, it will be the first one in the *Monumenta* series published by our new publisher, The Catholic University of America Press. The Institute is very grateful to the Director of the Press, Trevor Lipscombe, for enthusiastically accepting the *Monumenta* into its program, which already contains so much of interest for historians of canon law.

The Institute also wishes warmly to thank our director of many years, Joe Goering, who took on the heavy burden of reviewing the edition. But our greatest thanks go to the editor Sven Meeder for offering us this excellent edition and giving us a chance to get to know an interesting compiler. He has shown great patience with the many delays of the publication process.

Anders Winroth
President, Institute of Medieval Canon Law

PREFACE

The *Collectio CCCC capitulorum* first crossed my path as I conducted research for my doctoral dissertation on the spread and reception of Irish scholarship in centers across early medieval continental Europe, supervised by Prof. Rosamond McKitterick. I am immensely grateful for her guidance, wisdom, and inspiration as well as her encouragements for me to follow the various academic detours that presented themselves. This canonical collection has been a pleasantly distracting tangent to many research projects since. Much of the research time devoted to this work has been made possible by the generosity of the master and fellows of Trinity College Cambridge, the HERA project "Cultural Memory and Resources of the Past," the Dutch Research Council (NWO), and most recently the Gerda Henkel Stiftung.

I benefitted greatly from conversations with scholars and friends about either this collection in particular or canon law and medieval history in general. Special thanks go out to fellow students of medieval canon law Dr. Michael Elliot, Dr. Rob Meens, Dr. Christof Rolker, Dr. Danica Summerlin, and, in particular, Dr. Roy Flechner. For their time and erudition over coffee or other beverages, I am grateful to Dr. Shari Boodts, Prof. Maaike van Berkel, Dr. Maximilian Diesenberger, Prof. Stefan Esders, Dr. Robert Flierman, Dr. Lien Foubert, Dr. Clemens Gantner, Helena Geitz, Dr. Erik Goosmann, Prof. Olivier Hekster, Prof. Mayke de Jong, Dr. Sören Kaschke, Dr. Dominik Leyendecker, Dr. Britta Mischke, Prof. Walther Pohl, Dr. Richard Pollard, Clemens Radl, Dr. Carine van Rhijn, Dr. Gerda Rummel-Heydemann, Dr. Dominik Trump, Prof. Karl Ubl, Dr. Giorgia Vocino, Prof. Teresa Webber, and Prof. Ian Wood. I am grateful to the late Prof. Peter Landau who encouraged the publication of this collection early on, and to Prof. Joseph Ward Goering, who with Professor Landau proofread earlier versions of the edition with a meticulous eye for detail. Needless to say, should any errors stubbornly remain, I am solely responsible. I thank Prof. Anders

x   Collectio CCCC capitulorum

Winroth of the Stephan Kuttner Institute for seeing the edition through the lengthy publishing process with patience and confidence, and to Dr. Trevor Lipscombe for speeding up its last phase.

The book is dedicated to all who live by the lesson that the canonist regarded second to only one (chapter 2): to love one's neighbor.

ABBREVIATIONS

AASS		*Acta Sanctorum* (Antwerp, Venice, Paris, 1643–1940; repr. Turnhout, 1966–1971)
BM		Bibliothèque municipale
BnF		Bibliothèque nationale de France
CCSL		Corpus Christianorum, Series Latina
CSEL		Corpus Scriptorum Ecclesiasticorum Latinorum
EOMIA		C. H. Turner, *Ecclesiae Occidentalis Monumenta Iuris Antiquissima* (Oxford, 1899-1939)
J³		P. Jaffé, *Regesta pontificum Romanorum ab condita ecclesia ad annum post Christum natum MCXCVIII. Editio tertia*, revized by M. Schütz et al., 3rd ed. (Göttingen, 2016–2017)
MGH		Monumenta Germaniae Historica (Berlin, Hannover, Leipzig, Munich)
	Epp.	Epistolae (in Quart)
	Epp. sel.	Epistolae selectae
	LL	Leges (in Folio)
PL		J. P. Migne (pr.), *Patrologia cursus completus: series latina* (Paris, 1844–64)

INTRODUCTION

When Friedrich Maassen first described in detail the canonical collection now known as the *Collectio CCCC capitulorum*, he remarked that the text jumped abruptly from one subject to the other and that the arrangement was devoid of structure ("ohne Plan").[1] This sentiment was repeated by Hubert Mordek, who "with the best will in the world" could find no system in this collection either.[2] It is perhaps because of this apparent lack of system or other significant qualities that the collection currently carries the uninspiring title "Collection in 400 chapters," which Maassen introduced after counting four hundred chapters (although he noted some variation in the numbering of the chapters and in the list of rubrics).[3] Despite its flaws, however, there is evidence that the collection gained some popularity in the ninth century, apparently providing the basis for the *Poenitentiale Martenianum*, directly or indirectly influencing Hrabanus Maurus's *Paenitentiale ad Heribaldum*, and supplying material for the work of Benedictus Levita. The ninth-century appreciation is understandable, for, as one of the many products of the vigorous

---

1 Friedrich Maassen, *Geschichte der Quellen und der Literatur des canonischen Rechts im Abendlande bis zum Ausgang des Mittelalters* (Graz, 1870), 844 ("Es wird von einer Materie ohne innere Begründung plötzlich zu einer andern übergesprungen").

2 Hubert Mordek, *Kirchenrecht und Reform im Frankenreich: Die Collectio Vetus Gallica, die älteste systematische Kanonessammlung des fränkischen Gallien*, Beiträge zur Geschichte und Quellenkunde des Mittelalters (Berlin/New York, 1975), 163. For the same assesment, see also Paul Fournier and Gabriel Le Bras, *Histoire des collections canoniques en occident dépuis les Fausses Décrétales jusqu'au Décret de Gratien* (Paris, 1931; repr. Aalen, 1972), 90; and Raoul Naz, "Quatre cents chapitres (Collection en)," in Raoul Naz and Antoine Villien (eds.), *Dictionnaire de droit canonique, contenant tous les termes du droit canonique, avec un sommaire de l'histoire et des institutions et de l'état actuel de la discipline*, 7 vols. (Paris, 1935–65), VII: col. 425.

3 Maassen, *Geschichte der Quellen*, 844 ("Ich habe 400 Capitel gezählt und die Sammlung danach benannt"). As per usual, the manuscript witnesses do not preserve a title for the work: Vienna, Österreichische Nationalbibliothek MS lat. 522 (I) simply refers to "kanones."

xiv Collectio CCCC capitulorum

canonical activity of the eighth and ninth centuries, the *Collectio CCCC capitulorum* impresses in its handling of the canonical material as well as the breadth of sources and the topics covered.

The *Collectio CCCC capitulorum* (hereafter *Collectio CCCC*) is a systematically arranged collection of canons organized according to themes. It thereby differs from chronologically arranged collections, such as the *Collectio Dionysiana* and the *Collectio Hispana*, which present the canons of councils and synods in their original order and context and usually in their entirety. The 404 chapters in the *Collectio CCCC*, by contrast, each sport a descriptive heading and are made up of one or several statements taken from a variety of authoritative sources. These authoritative statements, the "canons," are not seldom altered or trimmed to serve the compiler's purpose. The systematic organisation of the collection testifies to the innovative notion that authoritative works, such as papal decretals and synodal acts, did not have to be transmitted intact but could be mined for individual rules and passages and that such canons retain their authority even outside of their original context. As rulings with universal significance, they could thus be brought to bear on contemporary concerns.

Although the systematic juxtapositioning of extracts from different authoritative texts constituted an important innovation in seventh- and eighth-century legal thought, the general principle was not alien to other genres. Medieval textual culture is full of examples of works featuring interwoven passages from authoritative texts that are refashioned into generalized rules and applied to wholly alien topics. The most obvious manifestation is the chronic use of Bible citations by medieval authors of any genre to bolster the points they try to make. In fact, Christian exegesis is mainly built on this mechanism exactly: extracts of learning taken from various (textual) authorities, including of course the Bible, engage with each other in order to elucidate the wisdom of God. There is reason to believe that the canonical innovators of the seventh and eighth centuries took their cues from the exegetical genre.[4]

---

4 On the relation between systematic canonical collections and exegesis, see Roy Flechner, "The Problem of Originality in Early Medieval Canon Law: Legislating by Means of Contradictions in the Collectio Hibernensis," *Viator* 43:2 (2012), 29–47.

Introduction

xv

Systematic collections, furthermore, allow the use of a much larger corpus of authoritative texts. In addition to the conventional canonical works, such as synodal decrees and papal decretals, systematic collections feature a host of hitherto unutilized sources, in particular the (exegetical) texts of Church Fathers and the Bible itself. In fact, it is worth asking the question whether the invention of systematic collections inspired canonical scholars to use different authoritative sources or vice versa—whether the desire to include other Christian texts provided the impetus for this legal innovation. Either way, the introduction of these novel canons meant that collections could now offer canonical guidance on topics and themes that were only sparsely touched on by the traditional canonical authorities, in particular issues of morality. Furthermore, the juxtaposition of canons on a similar subject under one thematic heading could demonstrate the unity of Christian law or, conversely, facilitate debates between different authorities and conversations about the subtle differences in the rules. By including passages from a greater variety of genres to participate in this conversation the concept of a single (if not wholly known) divine order in religious law and thought was reinforced.

The *Collectio CCCC* is an instructive, if unpolished, exponent of this important development in Western legal thought. Although some crude systematic collections existed before the seventh century— notably the fifth-century *Statuta Ecclesiae Antiqua* and the (now lost) precursor to the *Collectio Vetus Gallica*—the genre was given decisive impetus by canonical scholars from the British Isles in the late seventh and early eighth centuries. The most influential results were the collection of canonical and penitential prescriptions inspired by Archbishop Theodore of Canterbury (ob. 690) compiled by the *Discipulus Umbriensium* and, especially, the elaborate Irish collection known as the *Collectio canonum Hibernensis*, probably compiled in the first quarter of the eighth century.[5] The *Collectio CCCC* owes much to these insular innovations. It contains a large number of Theodorian

---

5 On both the Theodorian canons and the *Hibernensis*, and the underlying insular tradition, see Roy Flechner, "An Insular Tradition of Ecclesiastical Law: Fifth to Eighth Century,", in James Graham-Campbell and Michael Ryan (eds.), *Anglo-Saxon/ Irish Relations before the Vikings*, Proceedings of the British Academy 157 (Oxford, 2009), 23–46.

xvi   Collectio CCCC capitulorum

canons and draws on some of the same sources as the *Hibernensis*. That is to say, in addition to the more traditional sources, such as the acts from ecumenical councils and synods and papal letters, the *Collectio CCCC* includes rules taken from Gallic synods, Irish and Anglo-Saxon penitentials, patristic theological treatises, Roman secular law, and, importantly, the Bible. The latter source appears to have inspired the guiding principle of the first quarter of the *Collectio CCCC*.

The collection has unjustly been neglected by modern scholars. The collection's bold selection of canons provides an important witness to the creativity and open-mindedness of canonists (and copyists) in the heady days of the eighth and ninth centuries. The obscurity of the plan behind the canons' arrangement, furthermore, may in future research prove to represent an intermediate stage of the process of composing a systematic collection, thereby shedding light on the scholarly practice of an ambitious eighth-century canonist (or canonists). The *Collectio CCCC* is also a valuable product of the connections between continental and insular learning and between different canonical texts. In addition, despite its survival in just three manuscripts, there are indications that its influence in the ninth century was significant and that the *Collectio CCCC* provided important material for younger collections, including the *Poenitentiale Martenianum* and the *capitularia* of Benedictus Levita.

MANUSCRIPTS

Munich, Bayerische Staatsbibliothek, Clm 4592 (M)

Folios and size: Three units; I (fols. 1–75); II (fols. 76–117); III (fols. 120–207 = 87 fols., 235 x 16 mm (190 x 115 mm), 24 ll. (list of rubrics in two columns)
Date: I: *saec.* xii; II: *saec.* xiii$^{1/2}$; III: *saec.* ix$^{2/4}$
Origin: III: Southeast Germany[6]
Provenance: Benediktbeuern

---

6 Mordek, *Kirchenrecht und Reform*, 162, n. 304; see Bernhard Bischoff, *Die südostdeutschen Schreibschulen und Bibliotheken in der Karolingerzeit*, 2 vols. (Wiesbaden, 1974–80), I, 46.

Introduction   xvii

Contents: part III:

- 120r–157v *Collectio 250 capitulorum*[7] (preceded by an *index titulorum*)
- 157v–r Bede, *De temporum ratione* § 66 (on the first six ecumenical councils); *inc.* "Prima enim uniuersalis synodus in Nicea congregata est contra Arrium"; *expl.* "Sexta item Constantinopoli temporibus papae Agathonis sub Constantino principe filii Constantini."[8]
- 158r–207v *Collectio CCCC capitulorum* (preceded by an *index titulorum*); incomplete; *expl.* "cum disceptarent aduersum me" (c. 404).

Description: Munich, Clm 4592 is a composite manuscript comprising three codicological units. The ninth-century unit (III) contains the canon law collection known as the *Collectio 250 capitulorum*, a short excerpt from Bede's *De temporum ratione*, and the *Collectio CCCC*. This part of the manuscript was written by two scribes writing a Caroline minuscule with frequent occurrence of *cc*-shaped *a*, as well as high *r*-ligatures and *ct*-ligatures. Rubrics are entered in flourished half-uncials (consistently using *cc*-shaped *a*), in black and two shades of red, a practice that points to an origin in Salzburg or its vicinity according to Bernhard Bischoff.[9] Palaeographical evidence suggests a date for the manuscript in the second quarter of the ninth century.[10] Unit III is missing certain folios through loss.

Literature: Günter Glauche, *Katalog der lateinischen Handschriften der Bayerischen Staatsbibliothek München: Die Pergamenthandschriften aus Benediktbeuern: Clm 4501–4663* (Wiesbaden, 1994), 146–49; Bernhard Bischoff, *Die südostdeutschen Schreibschulen und Bibliotheken in der Karolingerzeit*, 2 vols. (Wiesbaden, 1974–80), I, 46, and II, 159–60;

---

7 The *Collectio 250 capitulorum* is a derivative text of the *Collectio canonum Hibernensis*; see August J. Nürnberger, "Über die Würzburger Handschrift der irischen Canonensammlung," *Archiv für Katholisches Kirchenrecht* 60 (1888), 1–84, at 71–74.

8 Beda Venerabilis, *De temporum ratione*, § 66, ed. C. W. Jones, *Bedae Venerabilis Opera, Pars II, Opera Didascalica*, CCSL 123B (Turnhout, 1977), 263–544, at 528; CPL 2320. See also Vatican, MS Reg. lat. 421, fol. 24v (*saec.* ix[med]), and Munich, Bayerische Staatsbibliothek, Clm 19413, fol. 120v.

9 Bischoff, *Schreibschulen*, I, 46.

10 Bernhard Bischoff, *Katalog der festländischen Handschriften des neunten Jahrhunderts (mit Ausnahme der wisigotischen)*, 3 vols. (Wiesbaden, 1998–2014), II, 229 (no. 2976).

xviii   Collectio CCCC capitulorum

Hubert Mordek, *Kirchenrecht und Reform*, 162–64; Roger Reynolds, "Unity and Diversity in Carolingian Canon Law Collections: The Case of the Collectio Hibernensis and Its Derivatives" in U.-R. Blumenthal (ed.), *Carolingian Essays: Andrew W. Mellon Lectures in Early Christian Studies* (Washington, DC, 1983), 99–135, at 110–11.

Vienna, Österreichische nationalbibliothek, MS lat. 522 (I)

Folios and size: 205 fols, 235 x 160 mm, 20–23 ll.
Date: *saec.* ix²ᐟ³
Origin: Salzburg[11]
Provenance: Salzburg
Contents:

- 1v–2v Teachings on the Gospel, *inc.* "Incipiunt nomina euangelii"[12]
- 2v–3r *Versus de conditore templi cuiusdam*, inc. "Culmina ampla uides"[13]
- 3r–29r Beda Venerabilis, *De natura rerum*[14]
- 29r–57r *Concordia quorumdam testimoniorum Sancti Gregorii*[15]
- 57r–113r *Collectio 250 capitulorum* (preceded by an *index titulorum*)
- 113v–192v *Collectio CCCC capitulorum* (preceded by an *index titulorum*)
- 192v–205r Bede, *De temporum ratione*, §§ 67–71[16]

---

11 Mordek, *Kirchenrecht und Reform*, 162.

12 Bernhard Bischoff, "An Hiberno-Latin introduction to the Gospels," *Thought: A Review of Culture and Idea* 54 (1979), 233–37; Michael Lapidge and Richard Sharpe, *A Bibliography of Celtic-Latin Literature 400–1200* (Dublin, 1985), C765 ("s. 8 p.c.")

13 Ed. E. Dümmler, MGH Poet. 2 (Berlin, 1884), 647 (*Carm.* 14).

14 Beda Venerabilis, *De natura rerum*, ed. C. W. Jones, *Bedae Venerabilis Opera, Pars I, Opera Didascalica* CCSL 123A (Turnhout, 1975), 189–234; CPL 1343.

15 Irénée Fransen, "Trente-Quatre Questions Sur Saint-Paul Passés Sous le Nom de Saint Grégoire," *Revue bénédictine* 73 (1963), 244–76; *PL* 97, cols. 659–78. See Roger Reynolds, "Unity and Diversity in Carolingian Canon Law Collections: The Case of the Collectio Hibernensis and Its Derivatives," in: U.-R. Blumenthal (ed.), *Carolingian Essays: Andrew W. Mellon Lectures in Early Christian Studies* (Washington, DC, 1983), 99–135, 106.

16 Beda Venerabilis, *De temporum ratione*, §§ 67–71 (535–44).

Introduction   xix

Description: Vienna 522 was written by several scribes writing a tidy, upright or slightly rightward-leaning Caroline minuscule. There are some occasional occurrences of the *cc*-shaped form of *a*. The rubrics are in red uncials, rustic capitals or mixed capitals, and initials are in black, red, or blue, sometimes with red, blue, yellow, or green backgrounds. There are some instances of Greek words in the canon law sections, which, according to Bischoff, might be traced back to an Irish manuscript.[17] On two occasions the scribe attempted to copy the insular symbol for *autem* (folios 188r and 189r); the shape of the abbreviations betrays an unfamiliarity with the symbol. The manuscript is thought to have been written at Salzburg and the script has been dated to the middle of the ninth century, during the archepiscopacy of Liuphram (836–859).[18]

Literature: *Tabulae codicum manu scriptorum praeter graecos et orientales in Bibliotheca Palatina Vindobonensi asservatorum* (Vienna, 1864–1899), I, 88–89; O. Mazal, "Die Salzburger Dom- und Klosterbibliothek in karolingischer Zeit," *Codices Manuscripti 3* (1977), 44–61; W. Hartmann, *Kirche und Kirchenrecht um 900. Die Bedeutung der spätkarolingischen Zeit für Tradition und Innovation im kirchlichen Recht*, MGH Schriften 58 (Hannover, 2008), 330.

Paris, Bibliothèque nationale de France, MS lat. 2316 (L)

Folios and size: Two units; I (fols. 1–25); II (fols. 26–133), 107 fols., 245–57 x 175–80 mm (200–201 x 130–45 mm), 24–26 ll.

Date: I: *saec.* xii; II: *saec.* ix$^{2/4}$

Origin: II: France ("mehr südlich"[19])

Provenance: St-Martial, Limoges (*saec.* xiv)

---

17 Bischoff, *Schreibschulen*, II, 159–60.

18 Bischoff, *Schreibschulen*, I, 46; and Bischoff, *Schreibschulen*, II, 159–60; Bischoff, *Katalog*, II, 229 (no. 2976); Günter Glauche, *Katalog der lateinischen Handschriften der Bayerischen Staatsbibliothek München: Die Pergamenthandschriften aus Benediktbeuern: Clm 4501–4663* (Wiesbaden, 1994), 146–51; and Roger E. Reynolds, "Canon Law Collections in Early Ninth-Century Salzburg," in: S. G. Kuttner and K. Pennington (eds.), *Proceedings of the Fifth International Congress of Medieval Canon Law, Salamanca 21–25 September 1976* (Vatican City, 1980), 15–34, at 32.

19 Mordek, *Kirchenrecht und Reform*, 283.

xx   Collectio CCCC capitulorum

Contents: part II:

- 26r–35v *index titulorum*
- 36r–83v *Collectio Dionysiana* (fragmentary)
- 84r *Collectio Vetus Gallica* XXXIII.5–6, XXIV.4[20]
- 84r–118v *Collectio CCCC Capitulorum*
- 118v–120r Pope John II, *Epistula* III[21]
- 120r–121v *Breuiarium apostolorum*[22]
- 121v–122v Council of Aachen (801), c. 3, 8, 4, 6, 7, 5, 1, 2, 9–16, 18–22[23]
- 122v–133 Theodulf of Orléans, *Capitula ad presbyteros parochiae suae* (797)[24] (fol. 133 damaged)

Description: Paris 2316 is a composite manuscript of two codicological units. The first folio of the ninth-century unit (unit II) is of a very worn, dark parchment, indicating heavy use. This part of the manuscript was copied by several scribes, all writing an upright, somewhat square early Caroline minuscule (with occasional slightly rightward or leftward slanting) with clubbed ascenders on *d, l, b* and interchanging Caroline *a*, (open) *cc*-shaped *a*, and occasional *ic*-shaped *a*. The script often features a short *s*, occasionally a round *s*, and a curly cross-bar on *t*.

The *index titulorum* on folios 26r–35v gives a selection of headings from the *Collectio Dionysiana*, the *Collectio Vetus Gallica* (some of it lost due to a lacuna) and a selection of headings of the *Collectio CCCC* (see appendix). The manuscript is missing some leaves through loss, though not in the quires containing the text of the *Collectio CCCC*. The *Collectio CCCC* was copied by one scribe, whose hand includes the same contraction sign for *-us* and *-ur* (a hook over the last minim), some instances of round *d*'s, some *i-longa*'s; numerous ligatures, including *ra*-ligature. There are some instances of homeoteleuton (line skip),

---

20 The text comprises canon 31 of the third synod of Orléans (538) and canons 26 and 27 of the first synod of Orléans (511); see Mordek, *Kirchenrecht und Reform*, 283–85.

21 Iohannes II papa, *Epistulae iii*, ed. C. de Clercq, CCSL 148A (Turnhout, 1963), p. 89–94 (different form).

22 *Breuiarium apostolorum*, ed. H. Quentin and H. Delehaye, *AASS*, Nov., II, 2 (Bruxelles, 1931), 3–4.

23 Ed. A. Boretius, MGH Capit. I (Hannover, 1883), 105–7.

24 Ed. P. Brommer, MGH Capit. episc. I (Hannover, 1984), 103–41.

Introduction

xxi

which is consistent with the general impression that the scribe copied the text without reading along critically. He or she appears to have had a rather dubious feeling for grammar, resulting in a multitude of grammatically unsound sentences and varying spellings for the same word. This may have been caused or compounded by the careless reading of an exemplar in a somewhat cramped script. There is no evidence that the scribe identified the beginnings and endings of individual sentences or even individual canons.[25] There are some examples of the insular symbol for *autem* on folios 102v and 115r. In two other occasions, the symbol appears to have been entered by the scribe only to be erased at a later stage (folios 96r and 97r).

Literature: *Bibliothèque nationale: Catalogue général des manuscrits latins*, vol. 2 (Paris, 1940), 400–401; Mordek, *Kirchenrecht und Reform*, 283–85.

Metz, Bibliothèque municipale, MS lat. 236

Folios and size: Two units (I: 1–142 and II: 143–206); 142 + 63 = 206 ff
Date: I: *saec.* ix[ex]; II: *saec.* viii[ex]/ix[in]
Origin: I: French (possibly Tours or St-Denis); II: Rhine region[26]
Provenance: St-Arnulf, Metz, destroyed in 1944
Contents:

- 3r–121v *Collectio Dacheriana*
- 121v–142v '*Appendix Dacherianae Mettensis*'
- ?–? *Collectio CCCC capitulorum* (fragment due to loss)[27]
- ?–? Book XLV (*De matrimonio*) of the *Collectio canonum Hibernensis*

Literature: A. Masson, *Manuscrits des Bibliothèques sinistrées de 1940 à 1944*, Catalogue général des manuscrits des bibliothèques publiques de France 53 (Paris, 1962), 12. Emil Seckel, "Benedictus Levita decurtatus et excerptus: eine Studie zu den Handschriften der falschen Kapitularien," in: *Festschrift für Heinrich Brunner zum fünfzigjährigen Doktorjubiläum* (Munich/Leipzig, 1914), 377–464, at 410–13; Mordek, *Kirchenrecht und Reform*, 162–63, n. 304; 262.

---

25 See, for instance, ch. 54 on fol. 92v.
26 Mordek, *Kirchenrecht und Reform*, 262.
27 Fournier and Le Bras, *Histoire des collections canoniques*, 90, n. 1.

xxii   Collectio CCCC capitulorum

THE COMPILER'S WORK

The *Collectio CCCC* is made up of 404 thematic chapters with descriptive headings, which hold one or multiple canons taken from one or multiple sources. In two manuscripts (I and M) a comprehensive list of numbered rubrics precedes the collection. Manuscript M repeats these rubrics in the main text above every single chapter, whereas the text proper of manuscript I only occasionally has rubrics accompanying the chapter numbers. Manuscript L has an *index titulorum* at the opening of the manuscript, which lists chapter headings for the various following texts. For the *Collectio CCCC* it lists only a selection of chapter headings (with numbers) ending abruptly with chapter 294 (*de sanctaemoniale forni-caria*).[28] Rubrics are sprinkled, seemingly rather erratically, throughout the main text, sometimes (but not always) corresponding to the chapter titles in the *index titulorum*. For all the differences between I and L, the rubrics in these copies, when present, often correspond, sometimes against the reading of M. This selection of rubrics in I and L is also found in the sections of the *Collectio CCCC* reproduced in the *Poeniten-tiale Martenianum* (see below). The fact that the arrangement of rubrics is present in I, L, and the exemplar of the *Martenianum* suggests that this represents an earlier archetype and that the fuller arrangement of rubrics in M reflects a later-stage innovation, rather than the other way around (see below).

The text proper of the collection is preceded by two prefatory chapters under the headings "excerptio synodum" and "praefatiuncula," respectively, which appear to comment on the compiler's method.[29] In the "excerptio synodum," the author—and there is no reason to doubt that this is the same person as the compiler—in rather tortuous Latin draws attention to his acts of selection and arrangement, referring to himself as the person "excerpting," "sifting," and "polishing" ("excerpens," "cribrans," and "limans"). The tone of the opening of this passage is remarkably combative: the author appears to be expecting criticism from certain elements of his readership. The points of contention seem to be

---

28 MS L, fols. 34v–35v (see appendix).

29 In manuscript M the heading of the "excerptio synodum" reads "incipit excerptio," and in manuscript L "Haec sunt precepta quod Dominus precepit Moyse caput xxxviii" (on which, see below).

Introduction   xxiii

the editorial choices of the compiler described above. Ostensibly in order
to prove his fitness for the job, the author remarks that he is "standing
in a sacred place," which must probably be understood to mean that he
is a religious man.

The main line of defence employed here is the reference to the aim
of the collection: the following text will provide its readership with
understanding of the canonical authorities that the author subsequently
lists. Beginning with the "dominicam sermocinationem," these include
the canons of the holy apostles, the ecumenical councils and Gallic
synods, various popes, and Augustine of Hippo. The latter is possibly
meant as a representative for patristic writers in general, while the
"dominicam sermocinationem" could be referring to Sunday's conversation or sermon, or perhaps—judging from its position at the top of
the list of authorities—it is to be understood more figuratively as the
Bible. The list is not an exhaustive catalogue of the authorities from
which canons are taken for this collection—the *Collectio CCCC* contains
excerpts from other works not mentioned in this list, particularly the
(Theodorian) penitential material and the excerpts from Roman secular
law, but this does not seem to have been the point of this passage.
The author states that the aim of the collection is to elucidate the said
authorities; the list is not meant to record the sources he used. In order
to clarify the meaning of the Bible, for instance, he may take recourse
to additional sources. Thus, the many canons taken from the *Iudicia
Theodori*, in this view, do not so much add further rules to the judgments
of earlier authoritative works, they merely clarify (and reformulate)
legal principles already laid down in the extensive tradition of religious
law. Finally, the author of the "excerptio synodum" concedes that his
selection only covers a portion of this rich legal heritage: the sources
(*causae*) for this collection have been chosen according to their usefulness
and "our" need. And while the "polisher" at times may have been forced
to alter the precise wording of his sources, he maintains that "those
[rules *or* principles] which they have upheld, we uphold."[30]

---

30 "Quos susceperunt suscipimus secundum iussionem summi sacerdotis": *Collectio
CCCC, praefatio* I ("Excerptio synodum"). See also Sven Meeder, "Biblical Past and
Canonical Present: The Case of the *Collectio 400 Capitulorum*," in Clemens Gantner,
Rosamond McKitterick, and Sven Meeder (eds.), *The Resources of the Past in Early
Medieval Europe* (Cambridge, 2015), 103–17. On the translation of *causae* as "sources"

xxiv   Collectio CCCC capitulorum

The unity of canonical, or rather religious, law proves a central theme in the *Collectio CCCC* as is also evinced in the subsequent "praefatiuncula." This chapter consists of three statements: a verse from the Old Testament, a New Testament extract, and a paragraph apparently from the author's own pen. The first statement, drawing on Deuteronomy 6:6–8, alludes to Moses's instructions to remember and honour God's commandments—an apt opening of a collection of religious law. The second item considers the translation of the law of the old covenant to the new Christian context by quoting 2 Corinthinans 3:6: "that letter killeth, the spirit quickeneth." The first two canons of the "praefatiuncula" thereby reflect the arrangement of the first chapters that will follow, which juxtapose Old and New Testament verses where the latter elucidates the desired Christian reception of the former. The combination demonstrates the relevance of Old Testament rules for contemporary Christians, with the important observation that where the Old Testament promises death to transgressors, the New Testament, through penance, offers the continued possibility of eternal life. This is the central message of the third statement, which—in tortured Latin—presses the message home that biblical and later Christian law constitutes a unity, centred on the primary commandment: to love God.[31]

The "praefatiuncula" thus provides a strong biblical context for the whole collection, something that is maintained over roughly the first ninety chapters, which are dominated by biblical material. The first thirty-eight chapters are almost exclusively composed of verses from the Old Testament (first) and an explanatory or contextualising New Testament excerpt (following). The scribe of manuscript L recognized this when he entered the rubric, "Haec sunt precepta quod Dominus precepit Moyse capitula XXXVIII," "These are the rules the Lord gave to Moses: 38 chapters." The same scribe, in fact, briefly restarted the numbering following chapter 38, although he realized at chapter 40 that this was in reality the same canonical collection. The combination of precepts from both Testaments resembles the exegetical method of juxtaposing (sometimes ostensibly contradicting) passages from

---

in a canonical context, see Roy Flechner, *The Hibernensis*, Studies in Medieval and Early Modern Canon Law (Washington DC, 2019), I: 67*–68*.

31 Meeder, "Biblical Past and Canonical Present".

Introduction   xxv

authoritative works in order to inspire users to engage with the texts and distill a sovereign principle, which, again, confirms the unity of religious law.[32]

The practice of juxtaposing various statements on the same topic in single chapters, so energetically introduced and started at the beginning, is not maintained throughout the collection. In fact, most chapters in the *Collectio CCCC* consist of a single ruling, and only a minority of chapters hold numerous canons from different authoritative sources. Chapters with multiple canons are particularly prevalent in the first part of the text, while most of the later chapters consist of single canons. The 404 chapters in the collection are not further arranged into larger thematic units and it is often impossible to detect a relationship between subsequent chapters, or at least a connection governed by their respective subject matter. The arrangement of the *Collectio CCCC* thus lacks the sophistication of some other systematic collections such as the *Hibernensis* in which chapters are further arranged into thematic books. Instead, the sequence of topics covered by the *Collectio CCCC*'s chapters often seems random, and as a result the rationale behind the organization of the chapters has remained unclear to its modern commentators (see above).

To the modern eye, the collection can be roughly divided into three uneven parts: the first 86 chapters almost all include a verse taken from the Old Testament, with occasional parallels in the New Testament or other canonical texts; the second block, from about chapter 87 to 266, is comprized of material from the more traditional canonical sources and thus include a variety of conciliar canons, synodal rules, and passages from papal letters and the occasional patristic text; the chapters of the last block, from 266 to 400, are mostly statements from the penitential canons of Theodore of Canterbury (the last four chapters have a slightly different character). Later in the collection, the chapters usually appear in clusters of canons taken from the same source. At times, it seems that the compiler simply copied the statements from his exemplars in the sequence in which they appeared in his source. For example, chapters 115 to 124 feature canons taken from the *Statuta ecclesiae antiqua* in their original sequence. Similar batches are made up of material from

---

32 See Roy Flechner, "The Problem of Originality," 43–47; and Meeder, "Biblical Past and Canonical Present."

xxvi   Collectio CCCC capitulorum

the *Canones apostolorum*, the Irish *Synodus II S. Patricii*, the Theodorian penitential decrees, and papal decretals and conciliar canons drawn from the *Collectio Sanblasiana*. There are, however, some instances in which this is demonstrably not the case. The progressive lack of complexity in the collection may suggest that the later portions of the collection had not (yet) received the same level of redaction when the work was committed to parchment. Possibly, the *Collectio CCCC* as we now have it represents work-in-progress, in which the first quarter (or so) is closer to the finished stage than the later parts.

The selection and arrangement of the canons is an obvious instrument with which the compiler determined how the canonical rules were presented to his audience. The collection generally gives the names of the authorities from which it draws its canons, with the exception of most of the penitential material, which is often simply introduced as "in alio," "alii," or (interestingly) "in nouo" or "canones nouae." The compiler appears to have made a deliberate effort to present the rulings as universally applicable and to omit elements that could refer to the original (textual) context of the source material. Through the omission of words or phrases or the introduction of new words or phrases the tenor of a canon could be altered. In addition, the wording of the rubric also influenced the context in which a chapter was read. It would go too far to analyze every instance of the compiler's recontextualizing handiwork, but one example may elucidate the extent of his actions.

In chapter 129 ("De confessione uera criminis et mendatii," "Concerning the true confession of a crime and of a lie") we find a ruling made universal despite its close relationship to a specific historical context. It takes its ruling from the fourth canon of the synod of Valence (374), which proclaims that bishops, priests, or deacons who themselves admit that they are stained by a mortal crime should be degraded, since they either tell the truth and are guilty of the offense, or they are lying, which constitutes an offense in itself. While it is hard to imagine that clergymen confessing to crimes, truthfully or falsely, was a common, rampant problem in the early medieval church, the canon's relevance becomes clear in light of its historical (and synodal) context. The sole subject of the deliberations at Valence, in fact, was the matter of the ordination of a certain Acceptus of Fréjus who was surrounded by "scandalum" and who

Introduction   xxvii

tried to escape the episcopal dignity by confessing to imaginary crimes. At the synod the canon functioned in a very specific context, while in the chapter in the *Collectio CCCC* the rule is presented as applying to all deacons, priests, and bishops, including those already ordained and established. The synodal ruling alludes to the precise historical context, which was discussed in the preceding canons, with an explanatory phrase, "Nec illud, fratres, scribere alienum ab ecclesiae utilitate censuimus," "And we do not feel, brothers, that we are writing something outside the interest of the church." This sentence is omitted in the *Collectio CCCC*. It leaves the readers of this collection with a generalized rule on clerics falsely or truthfully confessing to crimes.

SOURCES

The *Collectio CCCC* owes much to the insular innovations of systematic canonical collections, not least with regard to the great variety of sources. In addition to the more customary canonical texts, such as the acts of the ecumenical councils and the decrees from papal letters, the compiler of this collection drew his canons from the Bible (the Vulgate),[33] Roman secular law texts, the *Canones Apostolorum*, Gallic synods, and patristic works as well as Frankish and Insular penitential texts. It is useful to study some of the sources in detail.

Roman Law

One of the more unusual features of the *Collectio CCCC* is the use of excerpts taken from Roman law. In particular, the citation from the *Epitome Gai* in chapter 40 has raised attention, since it is one of only two attestations of this work in a medieval scholarly work.[34] Both the *Epitome Gai* (or *Liber Gai*), an abbreviated version of Gaius's

---

33 But see the version of Wisdom 14:21–4 in *Collectio CCCC capitulorum*, c. 7b.

34 Max Conrat (Cohn), *Geschichte der Quellen und Literatur des römischen Rechts im frühen Mittelalter* (Aalen, 1891), 46. See also Jean Gaudemet, "Survivances romaines dans le droit de la monarchie francque du Ve au Xe siècle," *Tijdschrift voor Rechtsgeschiedenis* 23 (1955), 149–206, at 169–70; the other attestation is in Regino of Prüm, *De Synodalibus Causis et Disciplinis Ecclesiasticis*, I. 429, ed. F.G.A. Wasserschleben (Leipzig, 1840; repr. Graz, 1964), at 194 (= *Epitome Gai*, I.4: 8).

xxviii   Collectio CCCC capitulorum

Institutes in two books, and the *Breviarium Pauli* (or *Sententiae Pauli*) are part of the *Breviarium Alaricianum* (or *Lex Romana Visigothorum*), the collection of Roman law promulgated by the Visigothic king Alaric II in 506.[35] In addition to the texts cited in the *Collectio CCCC*, the *Breviarium Alaricianum* contains other works of Roman secular law including the whole of the *Codex Theodosianus*.[36] It enjoyed a wide circulation early, as evident from the over seventy medieval manuscript copies surviving. This voluminous collection was itself subject to abbreviation in various *Epitomae*. The citations in the *Collectio CCCC* do not seem to stem from relatives of any of the known derivatives and may have been drawn from a source related to the *Breviarium Alaricianum* proper.

The rubric introducing chapter 39, the first chapter with Roman legal material, sheds some light on the place of Roman law within the canonical legal tradition, at least in the compiler's mind. The contents of this chapter, on the seven degrees of consanguinity, is taken from *Sententiae Pauli* 4.10. It is introduced by the rubric, "Moses turpitudinem multiplicius consanguinitatis quam leges Theodosi et Romanorum," which translates roughly as "Moses [described] the disgrace of consanguinity in a more complex way than the laws of Theodosius and the Romans."[37] The phrase explicitly connects Roman law with (the law of) Moses and seems to offer an explanation as to why the compiler chose to cite Roman law on the topic of consanguinity rather than biblical law. Apparently, the Roman legal tract was considered less complicated for his readership but equally acceptable for inclusion within a collection of canon law.[38] In addition to his high esteem of Roman secular legal tradition, this rubric demonstrates the compiler's ambition to produce a functional work that was not more difficult to use than strictly necessary.

---

35 Edition by Max Conrat (Cohn), *Breviarium Alaricianum* (Leipzig, 1903).

36 Gian Gualberto Archi, *"L'Epitome Gai," Studio sul tardo diritto romano in occidente* (Milan, 1937; repr. Naples, 1991); and A. Arthur Schiller, *Roman Law: Mechanisms of Development* (The Hague/New York, 1978), 43–48.

37 *Collectio CCCC capitulorum*, c. 39 (I and L; M now lacks the leaves that would have had these chapters).

38 Meeder, "Biblical Past and Canonical Present," 111.

Introduction   xxix

Chapter 40, which Maassen printed as an excerpt of an unidentified source,[39] is in fact a passage from the *Epitome Gai*. The fact that the two chapters drawing on Roman law are consecutive strongly suggests that the compiler of the *Collectio CCCC* worked from an exemplar in which both texts were present, probably a (partial) copy of the *Breviarium Alaricianum*.

Synodus II S. Patricii

While Maassen already noted the inclusion of Irish canons in the *Collectio CCCC*,[40] it was Paul Fournier who first identified the canons as stemming from the *Synodus II S. Patricii*, or "Second Synod of St. Patrick" (hereafter *Synodus II*).[41] Introduced as "Interrogandae romanis" and "Interrogatio romanis" respectively, the *Collectio CCCC* contains two clusters of, in total, eight canons from the Second Synod: canons 260 (*Synodus II S. Patricii* §§1, 4), 261 (*Synodus II S. Patricii* §3), 262 (*Synodus II S. Patricii* §5), 263 (*Synodus II S. Patricii* §10), 264 (*Synodus II S. Patricii* §18), and canons 326–27 (*Synodus II S. Patricii* §§23–24). It is worthwhile to look more closely at the text tradition of the *Synodus II* used by the compilers of the *Collectio CCCC*.

The *Synodus II* survives in two versions; one appended to the *Collectio Vetus Gallica*, the other circulating independently and surviving in two southern German manuscripts (the so-called "BV-version").[42] The version of the canons in the *Collectio CCCC* is related to the recension of the

---

39 Maassen, *Geschichte der Quellen*, 972 (appendix XXV).

40 *Ibid.*, 845. Maassen refers to an "Irish collection" preserved in Munich, Bayerische Staatsbibliothek, Clm 14468 and Vienna, Österreichische Nationalbibliothek, lat. 2232.

41 Paul Fournier, "Le Liber ex lege Moysi et les tendances bibliques du droit canonique Irlandais," *Revue Celtique* 30 (1909), 221–34, at 227, n. 2; 229–30, n. 2.

42 The *Vetus Gallica*–version was edited and translated by Ludwig Bieler, *The Irish penitentials*, Scriptores Latini Hiberniae 5 (Dublin, 1963), 184–97; the so-called BV-version, as preserved in Munich, Bayerische Staatsbibliothek, Clm 14468, and Vienna, Österreichische Nationalbibliothek, lat. 2232, was edited and translated by Aidan Breen, "The date, provenance and authorship of the pseudo-Patrician canonical materials," *Zeitschrift der Savigny-Stiftung für Rechtsgeschichte, Kanonistische Abteilung* 112:125 (1995), 83–129, at 112–21. Both versions originate from Ireland, I argue in "Text and Identities in the Synodus II S. Patricii," *Zeitschrift der Savigny-Stiftung für Rechtsgeschichte, Kanonistische Abteilung* 98 (2012), 19–45.

xxx   Collectio CCCC capitulorum

Synodus II circulating with the *Vetus Gallica*, rather than the BV-recension:[43] the text of the *Collectio CCCC* preserves words from the *Vetus Gallica*–version, which are absent in the BV-version.[44] It also accords with the word order in the *Vetus Gallica*–text, against the BV-version, in its versions of canon 5, 10, and 18.[45] At the same time, the chapters in the *Collectio CCCC* mostly omit readings peculiar to the BV-version: an important case in point is the absence of the words "episcopus uel" in canon 261, corresponding to the *Vetus Gallica*–recension reading of canon 3.[46]

At the same time, the text of the *Synodus II* canons in the *Collectio CCCC* has certain peculiar readings and additions: the collection's rendering of canon 4, in chapter 260, has the word "ethnicus" for "gentilis" in the phrase "Si te non audierit, sit tibi sicut ethnicus et publicanus."[47] The collection's reading of canon 3 (chapter 261) has "lacrimis" for "fletu" in the *Synodus II*.[48] Chapter 327 in the *Collectio CCCC* has the word "dominatur" for "amatur," and the verb "adiurat" is in the active voice, against the passive in both versions of the *Synodus II*.[49] Moreover, the compiler of the collection split this single *Synodus II* canon (§ 23) in two chapters:

---

43 Cf. Mordek, *Kirchenrecht und Reform*, 162–63 who argued the opposite; Mordek's assesment was repeated by Donnchadh Ó Corráin, "Synodus II Patricii and vernacular law," *Peritia* 16 (2002), 335–43, at 337–38; see also Meeder, "Text and Identities," 21, n. 6.

44 *Collectio CCCC capitulorum*, c. 260, cf. *Synodus II S. Patricii*, c. 4 ("et missa"); *Collectio CCCC capitulorum*, c. 326, cf. *Synodus II S. Patricii*, c. 23 ("uiuit Dominus et uiuit anima mea").

45 *Collectio CCCC capitulorum*, c. 262, cf. *Synodus II S. Patricii*, c. 5 ("diem iuditii"); *Collectio CCCC capitulorum*, c. 263, cf. *Synodus II S. Patricii*, c. 10 ("a conspectu Dei peccans"); *Collectio CCCC capitulorum*, c. 264, cf. *Synodus II S. Patricii*, c. 18 ("omnibus omnia").

46 *Collectio CCCC capitulorum*, c. 261; cf. *Synodus II S. Patricii*, c. 3; for a detailed comparison between the various readings of most canons, see the table in Meeder, "Text and Identities," 42–45.

47 *Collectio CCCC capitulorum*, c. 260 (MS I); cf. *Synodus II S. Patricii*, c. 4. MS L reads "et inimicus," which may represent a misreading of the word "ethnicus." Due to a loss of leaves, this canon is absent in MS M.

48 "Statuitur ut abbas uideat, cui a Deo tribuitur potestas alligandi et soluendi. Sed aptior est ad ueniam, iuxta scripturae exempla, si cum lacrimis et lamentatione et lugubri ueste sub custodia melior est penitentia breuis quam longa et remissa cum tempore mentis," *Collectio CCCC capitulorum*, c. 261; cf. *Synodus II S. Patricii*, c. 3.

49 *Collectio CCCC capitulorum*, c. 327; cf. *Synodus II S. Patricii*, c. 23.

Introduction   xxxi

Synodus II S. Patricii §23–24 (Vetus Gallica–version):	Synodus II S. Patricii §23–24 (BV-version):	Collectio CCCC, ch. 326–27:
§23 De iuramento	*§23 De iuramento*	*CCCXXVI Interrogatio Romanorum[a]*
Non iurare omnino: de hoc consequens lectionis series docit non adiurandam esse creaturam aliam sed Creatorem, ut prophetis mos est: Uiuit Dominus et uiuet anima mea, et: Uiuit Dominus, cui adsisto hodie.	Non iurare omnino; de hoc consequentia lectionis docet non iurandum esse creaturam aliam sed creatorem, ut prophetis mos erat: uiuit Dominus cui adsto hodie.	De iuramento: Non iurare omnino: hoc consequentia lectionis docet non adiurandum esse per creaturam aliam, sed per Creatorem, ut mos est prophetis: Uiuit Dominus, cui adsisto hodie.
		CCCXXVII De contradictione[b]
Finis autem contradictionis adiuramentum est, sed [in] Domino; omne enim quod amatur hoc [enim] et [ad]iuratur.	Finis contradictionis iuramentum, sed Domino. Omne enim quod amatur hoc adiuratur.	Finis autem contradictionis adiuramentum est, sed Domino: Omne enim quod dominatur hoc et adiurat. Alii periures III annis peniteat.
§24 De contentionem duorum absque testibus Statuunt ut per sancta quattuor euangelia antequam communicet testetur qui [a]d-probatur et deinde sub iudice[s] flamma relinquatur.	*§24 De contentione duorum absque testibus* Statuunt post IIII[or] euangelia antequam communicet testetur qui adprobatur, et deinde sub iudice flamma relinquatur.	De contraditionis duorum absque testibus: Statuunt ut per sancta IIII euangelia antequam communicant testantur, qui adprobantur et deinde sub iudice flamma relinquantur.

---

[a] In interrogatione Romanorum de confirmatione iuramenti M
[b] De contradictione iuramenti M

Chapter 326 contains the first half of *Synodus II*'s canon 23, under the same rubric as in the *Vetus Gallica* and BV-recensions: "De iuramento." It states that one should not swear an oath by any other creature than xxxii

God. The second half of canon 23 is represented in the first part of the collection's chapter 327, which bears the title "De contradictione." Paraphrasing Paul in his letter to the Hebrews, this sentence states that an oath is the end of controversy, and that one swears an oath by all or on all that (one?) is ruled over. Preserving the rubric, "De contraditionis duorum absque testibus," the second part of chapter 327 is made up of *Synodus II*'s canon 24. The thematic connection between the two *Synodus II* canons is clear.

In the middle of chapter 327, following the statement that one must not swear by any creature but only by God,[50] the *Collectio CCCC* declares that "alii periures III annis penitent," "other oath-breakers should do penance of three years." This phrase is not attested in the surviving complete copies of *Synodus II*. It seems to refer to the text of canon 328 of the *Collectio CCCC*, sourced from an unknown penitential, which states that forced or unknowing perjurers should do penance for three years.[51] The added phrase to canon 24 is thus clearly aimed at connecting it with the following chapter in the collection and it appears that this particular reading was introduced by the compiler of the *Collectio CCCC*. Whether this is also the case for changing "amatur" for "dominatur" in canon 24 (chapter 327) remains unclear to me.

An altered arrangement of some *Synodus II* canons also occurs in chapter 260, which comprises both a part of *Synodus II* canon 1 and canon 4 (including the rubric "de excommunicationem" for the latter canon). The pairing of these two rulings is not illogical: the first concerns how to act toward sinful brethren while the latter canon focuses on how to treat excommunicates. The treatment of the *Synodus II* canons demonstrates the ambition of the compiler (even in the less-organized later parts of the collection) to produce a unified, coherent collection.

As stated, the version of *Synodus II* canons found in the *Collectio CCCC* resembles the recension appended to the *Vetus Gallica* more closely than any other surviving recension of the *Synodus II*. Since there is no

---

50 Judging by the evidence from the so-called *Liber ex lege Moysi* and the "First Synod of St Patrick," this topic enjoyed particular interest of Irish legal scholars: cf. *Liber ex lege Moysi*, Ex. 20:7, ed. Sven Meeder, "The Liber ex lege Moysi: notes and text," *Journal of Medieval Latin* 19 (2009), 173–218, at 191 (cf. 176). *Synodus I S. Patricii*, c. 14, ed. and transl. Bieler, *Irish penitentials*, 54–59, at 56.

51 *Collectio CCCC capitulorum*, c. 328: "Si quis periurauerit, VI annis peniteat, III integros, ut et iuret numquam postea. Si quis coactus pro qualibet necessitate aut nesciens periurauerit, tribus annis peniteat, I integrum" (MS I, fol. 186v).

Introduction   xxxiii

convincing evidence for the use of texts from the *Vetus Gallica* proper in the *Collectio CCCC*,[52] it appears that the compiler did not obtain his *Synodus II* material from a copy of the *Vetus Gallica* including its appendix, but more likely from a copy in which the *Synodus II* was (still) separated from the canonical collection. The material probably did not reach the compiler of the *Collectio CCCC* directly or indirectly from Corbie, where the *Vetus Gallica* was revised, but rather arrived at the compiler's workplace independently, possibly along with other insular canonical texts (notably some version of the *Iudicia Theodori*).

Collectio Sanblasiana

Maassen remarked that, in addition to a collection of Gallic councils and penitential sources, the compiler of the *Collectio CCCC* seemed to have used the *Collectio Sanblasiana* "either as an immediate exemplar or otherwise."[53] Eckhard Wirbelauer recently confirmed Maassen's suspicion.[54] In fact, the text of the papal and conciliar material in the *Collectio CCCC* points to one manuscript witness of the *Sanblasiana* in particular: Cologne, Dombibliothek MS 213.

The *Collectio Sanblasiana*, a chronologically arranged canon law collection, is dated to the beginning of the sixth century (possibly compiled under Pope Hormisdas, 514–23) and was probably composed in Italy, perhaps Rome.[55] It comprises conciliar decrees and papal decretals, including the Symmachian forgeries.[56] For the conciliar section of the

52 Mordek concluded that the two instances of possible dependence (chapters 246 and 247) constitute too little evidence to argue for a direct connection. See Mordek, *Kirchenrecht und Reform*, 163.

53 Maassen, *Geschichte der Quellen*, 846.

54 Eckhard Wirbelauer, *Zwei Päpste in Rom: Der Konflikt zwischen Laurentius und Symmachus (498–514). Studien und Texte* (Munich, 1993), 122–28.

55 The collection received its name after one of its manuscript witnesses, which at one time was preserved in the monastery of Sankt Blasien in Austria (now Sankt Paul im Lavanttal, Stiftsbibliothek, Codex 7/1). See Wirbelauer, *Zwei Päpste*, 504–12. Work on the context of the *Sanblasiana's* composition (in particular with regard to the Symmachian material) has recently been done by Wirbelauer, *Zwei Päpste*, 122–28; and Idem, "Zum Umgang mit kanonistischer Tradition im frühen Mittelalter: Drei Wirkungen der Symmachianischen Documenta." in: Ursula Schaefer (ed.), *Schriftlichkeit im frühen Mittelalter* (Tübingen, 1993), 207–28.

56 There is no critical edition of the complete *Collectio Sanblasiana*. An (incomplete) edition of the various Latin versions of the *Canones apostolorum* and the councils of Nicaea, Ancyra, Neocaesarea, Gangra, Antioch, and Sardica is C. H. Turner,

xxxiv   Collectio CCCC capitulorum

collection it is mainly based on the fifth-century so-called Latin *"prisca"* translations, but we also find councils in the *versio Isidori* translation, as well as material taken from the collection of Dionysius Exiguus.[57] It is this same combination of different Latin versions that we find in the *Collectio CCCC*.

Cologne, Dombibliothek MS 213 is an early eighth-century Northumbrian manuscript and possibly the oldest extant copy of the *Sanblasiana*.[58] Its version of the *Sanblasiana* appears to represent a tradition that has undergone modifications as a result of comparison with other canon law collections.[59] This resulted in some unique readings, especially in the Symmachian material, that are seemingly the result of glosses in the exemplar, which were incorporated in the text proper by earlier scribes.[60] In his study of this Symmachian material, Wirbelauer demonstrated the dependence of the *Collectio CCCC* on the *Sanblasiana*. Chapters 212–17 of the *Collectio CCCC* contain material from the *Constitutum Silvestri*, purportedly a record of a Roman council held under Pope Silvester and Emperor Constantine in 324 but in reality a product of forgerers supporting Pope Symmachus (r. 498–514) in his

---

Ecclesiae occidentalis monumenta iuris antiquissima: canonum et conciliorum Graecorum interpretationes Latinae, 2 vols. in 7 pts. (Oxford, 1899–1939). Five manuscript witnesses for the *Sanblasiana* are included in these editions (siglum "S"). The Symmachian documents in the *Sanblasiana* and elsewhere are edited by Wirbelauer, *Zwei Päpste*, 228–300. For the decretals in the Sanblasiana, see Hubert Wurm, *Studien und Texte zur Decretalensammlung des Dionysius Exiguus* (Rome, 1939), 88–94.

57 The *Sanblasiana* and its contents (in particular with regard to the Cologne manuscript) are described by Michael D. Elliot, "Canon Law Collections in England ca. 600–1066: The Manuscript Evidence" (Unpubl. PhD thesis, University of Toronto, 2013), 228–44.

58 The *Sanblasiana* survives in Cologne, Erzbischöfliche Diözesan und Dombibliothek 213 (saec. viii^{in}); Lucca, Biblioteca Capitolare Feliniana 490 (saec. viii–ix); Paris, BN lat. 1455 (saec. ix²); Paris, BN lat. 3836 (saec. viii²); Paris, BN lat. 4279 (saec. ix^{med}); and Sankt Paul im Lavanttal, Stiftsbibliothek 7/1 (saec. viii), Lotte Kéry, *Canonical Collections of the Early Middle Ages (ca. 400–1140): A Bibliographical Guide to the Manuscripts and Literature*, History of Medieval Canon Law (Washington, DC, 1999). On the Cologne manuscript being the oldest, see Rosamond McKitterick, "Knowledge of Canon Law in the Frankish Kingdoms before 789: The Manuscript Evidence," *Journal of Theological Studies* 36 (1985), 97–117, at 111–12.

59 A detailed description of the textual content of Cologne 213 is provided by Elliot, "Canon law collections," 244–50.

60 Wirbelauer, "Zum Umgang," 214–17. Note that the text in Cologne 213 itself is also glossed, see Elliot, "Canon Law Collections," 248, n. 274.

Introduction   xxxv

dispute against Laurentius and his supporters.[61] Wirbelauer noted that a peculiar variant in Cologne 213, apparently the result of a gloss in its exemplar, was reproduced (though differently) in chapter 213 of the *Collectio CCCC*.

Constitutum Silvestri (ed. Wirbelauer, ll. 114–16)	*Constitutum Silvestri* (Cologne 213, fol. 79r)	*Collectio CCCC capitulorum,* c. 213 (MS I)
...nisi sicut scriptum est, in septem testimonia filios et uxores habentes et omnino Christum praedicantes. sic datur mistica ueritas.	...nisi sicut scriptum est **ii uel iii in testimonia** filios et uxorem habentem et omnino Christum predicantem sic datur mystica ueritas	...nisi, sicut scriptum est, **ii uel tria**. Sic datur mistica ueritas **in testimonia**.

Wirbelauer argues that the readings in Cologne 213 and the *Collectio CCCC* reflected two different interpretations of a gloss, which itself was the product of a comparison of this passage with I Tim 5:19 or with a later recension of the *Constitutum Silvestri*.[62] This passage demonstrates the connection between Cologne 213 and the *Collectio CCCC*, yet the difference between both readings might indicate that the copy of the *Sanblasiana* used by the compiler of the *Collectio CCCC* still had these words as a gloss—that is, in a form that could be misunderstood—and that the compiler did not have access to Cologne 213 immediately, but rather to an earlier witness to its tradition (possibly its immediate exemplar).

Closer study of peculiar readings in Cologne 213 of non-Symmachian material confirms this connection between the *Sanblasiana* tradition of Cologne 213 and the *Collectio CCCC*. This includes the material strewn throughout the collection, such as the *Canones Apostolorum* and the canons from Nicaea, as well as the other material taken from the *Sanblasiana*, which often occurs *en bloc*.[63]

---

61 Wirbelauer, *Zwei Päpste*. An edition (and German translation) of the *Constitutum Silvestri* is found on pp. 228–47.

62 Wirbelauer, 'Zum Umgang', 215, n. 28.

63 Another example is Nicaea (325), c. 10 (*Isidori*): *Sanbl.*: ...et per ignorantiam ordinati sunt uel contemptu eorum...; cf. Cologne 213: ...et per ignorantiam ordinati sunt uel contemptu **aut desimulatione ordinantium** eorum...; cf. *Coll. 400*, c. 147 (I): ...et per

xxxvi   Collectio CCCC capitulorum

Statuta Ecclesiae Antiqua

The text known as the *Statuta ecclesiae antiqua* is a small collection of
102 canons on church discipline. Although often misattributed to the
fourth council of Carthage (389) throughout the Middle Ages, historians
have identified that it originated in southern Gaul in the last quarter of
the fifth century. Its most recent editor, Charles Munier, proposed that
its author was Gennadius of Marseilles (*ob. c.* 496) based on obvious
parallels with the latter's writings on church life, in particular his tract
De ecclesiasticis dogmatibus.[64]

The *Statuta* feature in a large number of canonical collections,
especially in the *Collectio hispana* and its revised version known to
scholars in Gaul, the *Hispana Gallica Augustodunensis*. In Ireland the
text was known by the compilers of the *Hibernensis*,[65] and it also became
part of the Pseudo-Isidorian forgeries. The *Statuta* survive in over forty
manuscripts, twenty-two of which are used by Munier in his edition.[66]
He identified three main textual traditions of the collection: the Spanish,
Gallic, and Italian. The latter often carries the title "Statuta antiqua
orientis" or "Constituta antiqua orientis," whereas the Spanish and Gallic
are often referred to in manuscript witnesses as the canons from the
Carthaginian council, or as the "Statuta ecclesiae antiqua," or both. In
the *Collectio CCCC* the *Statuta ecclesiae antiqua* is consequently referred to
as "unica ecclesia," "the single church" or the "sole church," or "Statuta
ecclesiastica unica." Maassen assumed that "unica" was a corrupted form
of "antiqua."[67]

The version of the *Statuta* used by the compiler of the *Collectio
CCCC* is not easily determined. The title given to the *Statuta* canons
suggests that his exemplar was not a member of the Italian tradition,

---

ignorantiam ordinati sunt uel contemptu **aut disimulatione ordinantium** eorum... (see
Klaus Zeckiel-Eckes (ed.), *Concordia canonum des Cresconius. Studien und Edition* (Frankfurt
am Main, 1992), II, 176 n. 15, cited by Elliot, "Canon law collections," 246).

64 Charles Munier, *Les statuta ecclesiae antiqua. Édition, études critiques*, Bibliothèque
de l'Institut de Droit Canonique de l'Université de Strasbourg 5 (Paris, 1960), 107–24,
209–36.

65 For a table of the *Statuta ecclesiae antiqua* canons in the *Hibernensis*, see Luned
Mair Davies, "Statuta ecclesiae antiqua and the Gallic councils in the Hibernensis,"
Peritia 14 (2000), 85–110, at 101–3.

66 A description of the manuscripts is found at Munier, *Statuta*, 29–54.

67 Maassen, *Geschichte der Quellen*, 845, n. 14.

Introduction   xxxvii

and the textual evidence confirms this suspicion: very few of the variants peculiar to this tradition are shared with the *Collectio CCCC*. Distinguishing between the Spanish and Gallic traditions is more difficult. The *Collectio CCCC* preserves many variants not paralleled by manuscript witnesses of the *Statuta* proper. There are a few exceptions, including the version of canons 3 and 4 of the *Statuta* in chapter 99 of the *Collectio CCCC*. In this chapter the reading of the *Statuta* canons omits the words "et mensam."[68] In Munier's edition two manuscripts preserve the same omission, namely the late eighth-century manuscript Brussels, Bibliothèque royale, MS 8780–8793 and the ninth- or tenth-century manuscript Paris, Bibliothèque nationale, MS lat. 1454.[69] Both manuscripts are members of a separate group of the Gallic tradition, according to Munier. One of the characteristics of the group is the omission of canons 11 and 71. The *Collectio CCCC*, however, preserves canon 11 (chapter 116). A manuscript from this particular Gallic group of the *Statuta* therefore cannot have been (the only) exemplar used by the compiler.

A few canons demonstrate an intriguing connection with the *Statuta ecclesiae antiqua* tradition drawn upon by the compilers of the *Hibernensis*. Chapter 225, concerning bishops not reading the books of heretics and pagans, reads: "Episcopus gentilium libros non legat hereticorum autem pro necessitate et tempore perlegat." The final word, "perlegat," is not present in any of the *Statuta ecclesiae antiqua* witnesses, but it does feature in the *Hibernensis*.[70] More striking is the version of *Statuta ecclesiae antiqua* §75 in chapter 235. In the *Statuta* it is stated that a cleric who sings between courses is to be punished with the same severe sentence as is outlined in the previous canon (i.e., *Statuta ecclesiae antiqua* §74), namely excommunication.[71] The *Collectio CCCC*, which

---

68 "Et in unica ecclesia: Ut episcopus nullam rei familiaris curam ad se reuocet, sed ut lectioni et orationi et uerbi Dei predicationi tantum uacet, et uilem subpellectilem **et mensam** ac uictum pauperem habeat, et dignitatis suae auctoritatem fide et uitae meritis quaerat," *Collectio CCCC capitulorum*, c. 99; cf. *Statuta ecclesiae antiqua*, §§3–4 (text in bold is from *Statuta ecclesiae antiqua* but omitted by *Collectio CCCC*).

69 See Munier, *Statuta*, 31–32, 40–41.

70 *Collectio CCCC capitulorum*, c. 225; *Collectio canonum Hibernensis*, 1.10(e), ed. Flechner, I:11, ll. 16–17.

71 "Clericum inter epulas cantatem supradictae sententiae seueritate coercendum"; *Statuta ecclesiae antiqua*, §75.

xxxviii Collectio CCCC capitulorum

does not include canon 74, paraphrases and elaborates: "Clericus inter epulas cantans, fidem utique non edificans, sed auribus tantum pruriens, excommunicetur."[72] The same canon is copied by the compilers of the *Hibernensis*, in their book 10, under the heading "De multimodis causis clericorum: Synodus Kartaginensis."[73]

The unique embellishment of the *Statuta*'s §75 in both the *Hibernensis* and the *Collectio CCCC* demonstrates some connection between their respective exemplars. Not all *Statuta ecclesiae antiqua* canons used by the compiler of the *Collectio CCCC* are preserved in the *Hibernensis*, however, so he cannot have taken his *Statuta ecclesiae antiqua* material solely from the *Hibernensis*. In her research on the *Statuta ecclesiae antiqua* in the *Hibernensis*, Luned Mair Davies was unable to determine from which of the three textual traditions the *Hibernensis* compiler drew his canons when she concluded the compiler probably had access to "either the Gallic and the Spanish recensions of the *SEA* and possibly also the Italian, or to a fused version of all three recensions—perhaps in some cases via Irish synodal decrees."[74] Such a "fused version," either insular or otherwise, including its unique version of canon 75, may also have been at the basis of the *Collectio CCCC*.

Collectio Canonum Hibernensis

There are four instances in the *Collectio CCCC* in which canons resemble material from the *Hibernensis*. These are found in chapters 60 (*Hibernensis* 17.9), 242 (*Hibernensis* 39:14), 403 (*Hibernensis* 25.10), and 404 (*Hibernensis* 33:11). All instances represent material sourced by the *Hibernensis* compilers from different authorities: a synod of the Irish *Romani*-faction, a "Sinodus Alexandrina," Ambrose, and Jerome respectively. With the variety in sources, topics, and a lack of structural correspondence, it is doubtful that the compiler of the *Collectio CCCC* had a complete copy of the *Hibernensis* at his disposal. Contrary to the statement by Naz,[75] it is more plausible that he made use of texts that, in some shape or form, were also used by the compilers of the *Hibernensis*.

---

72 *Collectio CCCC capitulorum*, c. 235.
73 *Collectio canonum Hibernensis*, 10(i), ed. Flechner, I:45, ll. 1–2.
74 Davies, "Statuta ecclesiae antiqua," 101.
75 Naz, "Quarte cents chapitres."

Introduction   xxxix

Iudicia Theodori

A large portion of the collection is made up of material taken from the penitential and disciplinary pronouncements of Theodore of Canterbury (602–690). In fact, the *Iudicia Theodori* dominate the last 140 chapters of the collection, although earlier in the text we find two pockets of chapters with concentrations of Theodorian sentences, namely chapters 59–85 and 163–75. Almost without exception, these rulings can be found in the recension of Theodore's penitential as collected by the so-called *Discipulus Umbriensium* (Finsterwalder's U recension).[76] This recension is the most extensive version and, judging from the extant manuscript evidence, it was also the most popular.[77] The precise date of the *discipulus's* activity is unclear, but his work was certainly available in mainland Europe by the first half of the eighth century, when the redactors of the *Collectio Vetus Gallica* at Corbie drew from it for the collection's supplement. In fact, of the extant eighth-century copies of the U recension, all but one are attributed to scriptoria in northern and northeastern France.[78] The same recension was also used for the eighth-century *Paenitentiale Remense* and the *Excarpsus Cummeani* (also from Corbie).[79]

The *Collectio CCCC* in two instances contains some Theodorian material that is unique to the U recension. Chapter 270 preserves the canon II.12.33 in U, which has no direct parallel in any other extant

---

76 P. W. Finsterwalder, *Die Canones Theodori Cantuariensis und ihre Überlieferungsformen*, Untersuchungen zu den Bußbüchern des 7., 8. und 9. Jahrhunderts 1 (Weimar 1929); see Michael Elliot's edition online http://individual.utoronto.ca/michaelelliot/manuscripts/texts/iudicia_theodori.html (accessed December 2022). On the different recensions, see Raymund Kottje, "Paenitentiale Theodori," in *Handwörterbuch zur deutschen Rechtsgeschichte 3* (Berlin 1984), cols. 1413–16; and Flechner, "The Making of the Canons of Theodore," *Peritia* 17/18 (2002–2003), 121–43; and T. Charles-Edwards, "The Penitential of Theodore and the *Iudicia Theodori*," in Michael Lapidge (ed.), *Archbishop Theodore: Commemorative Studies on His Life and Influence* (Cambridge 1995), 141–74.

77 The twenty-five surviving manuscript copies are listed by Rob Meens, *Penance in Medieval Europe, 600–1200* (Cambridge, 2014), 227–28.

78 The other is Vienna, Österreichische Nationalbibliothek, lat. 2195 (end of the eighth century, Salzburg).

79 Ludger Körntgen, "Der Excarpsus Cummeani, ein Bußbuch aus Corbie," in O. Münsch and T. Zotz (eds.), *Scientia veritatis. Festschrift für Hubert Mordek zum 65. Geburtstag* (Ostfildern 2004), 59–75.

xl   Collectio CCCC capitulorum

recension, although traces are detected in the fragments of canon 103d in the sole surviving manuscript of the Theodorian tradition known as *Capitula Dacheriana* (D).[80] Some other canons in our collection, however, more closely reflect a reading in the recension of Theodore's rulings known as the *Canones Gregorii* (G). A case in point is chapter 70:

Collectio CCCC capitulorum, c. 70	Iud. Theod. G 78	Iud. Theod. U II.12.26–7
LXX De propinquitate In **quarta** propinquitate carnis secundum Grecos licet nubere sicut in lege scriptum est. In quinta secundum Romanos. Tamen in **tertia**ᵃ non soluunt coniugium postquam factum fuerit.	Secundum Gregos in **quarta** propinquitate carnis licet nubere, sicut in lege scriptum est; secundum Romanos in V, in **IIII** tamen non soluunt cumiugium postquam factum fuerit.	In **tertia** propinquitate carnis licet nubere secundum Grecos, s‹icut› in lege scriptum est; in V secundum Romanos, tamen in **III**‹I› non soluunt postquam factum fuerit.
		Ergo: in Va generatione coniungantur; IIII si inuenta fuerint, non separentur; III separentur.
In tertia tamen propinquitate non licet uxorem alterius accipere post obitum eius.	In tertia tamen propinquitate non licet uxorem alterius accipere post obitum eius.	In tertia propinquitate non licet uxorem alterius accipere post obitum eius.

ᵃ quarta M

Another, different example is provided by chaper 85, where the reading in the *Collectio CCCC* does not seem to correspond to any of the recensions of the *Iudicia Theodori*, but instead seems to align with various recensions at different places.

---

80 See Michael Elliot's edition of D on http://individual.utoronto.ca/ michaelelliot/manuscripts/texts/transcriptions/pthd.pdf (p. 10) (accessed December 2022).

Introduction   xli

Collectio CCCC capitulorum, c. 85	Iud. Theod. B 74	Iud. Theod. G 154	Iud. Theod. U I.7.2
LXXXV De pecunia aliena De pecunia quae in aliena prouintia ab hoste **alterum** superantium rapta fuerit: tertia pars ad ecclesiam tribuatur **uel pauperibus** et xl diebus penitentia, quia iussio regis erat.	De pecunia quæ in aliena prouincia ab hoste **alterum** superante rapitur, tertia pars ad ecclesiam tribuatur et XL diebus peniteat, quia iusio regis erat.	De pecuniam que in aliena prouintia ab aste **alterum regem** superante rapta fuerant, et tercias pars ad ecclesiam retribuatur et XL dies peniteat, quia iussi regis erat	De pecunia quae in aliena prouincia ab hoste superato rapta fuerit, **id est rege alio superato**, tertia pars ad ecclesia‹m› tribuatur **uel pauperibus** et XL diebus agatur penitentia, quia iussio regis erat.

Chapter 60 reveals an equally muddled lineage (now including parallels with the so-called *Canones Cottoniani* (C) version):

Collectio CCCC capitulorum, c. 60	Iud. Theod. C 199–200	Iud. Theod. G 44	Iud. Theod. U II.6.9
LX De abbate Qui uouerit uotum sine permissu abbatis commotetur ab abbate et uideat abbas. In alio loco: Monacho non licere uotum uouere sine **consensu** abbatis sui. **Sin minus frangendum est, si iusserit abbas.**	Monacho non licet uotum uouere sine licentia abbatis. Si uoluerit, sic dimittendus est **si iusserit abbas.**	Monacho non licet uotum facere sine licentia abbatis. Si uouerit, sic dimitendus est **si iusserit abbatis.**	Monacho non licet uotum uouere sine **consensu** abbatis; **sin minus frangendum est.**

xlii   Collectio CCCC capitulorum

Chapter 335 contains a canon only represented in the *Capitula Dache-riana* (D) tradition without parallels in other versions of the *Iudicia*. This recension is best known for the fact that it is closest to the text drawn on by the compilers of the *Hibernensis*.[81] This particular ruling, however, is not represented in the Irish collection, which can therefore not have been the source of the compilers of the *Collectio CCCC capitulorum* for this particular canon.

Collectio CCCC capitulorum, c. 335	Iud. Theod. D 89	Iud. Theod. U I.15.57
Qui non conposuit furtum aut homicidium		Qui sepe furtum fecerit, VII annis penitentia eius est uel quomodo sacerdos iudicauerit,
Qui homicidium uel furtum commiserit et non conposuit illis quibus nocuit, quando confessus fuerit episcopo uel presbitero peccata sua, debet illis aut propria reddere uel conponere. Si uero non habuerit substantiam unde conponere potest uel nescierit quibus nocuerit, **plus augeat penitentia**.	Qui homicidium uel furtum comiserit et non conposuit illis quibus nocuit, quando confessus fuerit æpiscopo uel presbitero peccata sua, debet illis aut propria reddere uel ponere. Si uero non habuerit substantiam unde conponere potest, uel nescierit quibus nocuit, **penitentia plus augetur**.	id ‹est iuxta quod› conponi possit quibus nocuit.

Chapter 371 preserves a canon only present in G (G30) regarding a cleric rushing to and baptising a sick pagan. Likewise, chapters 346–47 replicate material that, in this form and order, only survives in G (G118), while in chapter 265 canons G38b and G39 are combined.[82] A similar

---

81 Flechner, "The Making of the Canons of Theodore," 134, who qualifies the argument of T. Charles-Edwards, "The penitential of Theodore," 142; and Henry Bradshaw in Hermann Wasserschleben, *Die irische Kanonensammlung* (rev. edn. Leipzig, 1885, repr. Aalen, 1966), lxiii–lxxv, at lxx.

82 The joining of these two canons seems to reflect the difficulty for the compiler of the *Collectio CCCC* to separate correctly the decrees of Theodore. The same combination, however, is also found in the St. Gall tripartite penitential (II.29) and the *Capitula Iudiciorum* (XII.2), which draws on the *Paenitentiale Sangallense Tripartitum*. The

Introduction   xliii

instance is found in chapter 350, concerning rulings about drunk priests
vomiting, which resembles those in G122 or (in a wholly different order)
U I.1.3, I.1.2 and I.1.5. Since none of the extant recensions of the *Iudicia
Theodori* contains all the Theodorian material present in our collection
or is in complete agreement with the wording in the *Collectio CCCC*, it
is impossible to determine which served as an exemplar to its compiler.
It seems likely that the compiler had access to multiple recensions or to
a version of the *Iudicia* that no longer survives.

THE *COLLECTIO CCCC* IN OTHER TEXTS

Poenitentiale Martenianum and the Paenitentiale ad Heribaldum

The *Poenitentiale Martenianum* is a tripartite penitential named after the
eighteenth-century Maurist, Edmond Martène, who first published the
text in 1717.[83] Walther von Hörmann studied the work exhaustively
in the early twentieth century and provided the most recent edition of
the text.[84] He identified 26 canons taken from Frankish penitentials,
40 from the penitential of Cummean, and 124 taken from Theodorian
sources.[85] Von Hörman and subsequent scholars have also found evidence
for the use of the penitentials attributed to Bede and Egbert as well
as the *Collectio canonum Hibernensis*, the *Collectio Vetus Gallica*, and the
Collectio CCCC capitulorum or a common source.[86] This amalgam displays,
in Cyrille Vogel's words, "une remarquable incohérence."[87]

Von Hörmann dated the composition of the *Martenianum* to
sometime between 802 and 813 while also arguing that the single
surviving manuscript witness, Florence, Biblioteca Medicea Laurenziana

---

first part, "Si quis uult [...] presbitero," was not supposed to be included in this canon
on theft, as explained by Meens, *Tripartite boeteboek*, 93.

   83 Edmond Martène, *Thesaurus novus anecdotorum* (Paris, 1717), vol. IV, p. 31–56.

   84 Walther von Hörmann, "Bußbücherstudien I," *Zeitschrift der Savigny-Stiftung
für Rechtsgeschichte, Kanonistische Abteilung* 1 (1911), 195–250; *idem*, "Bußbücherstudien
II," *Zeitschrift der Savigny-Stiftung für Rechtsgeschichte, Kanonistische Abteilung* 2 (1912),
11–181; *idem*, "Bußbücherstudien III," *Zeitschrift der Savigny-Stiftung für Rechtsgeschichte,
Kanonistische Abteilung* 3 (1913), 413–92; *idem*, "Bußbücherstudien IV," *Zeitschrift der
Savigny-Stiftung für Rechtsgeschichte, Kanonistische Abteilung* 4 (1914), 358–483.

   85 *Idem*, "Bußbücherstudien I," 219–20, 226, 248.

   86 Ibid., "Bußbücherstudien I," 232; ibid., "Bußbücherstudien II," 143–44, 158–74.
See Mordek, *Kirchenrecht und Reform*, 201.

   87 Cyrille Vogel, *Les "libri paenitentiales," Typologie des Sources du Moyen Âge
Occidental* 27 (Turnhout, 1978), 78.

xliv   Collectio CCCC capitulorum

Ashburnham 82 (32), is in fact the author's original copy.[88] The Fleury manuscript in question, however, has subsequently been dated to the third quarter of the ninth century.[89] Mordek, unconvinced by Von Hörmann's arguments for dating the text to the early ninth century but willing to accept that the sole surviving manuscript witness is in fact the text's original copy, put forward that the penitential was several decades younger than Von Hörmann suggested.[90] When Raymund Kottje determined that the *Martenianum* was used by Hrabanus Maurus for his *Paenitentiale ad Heribaldum*, written in 853, this provided a new, earlier *terminus post quem non* for the work.[91] Haggenmüller advanced a *terminus ante quem non* when he found that the compiler of the *Martenianum* drew from an early precursor of the *Paenitentiale Ps.-Bedae-Egberti*, which he dated to around 800.[92] On this basis, Meens concluded that the penitential was probably compiled in the second quarter of the ninth century somewhere in northeastern France, an important region of the Frankish penitential reforms.[93]

Much of the material in the *Martenianum* is found in more than one of its immediate sources, such as the various canons of the *Synodus II S. Patricii*, a text that survives not only in its entirety appended to the *Vetus Gallica*, but of which selections were also taken up in the *Hibernensis* and the *Collectio CCCC*.[94] In some instances there are easily identifiable markers evincing that the exemplar used is the *Collectio CCCC* or, theoretically, a shared source text. This is often demonstrated not only by the strong similarity in the wording of canons but also by the same

---

88 Von Hörmann, "Bußbücherstudien III," 442, 459, and 461.

89 Mordek, *Kirchenrecht und Reform*, 200.

90 Ibid.

91 Raymund Kottje, *Die Bussbücher Halitgars von Cambrai und des Hrabanus Maurus: Ihre Überlieferung und ihre Quellen* (Berlin/New York, 1980), 204–9.

92 Reinhold Haggenmüller, "Zur Rezeption der Beda und Egbert zugeschriebenen Bußbücher," in Hubert Mordek (ed.), *Aus Archiven und Bibliotheken. Festschrift für Raymund Kottje zum 65. Geburtstag, Freiburger Beiträge zur mittelalterlichen Geschichte, Studien und Texte 3* (Frankfurt am Main, 1992), 149–59, at 154–55.

93 Meens, *Het tripartite boeteboek*, 54–55; for the Carolingian reforms of penitential practice, see ibid., 60–69. Vogel suggested the region of Orléans, see *Les "libri paenitentiales,"* 78

94 *Synodus II S. Patricii* §29 (cited in *Poen. Martenianum* c. 33) is not found in the *Hibernensis* or the *Collectio CCCC*, which suggests that this canon is drawn from the version appended to the *Vetus Gallica*.

Introduction   xlv

combination and arrangement of groups of canons. The unique combination of Theodorian canons in *Martenianum* LXV.5–7, for instance, corresponds with the text in chapter 276 of the *Collectio CCCC*.[95]

In chapter XLIII of the *Martenianum* we encounter a canon purportedly from the Synod of Ancyra ("Sinodus Anquirinensium") that in reality is a canon from the *Iudicia Theodori* and corresponds with chapter 163 in our collection, where it is flanked by other precepts taken from Ancyra (*Collectio CCCC*, cc. 161, 162, 164). The relevant preamble to the canon in the *Collectio CCCC* "Et in alia...," which could have tipped the *Martenianum* compiler off that this sentence did not come from Ancyra, is not present in manuscripts L and M. An inattentive reader of this section of the *Collectio CCCC* could thus easily have understood this canon, like the ones before and after, to represent a pronouncement from Ancyra.

Collectio CCCC capitulorum	*Poen. Martenianum*	Source
163 *Qui abortiuum faciunt**	XLIII *In alio loco. Sinodus Anquirinensium*	
Et in alia[a]: Mulieres quae abortiuum faciunt	Mulieres quae abortiuum faciunt...	cf. *Iud. Theod.* U I.14.24; C 147 Ancyr. §21
162 *De necantibus partus suos** Mulieres uero quae fornicantur...[b]	XLIV *Et in alio* Mulieres uero quae fornicantur...	

[a] Et in alia] *deest* LM
[b] Mulieres uero quae fornicantur] Mulieres uero qui fornicantur I Et in alia: Mulieres uero qui fornicantur L

* title not in running text in IL

---

95 Namely *Iud. Theod.* U I.14.5; I.14.7; and II.12.31. See *Collectio CCCC capitulorum*, c. 276; and Von Hörmann "Bußbücherstudien IV," 435–36.

xlvi   Collectio CCCC capitulorum

The order of the two respective chapters in the *Martenianum* follows the sequence of the chapters in *Collectio CCCC*'s version of manuscript L, where chapters 162 and 163 are entered in reverse order. There are other indications that the compiler of the *Martenianum* had recourse to a version closest to L: the words 'Et in alio' in chapter XLIV correspond to the reading 'Et in alia', unique to L chapter 162. Moreover, the titles of the chapters, present in the *index titulorum* of I and M and in the running text of M, are absent in both L and the *Martenianum*.

The parallels between the two works in content, order, and titles is also clear from the *Martenianum* chapters LIII–LIV, which correspond to chapters 324–328 in the *Collectio CCCC*, especially (again) in the version of L.

Collectio CCCC capitulorum		*Poen. Martenianum*		Source
324	*De iuramento*	LIII	*De iuramento*	
	Periurium qui fecerit...	LIII §1	Periurium qui fecerit...	*Iud. Theod.* U I.6.1
325	*Necesse in manus*[a]			
325a	Qui uero...[b]	LIII § 2	Qui uero... Neces̄ in manus	*Iud. Theod.* U I.6.2
325b	Si uero iurauerit...	LIII §3	Si uero iurauerit...	*Iud. Theod.* U I.6.4
325c	Si quis iurauerit...	LIII §4	Si quis iurauerit...	*Iud. Theod.* U I.6.3
325d	Nos secundum Christum...	LIII §4	Nos secundum Christum...	Mt 12:37
326	*Interrogatio Romanorum* De iuramento...	LIII §5	*Interrogatio Romana* De iuramento...	*Syn. II Patr.* §23 (fragment)
327	*De contradictione*	LIV	*De contradictione*	
327a	Finis autem...	LIV §1	Finis autem...	*Syn. II Patr.* §23 (fragment)
327b	De contradictione ...	LIV §2	De contraditionis ...	*Syn. II Patr.,* §24
328	*De paenitentia iuramenti** Si quis periurauerit...	LIV §3	Si quis periurauerit...	cf. P. *Burg.* §§5–6; P. *Bobb.* §§6–7; P. *Slet.* §§5–6; P. *Flor.* §§5–6

a *Necesse in manus*] Necesse I Si iurauerit in manu episcopi M
b *This canon precedes*
c. *325 in L*
* title not in running text in IL

Introduction   xlvii

The scribe of L and the compiler of the *Martenianum* appear to have
had recourse to a common, or closely related, exemplar (the absence of
c. 172 in L means that it cannot have been the direct exemplar for the
Martenianum–see below). Chapters XXVIII–XLII, and in particular the
use (or not) of rubrics, provide more evidence for the correspondence
with L's version of the *Collectio CCCC*, that is, a version with a limited
number of rubrics in the running text.

Collectio CCCC capitulorum		*Poen. Martenianum*		Source
267	*De adultera*	XXXVIII	*De adulterio*	*Iud. Theod.* U I.14.4
268	*De lauatione matrimonii**	XXXIX	*Item*	*Iud. Theod.* U II.12.30
269	*De muliere adultera**	XL	*Item*	*Iud. Theod.* U II.12.11
270	*De uiro non posse nubere**	XLI	*Item*	*Iud. Theod.* U II.12.33
271	*Ab hostibus capta*	XLII	*Ab ostibus capta*	cf. *Iud. Theod.* U II.12.24–5

* title not in running text in IL

Martenianum chapters XLIII–XLIV (*Collectio CCCC*, cc. 162–63)
are not only interesting for their mistaken identification of Theodorian
sentences for Ancyrian material, as discussed above. Kottje observed the
peculiar spelling of "Anquirinensium" employed here; it is the preferred
spelling in the *Martenianum* and is also found in one peculiar instance in
Hrabanus Maurus's *Paenitentiale ad Heribaldum*, which otherwise would
refer to "concilio Ancyrano" (Migne's edition, printed below, corrected
the reading).[96] In fact, Kottje argued that this particular chapter (c. 25)
in Hrabanus's penitential drew on the *Martenianum*. Rather than the
Martenianum, however, the model for Hrabanus's penitential might just
as easily have been the *Collectio CCCC*; it also has "Synodus Anquirinentium" for the relevant chapters (see c. 161). Other chapters also
illustrate the strong parallels between the three works.

---

96 *Poenitentiale ad Heribaldum*, c. 25 (*PL* 110, col. 490A-B); Kottje, *Die Bussbücher*,
205–6.

xlviii   Collectio CCCC capitulorum

Collectio CCCC capitulorum	Paen. Martenianum	Paen. ad Heribaldum	Source
171 *Si mulier cum muliere fornicat*✱	LXXVII	XXV *De his quae inter se fornicantur, et de his quae semen uirorum suorum pro libidine cibo uel potui miscent*	
		De feminis quae inter se fornicantur in Ancyrano concilio scriptum est:	*Iud. Theod.* U I.2.12 (G 95)
Si mulier cum muliere, annis III,	§ 3 Si mulier cum muliere annos III,	Si mulier cum muliere fornicate fuerit, annos III poeniteat.	
id est, si mulier quasi more fornicatoris ad alteram coniunxerit, iii annis sicut fornicator peniteat.	id est, si mulier quae se more fornicatoris ad alteram coniunxerit III annos sicus fornicator pentiteat.	Item: Si mulier more fornicationis ad alteram coniunxerit, tres annos, sicut fornicator, poeniteat.	*Iud. Theod.* U I.14.15
172ª *Permiscens semen uiri sui*✱			
Sic et illa, quae semen uiri sui in cybo miscens, ut inde plus eius amorem accipiat, peniteat.	sic et illa quae semen uiri sui in cibo miscens ut inde plus eius amorem accipiat peniteat similiter.	Sic et illa quae semen uiri sui in cibo miscens, ut inde plus eius amorem accipiat, poeniteat.	*Iud. Theod.* U I.14.15

Introduction

xlix

	§ 4 Mulier si aliquid interimit arte malefica sua id est per poculum. aut per artem aliquam VII annos peniteat Si paupercula IIII annos peneteat.			cf. *Egb.* VII.7, 8.
173 *Qui cum uirginem fornicat**	§ 5			
Si quis fornicat cum uirgine iii annis.	al. 1 Si quis fornicator cum uirgine III annos peniteat.			cf. *Iud. Theod.* U I.2.1; D 82
174 *Si cum maritata fornicat**				
Si cum maritata, iiii annis: integros ii, alios ii, in xlmis tribus et tribus diebus in ebdomata peniteat.	si cum maritata IIII annos integros II, alios II quadragesimis tribus et tribus diebus ebdomadae peniteat.			cf. *Iud. Theod.* U I.2.1; D 82
175 *Si mulier cum se sola**	al. 2 (Si)			
Mulier sola cum se ipsa coitum habeat, iii annis peniteat.	Mulier sola cum se ipsa coitum habeat III annos peniteat.	Mulier sola, si cum se ipsa coitum habeat, tres annos poeniteat.		cf. *Iud. Theod.* U I.2.13; G 97

---

[a] *This chapter is omitted in L*

* title not in running text in IL

l   Collectio CCCC capitulorum

The table above demonstrates that rather than the *Martenianum*, Hrabanus Maurus could just as well have drawn on the *Collectio CCCC* for this material. This is also the case for chapter 29 of the *Paenitentiale ad Heribaldum*, which according to Kottje also drew on the *Martenianum*.[97] It is possible that instead of the *Martenianum*, Hrabanus drew on a version of the *Collectio CCCC* for this chapter of his penitential. It means that the *terminus post quem non* of 853 for the composition of the *Martenianum* (namely its use in the *Paenitentiale ad Heribaldum*) can no longer be upheld, which (again) opens up the possibility that the Florence manuscript indeed represents the compiler's original copy of the *Martenianum*, as Von Hörmann surmized.

Similarly, other purported borrowings from the *Martenianum* may be attributed to the *Collectio CCCC* instead. The Old English Confessional or *Confessionale Pseudo Egberti* (*c.* 950–1000), for instance, may have adapted material from the *Collectio CCCC* (c. 163), rather than from c. XLIIII of the *Martenianum* in its compilation of articles 16.19.i–16.19.k.[98] Similarly, Burchard's source for his *Decretum* c. 9.1 might have been chapter 74 of the *Collectio CCCC*, rather than *Martenianum* XXXVI.[99]

The Capitularies of Benedictus Levita

When Kottje described the connection between chapter 270 of our collection with *Martenianum* c. 29, he noted a parallel with a passage in the Capitularies of Benedictus Levita.[100] In this case it is possible that either the *Martenianum* or the *Collectio CCCC* provided the material

---

97 *Paenitentiale Martenianum*, c. XLI; *Collectio CCCC capitulorum*, c. 270; *Paen. ad Heribaldum*, c. 29 (*PL* 110, col. 490A-B). See Kottje, *Die Bussbücher*, 206–7, n. 178.

98 Cf. Marianne Elsakkers, "The Early Medieval Latin and Vernacular Vocabulary of Abortion and Embryology," in: Michèle Goyens, Pieter de Leemans, An Smets (eds), *Science Translated: Latin and Vernacular Translations of Scientific Treatises in Medieval Europe* (Louvain, 2008), 377–414, at 407–9. Zubin Mistry, *Abortion in the Early Middle Ages, C. 500–900* (York, 2015), 174–75.

99 See Hartmut Hoffmann and Rudolf Pokorny, *Das Dekret des Bischofs Burchard von Worms. Textstufen—Frühe Verbreitung—Vorlagen*, MGH Hilfsmittel 12 (Munich, 1991), 212. I thank Clemens Radl for this observation.

100 Capitularies of Benedictus Levita, II.LV; *PL* 97, col. 757C and 760C. At the time of writing, this canon was not yet included in the edition-in-progress of www.benedictus.mgh.de; see the edition of book II: http://www.benedictus.mgh.de/edition/aktuell/libII.pdf (13–14) (accessed September 2024).

Introduction

li

here for the Capitularies. There is, however, another instance in which Benedictus Levita very clearly seems to have drawn specifically upon the *Collectio CCCC*.

Collectio CCCC capitulorum	*Capitularies of Benedictus Levita*[101]	Source
80 De penitentia amborum abundanter*	II.CCVIIII *DE PROPINQUITATE*	
...	...	
80f Mulier quae subcubuerit cuilibet iumento simul interfitiatur cum eo.	Mulier, quae subcubuerit cuilibet iumento, simul interficiatur cum eo.	cf. Lev 20:16
80g In nouo: Illa sicut ille qui cum pecoribus coierit xv alii xi annis peniteat.	In nouo illa, sicut ille, qui cum pecoribus coierit, quindecim annis, alii undecim poeniteat.	cf. *Iud. Theod.* U I.2.3
81 *De coinquinatis animalibus** Animalia talia[a] coitu hominum polluta occidantur carnesque canibus proiciantur, sed coria adsumantur. Ubi autem dubium est, non occidantur.	Animalia coitu hominum polluta occidentur carnesque canibus proiciantur; sed coria eorum assumantur. Ubi autem dubium est, non occidantur	cf. *Iud. Theod.* G 139; C 123; U II.11.9; D 54

[a] talia] ad alia L *deest* M
* title not in running text in IL

Chapter CCVIIII in book II reproduces two canons from *Collectio CCCC* c. 80 (drawing from Leviticus and the *Iudicia Theodori* respectively), as well as the first statement of the following chapter (another Theodorian sentence). The combination and sequence of the three canons in both collections very strongly suggest that the compiler of the Capitularies of Benedictus Levita used the *Collectio 400*, especially

---

101 *PL* 97, col. 773B; and http://www.benedictus.mgh.de/edition/aktuell/libII.pdf (35–36).

lii   Collectio CCCC capitulorum

because they concern material from different textual sources.[102] The wording employed in both collections has shared differences compared to the *Iudicia Theodori*,[103] and the Capitularies in fact reproduce the words 'in nouo', which in the *Collectio CCCC* is sometimes used to denote the Theodorian canons.[104] In light of the other similarities with our collection, there is no reason to believe that the words "in nouo" in Benedictus Levita's collection represent a corruption of "item aliud," as the most recent editors assume.[105]

TEXT TRADITION, DATE, AND PROVENANCE

Determining the relationship between the three manuscript copies of the *Collectio CCCC* is extremely difficult. Its use by the compiler of the *Martenianum* and Benedictus Levita indicates that the collection enjoyed ample dissemination and must have been copied more times than the three surviving copies suggest, which means that we lack a great deal of evidence for a precise picture of its diffusion. Furthermore, the three extant copies contain considerable differences, especially in terms of grammar, orthography, and use of rubrics. The text in Paris, Bibliothèque nationale, MS lat. 2316 (L) has the most distinctive readings. Many of these variants are apparently due to the poor linguistic skills of the scribe, who does not always seem to have had a full grasp on the text he was copying, resulting in a multitude of grammatical infelicities and copying errors such as lineskip. While this need not mean that the copy is further removed from the original text (it is unwise to assume the archetype of the collection was grammatically flawless), it does indicate that it cannot have served as the direct exemplar of either of the other two surviving copies.

A canonical collection of mostly well-known authoritative texts such as the *Collectio CCCC* invites subsequent scribes and scholars to make small adjustments and corrections, since they may have had the source texts of the canons at their disposal in their libraries. Munich, Clm 4592 (M) seems the product of such deliberate attempts to correct

---

102 http://www.benedictus.mgh.de/edition/aktuell/libII.pdf (36).

103 For instance the omission of 'quod generant, sit in usu et' in between 'sed' and 'coria'; http://www.benedictus.mgh.de/edition/aktuell/libII.pdf (36, n. 323).

104 Also in chapter 58: "Canones nouae."

105 http://www.benedictus.mgh.de/edition/aktuell/libII.pdf (36, n. 320).

Introduction

the text and improve its readability. Many of its improvements are not shared with the other copies. Vienna, lat. 522 (I) takes a middle position here: it presents a conscientiously copied text, but without some of the enhancements in M. None of the witnesses is thus a direct copy of another. Each has its own significant variants and omissions. At the same time, all witnesses at times share errors with another copy against the third.

The different treatment of the descriptive chapter headings in the three witnesses suggests an evolution of this aspect of the collection and might even illustrate where to place the three manuscript copies in this development. Only the copy in M has rubrics for every chapter in the text proper as well as a full *index titulorum* preceding the collection. Witness I also has a full *index titulorum*, but only some of its chapters in the text proper are introduced by a rubric. The wording of these rubrics does not always correspond with the wording in the *index titulorum*. L has the same sporadic rubrics at the same instances as I and often in the same wording. The collection in L is preceded by an unmethodical list of random chapter headings, which are also found in the text proper (see appendix). The use of chapter titles in M, therefore, strikes us as the most sophisticated. Since it seems unlikely that subsequent scribes would decide to omit such a functional practice, it seems fair to assume that the chapter headings in M represent a later stage in the text tradition of the *Collectio CCCC*, when a scribe decided to enter the rubrics of the *index titulorum* in the text proper. This *index titulorum* had been compiled in an earlier stage, as demonstrated by its presence in I. The random rubrics in the text proper of the latter, however, do not seem to have any connection with the *index titulorum*. Instead, they appear to be remnants of an even earlier phase in which both the list of chapter titles and the headings within the text proper were apparently random and haphazard. This phase seems preserved in the arrangement in L. Despite the geographical and temporal proximity of I and M, neither is the direct exemplar of the other, although they could stem from a common exemplar, in which case the entering of the titles of the *index titulorum* as rubrics within the text was an innovation executed by the scribe responsible for M. A possible stemma of this development, based solely on the use of chapter titles, could look like this:

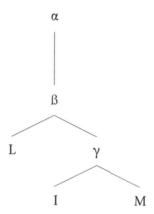

ß signifies a recension in which some descriptive headings are entered in the text proper, a list of which is added to the collection in L. In γ, this list of haphazard rubrics is replaced by an *index titulorum* with descriptive titles for each of the 404 chapters. The recension in I still retains the intermittent rubrics in the text proper. In M, these have been replaced by the titles as they appear in the *index titulorum*.

It is important to stress that this reconstruction of the development of the use of rubrics in the *Collectio CCCC* may mirror the progression of the text itself, but it is equally possible that these processes ran an entirely independent course. The stemma above therefore cannot claim to represent the relationships between the texts proper of the extant copies.

The *terminus post quem non* for the composition of the collection is provided by the date of its manuscript witnesses. The *Collectio CCCC* survives in three manuscripts from the first half of the ninth century: two south-Bavarian manuscripts (M and I), and one southern French manuscript (L). A fourth manuscript, containing perhaps only the preface to the collection and destroyed in the Second World War, may have been from an even earlier date as a product from the Rhine region. The three extant manuscripts demonstrate that by the early ninth century, the collection had already received some editorial attention from scribes, explaining the differences sketched above. The *terminus ante quem non* is provided by the sources used by the collection's compiler. The youngest datable source of the collection appears to be an unknown letter from

Introduction

lv

Pope Sergius (687–701) who is mentioned by name in chapters 159 and 160. This prompted Maassen, quite prudently, to propose a compilation date for the *Collectio CCCC* in the eighth century or after.[106] This *terminus* is also supported by the use of the various redactions of Archbishop Theodore's *Iudicia*, which are roughly contemporary to Sergius's papacy. The canons taken from the so-called *Vetus Gallica*–version of the Irish *Synodus II S. Patricii* seem to stem from the early years of the eighth century.[107] The collection can therefore safely be dated to the second quarter of the eighth century at the earliest, or the first half of the ninth century at the very latest.[108]

The absence of some other sources in the collection may suggest a date earlier rather than later in this timespan. The *Collectio CCCC* lacks clear connections with the *Collectio Vetus Gallica*, which became particularly influential following its redaction at Corbie in the second quarter of the eighth century.[109] There are, similarly, no direct overwhelming signs of influence from the the *Collectio canonum Hibernensis*, from the first quarter of the eighth century, or from canon law collections such as the *Dionysio-Hadriana*. One might expect the influence of works of Bede, or royal capitularies in a collection from the later eighth or early ninth centuries, and these are similarly missing. These observations, however, amount to nothing more than *argumenta e silentio* and only deserve the most cautious of considerations.

The workplace of the compiler of the *Collectio CCCC* must be a location where the peculiar combination of sources for the collection was available in the eighth century. That is to say: a good selection of continental as well as insular material. The most extensively used insular source is without doubt the *Iudicia Theodori*, apparently in the version resembling both the *Paenitentiale Umbrense* and the *Canones Gregorii*. The latter is attested in early eighth-century continental texts,[110] confirming its presence in northern Francia at that time. The

---

106 Maassen, *Geschichte der Quellen*, 846.
107 Meeder, "Text and Identities."
108 Mordek, *Kirchenrecht und Reform*, 162.
109 Ibid, 162–64.
110 I.e. the *Scarapsus* of Pirmin (see E. Hauswald, "Pirmins Scarapsus. Einleitung und Edition," unpubl. PhD diss. University of Konstanz, 2006, xv, 73); the *Excarpsus Cummeani* (see Körntgen, "Der Excarpsus Cummeani"), and the *Capitula Iudiciorum* (see

lvi   Collectio CCCC capitulorum

Paenitentiale Umbrense found its way to Corbie prior to the revision
of the *Vetus Gallica* before the middle of the eighth century, possibly
through the agency of Boniface.[111] The same collection is also our first
continental witness to the *Synodus II S. Patricii* in the version that was
used by the compiler of the *Collectio CCCC*.[112] The peculiar version of
the *Sanblasiana* drawn upon by the *Collectio CCCC* (uniquely preserved
in the Northumbrian manuscript Cologne, Dombibliothek MS 213) need
not have originated from the British Isles (although it might have): Italy
or Southern Gaul have been suggested as alternative origins.[113] The
compiler of the *Collectio CCCC* probably did not make direct use of the
Cologne manuscript (see above) and therefore could have drawn from a
different, possibly continental, manuscript copy now lost to us.

Given the richness of insular material (and connections) in northeastern France, I should like to propose an origin in this region some
time in the second half of the eighth century. The two Bavarian
manuscript witnesses suggest close ties with this area as well.[114] The
dominance of canons on the conduct of secular clergy, rather than
monks, would suggest an origin in an episcopal center rather than a
monastic center.

PRINCIPLES OF THIS EDITION

The main text in this edition of the *Collectio CCCC* is based on the
reading in I. This manuscript presents a relatively complete text
which appears to have been copied with care. Its text is, therefore, to
be preferred over the text in L, which preserves many erroneous and
idiosyncratic readings, apparently the product a careless copyist with
limited grammatical skills. The considerable lacunae in witness M are

---

Letha Mahadevan, "Überlieferung und Verbreitung des Bußbuchs 'Capitula Iudiciorum,'"
Zeitschrift der Savigny-Stiftung für Rechtsgeschichte, Kanonistische Abteilung 72 [1986],
17–75).

111 Mordek, *Kirchenrecht und Reform*, 86.

112 Meeder, "Text and Identities," 21.

113 See Elliot, "Canon Law Collections," 247–50.

114 Paul Fournier, "De l'influence de la collection irlandaise sur la formation
des collections canoniques,'" *Nouvelle revue historique de droit français et étranger* 23
(1899), 27–78, at 40–41; see also Reynolds, "Unity and Diversity," 111. Jean Gaudemet
suggested the collection may have been composed in Gaul: Gaudemet, "Survivances
romaines"; Kéry, *Canonical Collections*.

Introduction

lvii

the reason why this copy cannot serve as the basis for this edition, despite its orthographic and grammatical superiority.

Generally, the orthography, word order, and chapter numbering of manuscript I are thus privileged throughout the edition, except when I is clearly in error. This is reported in the apparatus criticus as a variant reading. I have tried to avoid constructing a mythical archetypical text, divorced from the shape and content of any of the extant copies. This editorial "light touch" means that the editorial interventions are mostly limited to obviously erroneous, nonsensical, or unnecessarily confusing readings in I. In these cases, I have provided a reading from L and/or M or, if these were unavailable, cautiously emended the text in light of the sources preserving I's orthography, based on the most common form of the word in manuscript I. In the edition, $ę$ (*e-caudata*) is expanded to *ae*. The majuscule *V* is only used for numbers, while minuscule *u* and majuscule *U* represent both the consonantal and the vocalic and semi-vocalic sounds. The punctuation does not follow the manuscripts' practice but leans toward modern usage with sparing use of commas. Here, I mostly follow the practice of modern editions of the source texts.

The exception to this privileging of I concerns its use of titles. Witness I only sporadically supplies rubrics in the text proper, like L, although it has a full *index titulorum* preceding the collection. Chapter titles in the running text, however, greatly enhance the accessibility of the text (as the scribe of M or M's exemplar recognized). For this reason, this edition has chapter titles in the text, introducing each chapter. These titles as supplied from M, following its usage of presenting the titles in the text proper, or, in case of a lacuna in M, the *index titulorum* in I. The sporadic titles in I are noted in the critical apparatus. The *index titulorum* as preserved in I (fols. 113v–123v) and M (fols. 158r–161r) is printed before the text proper. Manuscript L's nonconventional list of titles is printed in appendix 1.

Folio numbers are given in the margin. There are two apparatus on each page; a source apparatus and the critical apparatus. The former presents the sources from which the collection draws, generally in their most original form. Thus, for example, a passage taken from the acts of the Council of Nicaea is referred to as such and not to the *Collectio Sanblasiana*, wherein the compiler might have found his example. The canons mined from the *Iudicia Theodori* are listed with a reference to the recension (*U, C, B, D, or G*), which most closely reflects the reading in

lviii
Collectio CCCC capitulorum

our collection, but with a mention of other parallels. A "cf." preceding the reference indicates that the compiler quoted the passage only partly or in a substantially rewritten form. Quotes within a borrowed passage (often biblical verses) are generally ignored and quotation marks are only introduced when their use facilitates the understanding of the passage (for instance when the source introduces a dialogue or a question-and-answer format).

The apparatus criticus lists all variant readings in L and M and, whenever editorial emendation was called for, the original reading in I. It should always be possible for readers to reconstruct the particular reading in any of the three manuscripts. Whenever the original copyists or subsequent scribe made corrections, this is marked by an asterisk (*) when the corrected form is in the main text, or the form "x *corr.* y." It also lists the lacunae in the various witnesses due to the loss of leaves.

Collectio CCCC capitulorum

SIGLA

I   Vienna, Österreichische National Bibliothek, MS 522, fols 113v-192v (*saec.* ix^{med})

M   Munich, Bayerische Staatsbibliothek, Clm 4592, fols 120r-157v (*saec.* ix$^{2/4}$)

L   Paris, Bibliothèque nationale de France, MS lat. 2316, fols 84r-120r (*saec.* ix$^{2/4}$)

Collectio CCCC capitulorum

1

I 113v;		INCIPIUNT CAPITULA KANONUM	
M 158r	I	DE CONFIRMATIONE CARITATIS DEI	
	II	DE AMORE CONFIRMATA PROXIMI PER DEUM	
	III	DE DEO QUOD NON EST PERSONARUM ACCEPTOR	5
I 114r	IIII	DE PUBLICA INCREPATIONE ET DE FRATRE LUCRARE	
	V	DE OBLIUIONE ULTIONIS PRO DEO DIMITTENDUM	
	VI	DE CICATRICE CRIMINATORIS A DEO EIECTO	
	VII	DE MERCEDE AD DEUM CLAMANTIUM	
	VIII	DE HONORE CAECI ET SURDI	10
	VIIII	NON FURANDUM NEC MENTIENDUM	
	X	NON OCCIDENDUM NEQUE MOECHANDUM	
	XI	NON PERIURARE INANITER	
	XII	DE DILECTIONE AMICI ET ODIO INIMICI	
	XIII	DE OCULIS ET DENTIBUS ERUENDIS	15
	XIIII	ULTIONEM SEPTIES DIMITTENDUM	
	XV	DE MULIERE REPUDIATA	
	XVI	DE MARITO FIDELE	
	XVII	DE HONORE PARENTUM	
	XVIII	DE DIIS ALIENIS	20
	XVIIII	DE MUNERIBUS CECATIS	
	XX	NON ERIS ONEROSUS PEREGRINO	
M 158v	XXI	NON COMEDENDUM CARNEM PREGUSTATAM	
	XXII	DEOS NON DETRAHERE NEC PRINCIPES	
	XXIII	NEC CANTATORES SCISCITARE	25
	XXIIII	DE DECIMIS ET PRIMITIIS	
	XXV	DE SEGETE ET UINEA	
	XXVI	DE SERUIS EMPTICIIS	
I 114v	XXVII	DE FILIA FAMULATA	

---

2 INCIPIUNT CAPITULA KANONUM] *deest* M   **5** QUOD NON] NON I   **5** ACCEPTOR] DEUS
SED TIMENTIUM DEUM I   **6** ET DE] DE I   **6** FRATRE] FRATRES M   **8** EIECTO] ELECTO
I   **12** MOECHANDUM] MECHANDUM* I   **13** INANITER] INANTER* I   **14** DE DILECTIONE]
DILECTIO I   **14** ODIO] ODIUM I   **15** ET DENTIBUS] DENTIS I   **15** ERUENDIS] ERUENTIS
I   **21** CECATIS] CAECATIS M   **22** ONEROSUS] HONEROSIS* I   **23** COMEDENDUM] COMEDEN-
DAM M   **23** PREGUSTATAM] PREGUSTATA I PRAEGUSTATAM M   **24** PRINCIPES] PRINCIPEM I
25 SCISCITARE] SISCITARE* I   **26** PRIMITIIS] PRIMITIUIS IM   **28** EMPTICIIS] EMPTICIS M

Collectio CCCC capitulorum

XXVIII	DE UIRGINE SEDUCTA
XXVIIII	DE LUSCO SERUO UEL ANCILLA
XXX	DE PERCUSSIONE MANCIPIORUM
XXXI	DE PUGNO ET LAPIDE
XXXII	DE PREGNANTE PERCUSSA
XXXIII	DE ADPREHENSA UERECUNDA
XXXIIII	DE CORNUPETO PECODE
XXXV	SI CORNUPETIERIT FILIUM
XXXVI	DE UULNERATO BOUE
XXXVII	SI ANTE ERIT CORNUPETUS
XXXVIII	DE CISTERNA APERTA
XXXVIIII	DE SEPTEM GRADIBUS CONSANGUINITATIS
XL	DE MATRIMONIIS
XLI	DE PROPINQUITATE GREGORIUS RESPONDIT
XLII	DE FURTU BOUIS ET OUIS
XLIII	DE FURE EFFRINGENTE DOMUM
XLIIII	DE COMMENDATA PECUNIA
XLV	DE DIIS ADIURANTIBUS
XLVI	DE ASINO COMMENDATO
XLVII	QUOD NON SOLUM FUR IN MAGNIS
XLVIII	DE PECUNIA AECCLESIASTICA GREGORIUS
XLVIIII	DE LESIONE AGRI ET UINEAE
L	DE FOCO UAGO
LI	DE MUTUO POPULO DEI
LII	DE PIGNO ACCEPTO ET MOLA REDDENDA
LIII	DE DUABUS UEL TRIBUS TESTIBUS
LIIII	SI QUID FORTUITU ACCIDERIT
LV	SI FUERIT ALIQUA CAUSA APUD IUDICES
LVI	DE NOCTURNA POLLUTIONE LAICORUM SEU SACERDOTUM
LVII	DE UOTO UIRORUM ET UIDUARUM ET MULIERUM

I 115r (at line L)

M 159r (at line LIIII)

---

3 PERCUSSIONE⌉ PERCUSSORE I PERCUSSONE* M   **7** CORNUPETO⌉ CORNUPETE M   **8** SI⌉ DI* I
8 CORNUPETIERIT⌉ CORNUPETERIT M   **16** EFFRINGENTE⌉ EFFRIGENTE* I   **21** AECCLESIASTICA⌉
ECCLESIASTICA M   **22** LESIONE⌉ ELYMONIA M   **26** DUABUS⌉ DUOBUS M   **27** LIIII⌉ LV M (*praecedit* LIIII DE MENDACIS TESTIBUS M)   **27** ACCIDERIT⌉ ACCEDERIT* I   **28** LV⌉ LVI M   **29** LVI⌉
LVII M   **30** LVII⌉ LVIII M   **30** UOTO⌉ UOTU I

Collectio CCCC capitulorum   3

	LVIII	DE SOLUTIONE UOTIS AB EPISCOPO
	LVIIII	DE MONACHORUM UOTIS AB ABBATE
	LX	QUI SE UOUERIT ET ITERAUERIT
	LXI	DE MENSTRUATA AECCLESIAM INTRARE
	LXII	DE LAUACRO UIRORUM
	LXIII	DE CREANDIS LIBERIS
	LXIIII	DE INGRESSU MULIERIS AECCLESIAM
	LXV	DE PREGNANTE BAPTIZANDA
	LXVI	DE ABLACTATIONE INFANTIS
	LXVII	DE ABSTINENTIA ANTE PARTUM ET COMMUNIONE
	LXVIII	DE DUOBUS GERMANIS FRATRIBUS
	LXVIIII	DE PROPINQUITATE CARNIS
	LXX	DE AMBORUM LICENCIA SERUITUTIS DEI
	LXXI	QUOD LEX MULTA PROHIBEAT
	LXXII	DE HEREDIBUS MOSAICE RATIONE
I 115v	LXXIIII	LEO ANCILLARUM FILIOS DE HEREDITATE ABIECIT
	LXXV	LEO ANCILLAM A THORO ABIECIT
	LXXVI	LEO PUELLAS CONCUBINARUM PERCUSSIT
	LXXVII	APOSTOLUS MATRIMONIO LICENTIAM DEDIT
I 159v	LXXVIII	NON COMMISCENDUM CUM MASCULO
	LXXVIIII	NON COIRE CUM OMNI PECODE
	LXXX	DE PENITENTIA AMBORUM ABUNDANTER
	LXXXI	DE COINQUINATIS ANIMALIBUS
	LXXXII	DE PREDA DIUIDENDA
	LXXXIII	DE EQUALI PARTE PREDAE
	LXXXIIII	NON MORIATUR PATER PRO FILIO
	LXXXV	DE ALIENA PECUNIA

---

1 LVIII] LVIIII M   1 SOLUTIONE] DESOLUTIONE IM   2 LVIIII] LX M   2 ABBATE] ABBATO M
3 LX] LXI M   4 LXI] LXII M   4 AECCLESIAM] ECCLESIAE M   5 LXII] LXIII M   6 LXIII]
LXIIII M   7 LXIIII] LXV M   7 AECCLESIAM] ECLESIAE M   8 LXV] LXVI M   9 LXVI] LXVII
M   9 ABLACTATIONE] ABLATIONE I ABLUTIONE M   10 LXVII] LXVIII M   11 LXVIII] LXVIIII
M   12 LXVIIII] LXX M   13 LXX] LXXI M   13 LICENCIA] LICENTIA M   14 LXXI] LXXII M
15 LXXII] LXXIIII M   15 MOSAICE RATIONE] MOSAICE RATIONIS I deest M   16 ABIECIT] EIECIT*
I EIECIT M   17 ANCILLAM] ANCELLAM* I   22 PENITENTIA] PAENITENTIA M   22 ABUNDANTER]
HABUNDANTER I   23 COINQUINATIS] INCOINQUINATIS I   24 PREDA] PRAEDA M   25 EQUALI]
QUALE* I QUALE M

Collectio CCCC capitulorum

LXXXVI	DE HONORE UIDUAE FILIATIS
LXXXVII	DE UIDUA SINE LIBERIS
LXXXVIII	DE DIUERSITATE MORUM AECCLESIARUM
LXXXVIIII	DE ELECTIONE EPISCOPORUM ET EXAMINATIONE
XC	DE ORDINATIONE EPISCOPI
XCI	DE ORDINATIONE PRESBYTERI ET CETERORUM
XCII	QUO TEMPORE PASCHA CAELEBRATUR
XCIII	NON INUADENDUM ALIENA PARROCHIA
XCIIII	EPISCOPUS PRECIPITUR RES AECCLESIAE
XCV	DE HIS QUAE INDIGET AECLESIA
XCVI	DE USURIS EXIGENDIS
XCVII	UT CURA RERUM AECCLESIAE EPISCOPIS
XCVIII	DE CURA UIDUARUM EPISCOPIS
XCVIIII	NE AMANT SAECULARES RES
C	NON SUMENDUM PER PECUNIAM DIGNITATEM
CI	NE SUMAT PER POTESTATEM AECCLESIAM
CII	NON AUDENDUM EXTRA TERMINOS PROPRIOS
CIII	QUIS PRIMUS EPISCOPUS IN GENTE
CIIII	DE SACRIFICANTE ET NON MANENTE
CV	QUIA NON DEBEANT SACERDOTES PERCUTERE
CVI	QUIA DAMNATI OFFICIUM NON DEBEANT USURPARE
CVII	UT BIS IN ANNO CONCILIA EPISCOPORUM
CVIII	NULLUS EPISCOPUS <UEL> PRESBITER PEREGRINET SINE LITTERAM
CVIIII	DE EBRIETATE SACERDOTUM
CX	QUI CUM HERETICIS ORAUERIT DAMNETUR
CXI	DE BAPTISMO HERETICORUM
CXII	NON ITERUM BAPTIZANDUM
CXIII	DE HEREDITATE EPISCOPI IN OBITUM EIUS
CXIIII	DE DAMNATIONE GRADUUM AECCLESIA
CXV	NON ORDINANDUM SINE CONSILIO

I 116r

---

1 FILIATIS⌉ *deest* M   **2** UIDUA⌉ UIDUAE M   **3** AECCLESIARUM⌉ ECCLESIARUM M
7 CAELEBRATUR⌉ CELEBRATUR M   **9** EPISCOPUS⌉ EPISCOPI M   **9** AECCLESIAE⌉ ECCLESIAE
M   **10** AECLESIA⌉ ECCLESIA M   **12** AECCLESIAE⌉ ECCLESIARUM M   **12** EPISCOPIS⌉ EPISCO-
PUS HABEAT M   **13** EPISCOPIS⌉ EPISCOPI M   **15** DIGNITATEM⌉ DIGNITAT I   **16** NE⌉ NON M
16 AECCLESIAM⌉ AECCLESIAE I ECCLESIIS M   **19** MANENTE⌉ MANE I   **20** DEBEANT⌉ DEBENT M
21 OFFICIUM⌉ *deest* I   **21** USURPARE⌉ USURPARI I   **22** CVII⌉ *capitula* CVII…CCLXII *lacuna* M

Collectio CCCC capitulorum

5

	CXVI	Non uagandum per loca sacerdotibus
	CXVII	Episcopus sedenti et presbiteri eadem
	CXVIII	Episcopus numquam sine testibus iudicatur
I 116r	CXVIIII	Episcopus res aecclesia non utatur quasi sua
	CXX	Episcopus nullum prohibeat intrare aecclesia
	CXXI	Episcopi desidentes reconciliet
	CXXII	Episcopus discordantes per sinodus damnet
	CXXIII	Episcopus fratres ad pacem hortetur
	CXXIIII	Nullum absentem damnare
	CXXV	De altera aecclesia nullum elegatur si alterum est
	CXXVI	Nec alter alterius monachum ordinet
	CXXVII	Causae magnae ad sedem apostolicam
	CXXVIII	Nullus sacerdos canones ignorat
	CXXVIIII	De confessione uera criminis et mendatii
	CXXX	De ecclesia in morte episcopi
	CXXXI	De territorio episcopi in alterius parrochia
	CXXXII	Episcopus non damnetur in repetendo propriae iuris
	CXXXIII	De episcopo non faciente ministerium
	CXXXIIII	<De> propria parrochia relicta
	CXXXV	Segregato ab alio non recipi
	CXXXVI	Alter alterius non ordinet
	CXXXVII	Nemo episcopum contemnens
	CXXXVIII	Nemo in domo cum excommunicato
	CXXXVIIII	Nemo cum damnato clerico orauerit
	CXL	Laicus excommonicatus non recipiatur
	CXLI	Excommonicato protelletur correctio
I 117r	CXLII	Presbiteri propter episcopi licentiam nihil habentes
	CXLIII	Qui se ipsum castrauerit non potest esse clericus quia se ipsum amputauit
	CXLIIII	De clerico damnato amputato
	CXLV	De penitentia laici castrati

---

3 iudicatur] dicat I   **8** fratres] frater I   **14** De confessione uera criminis et men-
datii] De crimine uere confessio et mendatii I   **17** damnetur] damnet I   **24** clerico]
clero* I   **25** recipiatur] recipitur* I   **28** quia] qui I   **29** amputauit] amputabit I
30 De] *deest* I

Collectio CCCC capitulorum

CXLVI	DE UXORE REPUDIATA
CXLVII	DE ORDINATIS PER IGNORANTIAM
CXLVIII	ILLIS ALIQUA MISERICORDIA
CXLVIIII	DE ORDINATIS INDISCRETE
CL	NON PREFERENTUR DIACONI PRESBITERIS
CLI	SACERDOTI SECUM MULIERES NON HABENTES
CLII	QUI SINE ELECTIONE ORDINATI ABICIANTUR
CLIII	DE PROPOSITO MONACHI PROPRIO
CLIIII	DE PUELLIS NON CONSECRATIS
CLV	DE DISCIPULO BAPTISMATIS
CLVI	QUI NESCIUNT IN QUA SECTA BAPTIZANTUR
CLVII	DE BAPTIZATIS CAPTIUIS A GENTILIBUS
CLVIII	QUI IN PAENITENTIA MORIUNTUR
CLVIIII	SI ORDINETUR NON BAPTIZATUS
CLX	QUI AESTIMATIONE HABET QUOD BAPTIZATUS ESSET
CLXI	QUI ADULTERIUM CONMISERIT
CLXII	DE NECANTIBUS PARTUS SUOS
CLXIII	QUI ABORTIUUM FACIUNT
CLXIIII	QUI HOMICIDIUM FACIUNT
CLXV	QUI CASU HOMICIDIUM FACIUNT
CLXVI	SI MATER OCCIDAT FILIUM
CLXVII	DE PENITENTIA PAUPERCULAE
CLXVIII	QUI NECAT <FILIUM> SINE BAPTISMO
CLXVIIII	QUI AUGURIA ET AUSPITIA SERUAT
CLXX	QUI RETRO FACIT CUM MULIERE
CLXXI	SI MULIER CUM MULIERE FORNICAT
CLXXII	PERMISCENS SEMEN UIRI SUI
CLXXIII	QUI CUM UIRGINE FORNICAT
CLXXIIII	SI CUM MARITATA FORNICAT
CLXXV	SI MULIER CUM SE SOLA
CLXXVI	<DE> DISPONSA SORORE
CLXXVII	SI DUOBUS FRATRIBUS NUPSERIT

I 117r

---

3 ALIQUA MISERICORDIA] ALIQUAM MISERICORDIAM I   **8** PROPOSITO] PROPOSITU I
10 DISCIPULO] SCUPULO I   **15** QUOD BAPTIZATUS ESSET] BAPTISMA I   **23** SINE] SI NON
I   **31** SORORE] SORORICIA I

Collectio CCCC capitulorum

	CLXXVIII	Presbiter secundis nuptiis non debet inesse
	CLXXVIIII	Presbiter qui admiserit corporale peccatum
	CLXXX	Qui commonia ieiunia contemnit
	CLXXXI	De tribus gradibus continentium
	CLXXXII	Si clericus commodauerit
	CLXXXIII	Ut non sint sacerdotes procuratores
	CLXXXIIII	Ut episcopi trans mare non proficiscantur
	CLXXXV	Non licet episcopo uendere pretia ecclesiae
	CLXXXVI	De benedictione sponsi et sponsae
	CLXXXVII	De ueste sanctaemonialis feminae
I 118r	CLXXXVIII	De subdiacono
	CLXXXVIIII	Quid sit acholitus
	CXC	De exorcista
	CXCI	De lectore
	CXCII	De ostiario
	CXCIII	De cantatore
	CXCIIII	De dispendio uiduae
	CXCV	Ne quis clericus ad iuditia secularia \<eat\>
	CXCVI	Qui contra metropolitanu
	CXCVII	Peregrinus non ministrare
	CXCVIII	Ad abicienda crimina conspirationis
	CXCVIIII	Post mortem episcopi non licet predare
	CC	De monasteriis consecratis
	CCI	Non transgredi fidem sanctorum
	CCII	De principatu Constantinopolitani episcopi
	CCIII	\<De primatu\> Alexandrini episcopi
	CCIIII	De primatu Antiochenae \<episcopi\>
	CCV	De Ponto \<et\> Ponticae
	CCVI	De principatu barbaricis
	CCVII	Si depositus fuerit episcopus
	CCVIII	Nullus sollicitat alterius clericum
	CCVIIII	De accusato episcopo
	CCX	Si quis in aliquibus episcopus accusatus

---

9 benedictione⌉ benedictio* I   **10** feminae⌉ femina I   **19** metropolitanu⌉ metropolitano* I   **24** transgredi⌉ gredi* I   **33** episcopus⌉ episcopo* I

Collectio CCCC capitulorum

	CCXI	Ut nullus episcopus eligat successorem in exitum vitae	*I 119r*
	CCXII	Ut nullus gradus aduersus alium	
	CCXIII	Presbiter cum XLIIII testimoniis \<damnabitur\>	
	CCXIIII	Ut nullus gradus intrat in curia	
5	CCXV	Nemo clericum caedat	
	CCXVI	Si presbiter sumat coniugium post XII annum sacrificat	
	CCXVII	Nemo iudicabit primam sedem	
	CCXVIII	Nullus eligatur de altera \<ecclesia\>	
	CCXVIIII	Facultas resistendi	
10	CCXX	Episcopus ab omni labe securus	
	CCXXI	De ultima paenitentia	
	CCXXII	Nemo gradatis manus inponent	
	CCXXIII	Episcopus \<cum\> collegis sedeat nisi in aecclesia	
	CCXXIIII	Episcopus non longe ab aecclesia \<hospitiolum habeat\>	
15	CCXXV	Episcopus hereticorum libros non legat	
	CCXXVI	Episcopus in synodo non litiget	
	CCXXVII	Episcopus legatum mittat pro se ad synodum	
	CCXXVIII	De penitentia in infirmitate	
	CCXXVIIII	In fine uitae commonio non denegetur	
20	CCXXX	De auditorio nullus egrediatur	
	CCXXXI	Clericus se ipsum ubique ostendat	
	CCXXXII	De artifitio debet uestire	
	CCXXXIII	De artifitio uictum quaerat	
	CCXXXIIII	Qui episcopis contemnet recurrat ad synodum	*I 119v*
25	CCXXXV	Qui cantat in epulis clericus excommunicatur	
	CCXXXVI	Penitentes sepeliantur aecclesia	
	CCXXXVII	De honore confessoris	
	CCXXXVIII	De uidua adulescentula	
	CCXXXVIIII	De clerico adolatore	
30	CCXL	Maledictus degradetur	
	CCXLI	Populus docendus est	
	CCXLII	Si monachi procreantes filios	
	CCXLIII	De uirgines habitantibus in monasterio	

---

6 sacrificat⌉ sacrifiter I   **13** collegis⌉ colliga I   **16** litiget⌉ liget* I

Collectio CCCC capitulorum 9

	CCXLIIII	DE UIDUIS DIU PERMANSURIS
	CCXLV	QUI AB HERETICIS BAPTIZATI
	CCXLVI	QUI PASCHA UNO DIE CAELEBRATUR
	CCXLVII	DUO EPISCOPI NON SINT IN UNA CIUITATE
	CCXLVIII	DE AMENTIBUS
	CCXLVIIII	DE INERGUMINIS
	CCL	DE PUBLICIS ODIIS EXARSIS
	CCLI	DE LAICIS TRIBUS TEMPORIBUS NON COMMONICANT
	CCLII	MONASTERIUM EPISCOPO TESTE FUNDANDUM EST
	CCLIII	DE MONACHO UAGO
	CCLIIII	NULLUS ALTERIUS MONACHUM ACCIPIAT
	CCLV	NULLUS EPISCOPUM PRETER IN UILLA III TEMPORIBUS \<CELEBRAT\>
	CCLVI	EPISCOPUS CORRIGAT ABBATES
I 120r	CCLVII	DE DONO DATO PRO ANIMABUS
	CCLVIII	QUI MORTE DIGNUS SUBICIENDUS SERUITUTI
	CCLVIIII	DE INHABITANTE SINE UOTO
	CCLX	DE PECCATORIBUS EXCOMMONICATIS
	CCLXI	DE PENITENTIBUS POST RUINAS
	CCLXII	DE SUSPECTIS CAUSIS
	CCLXIII	DE LAPSIS POST GRADUM
	CCLXIIII	DE TRIBUS SEMINIBUS EUANGELIORUM
	CCLXV	DE FURTIS RESTITUENDIS
	CCLXVI	QUI POST RENUNTIATIONEM REUERSURUS
	CCLXVII	DE ADULTERA
M 160r	CCLXVIII	DE LAUATIONE MATRIMONII
	CCLXVIIII	DE MULIERE ADULTERA
	CCLXX	DE UIRO NON POSSE NUBERE
	CCLXXI	DE UXORE CAPTA AB HOSTIIS
	CCLXXII	SI IN CAPTIUITATEM PERDUCTA
	CCLXXIII	QUI UOUIT POST MORTEM UIRI
	CCLXXIIII	DE MULIERE MORTUA
	CCLXXV	DE UIRO MORTUO

---

7 EXARSIS] EXARDESCANT I   **20** GRADUM] GRADUUM I   **25** LAUATIONE] LABATIONE I
26 ADULTERA] ADULTER M   **28** HOSTIIS] HOSTIBUS M   **29** CAPTIUITATEM] CAPTIUITATE M
29 PERDUCTA] PRAEDUCTA M   **30** UOUIT] NOUIT I

Collectio CCCC capitulorum

10

CCLXXVI	DE UOTO UIRGINITATIS	
CCLXXVII	DE RECONCILIATIONE MULIERIS	
CCLXXVIII	DE PENITENTIA INTIMA	*I 120v*
CCLXXVIIII	UNA PENITENTIA PUELLAE ET UIDUAE	
CCLXXX	SI OCCIDAT FILIUM	
CCLXXXI	SI PAUPERCULA OCCIDAT	
CCLXXXII	SI MORITUR SINE BAPTISMO	
CCLXXXIII	QUI NECAT SINE BAPTISMO	
CCLXXXIIII	SI ALITER MORITUR SINE BAPTISMO	
CCLXXXV	DE PENITENTIA SI ALTERAM DUXERIT	
CCLXXXVI	SI MENSTRUO COIERIT	
CCLXXXVII	SI CUM SORORE	
CCLXXXVIII	SI CUM MATRE	
CCLXXXVIIII	SI SAEPE FACIENS FORNICATIONEM	
CCXC	SI SEMEN IN OS MISERIT	
CCXCI	DE GUSTANDO SANGUINIS	
CCXCII	DE ABSTINENTIA ANTE PASCHA	
CCXCIII	DESPONSATA PUELLA	
CCXCIIII	DE SANCTAMONIALE FORNICARIA	
CCXCV	DE FORNICARIA CUM ILLA	
CCXCVI	DE ILLA PENITENTIA	
CCXCVII	DE ESCIS INMUNDIS	
CCXCVIII	QUI A BESTIIS LACERANTUR	
CCXCVIIII	DE MORTICINIS	*I 121r*
CCC	DE PORCIS BIBENTIBUS SANGUINEM	
CCCI	DE PORCIS MANDUCANTIBUS CADAUERA	*M 160v*

---

3 PENITENTIA⌉ NITENTIA* I PAENITENTIA M **4** CCLXXVIIII⌉ *deest* M **4** PENITENTIA⌉ PAE-
NITENTIA M **5** CCLXXX⌉ CCLXXVIIII M **6** CCLXXXI⌉ CCLXXX M **7** CCLXXXII⌉ CCLXXXI M
7 BAPTISMO⌉ BAPTISMO BAPTISMO M **8** CCLXXXIII⌉ CCLXXXII M **9** CCLXXXIIII⌉ CCLXXXIII
M **10** CCLXXXV⌉ CCLXXXIIII M **10** PENITENTIA⌉ PITENTIA I PAENITENTIA M **10** ALTERAM⌉
ALTERA I **11** CCLXXXVI⌉ CCLXXXV M **11** MENSTRUO⌉ MENSTRO I **11** COIERIT⌉ COLERIT I
12 CCLXXXVII⌉ CCLXXXVI M **13** CCLXXXVIII⌉ CCLXXXVII M **14** CCLXXXVIIII⌉ CCLXXXVIII
M **14** SAEPE⌉ SEPAE I **15** CCXC⌉ CCLXXXVIIII M **16** CCXCI⌉ CCXC M **17** CCXCII⌉ CCXCI
M **18** CCXCIII⌉ CCXCII M **19** CCXCIIII⌉ CCXCIII M **20** CCXCV⌉ CCXCIIII M **21** CCXCVI⌉
CCXCV M **21** PENITENTIA⌉ PAENITENTIA M **22** CCXCVII⌉ CCXCVI M **23** CCXCVIII⌉ CCXCVII
M **23** BESTIIS⌉ BESTEIS M **24** CCXCVIIII⌉ CCXCVIII M **25** CCC⌉ CCXCVIIII M **26** CCCI⌉
CCC M

Collectio CCCC capitulorum   11

CCCII	DE PISCIBUS ET AUIBUS
CCCIII	SI ACCIPITER OBPRESSERIT
CCCIIII	DE EQUUM MANDUCANDUM
CCCV	DE ANIMALE GUSTATO A BESTIIS
CCCVI	SI APES OCCIDENT
CCCVII	DE PUELLA XVI ANNORUM
CCCVIII	DE PUERO XV ANNORUM
CCCVIIII	DE ORDINATIONE PUERI
CCCX	DE MONACHATO PUERI
CCCXI	DE SERUITUTE FILII
CCCXII	DE SERUITIO SEMETIPSIUS
CCCXIII	DE TESTIMONIO
CCCXIIII	DE PREGNANTE
CCCXV	DE ANCILLA PREGNANTE
CCCXVI	DE LIBERTATE MONASTERII
CCCXVII	DE PUGNATIONE SERUORUM DEI
CCCXVIII	DE INFIRMANTIUM ESU
CCCXVIIII	QUI OPERANTUR DIE DOMINICO
CCCXX	DE COMMUNIONE DIEBUS DOMINICIS
CCCXXI	DE ABSTINENTIA MARITORUM
CCCXXII	DE UEXATIONE DIABOLICA
CCCXXIII	DE DISPERATIONE
CCCXXIIII	DE IURAMENTO
CCCXXV	SI IURAUERIT IN MANU EPISCOPI
CCCXXVI	DE CONFIRMATIONE IURAMENTI
CCCXXVII	DE CONTRADICTIONE IURAMENTI

I 121v

---

1 CCCII⌉ CCCI M   1 ET⌉ DE I   2 CCCIII⌉ CCCII M   3 CCCIIII⌉ CCCIII M   3 EQUUM⌉ AE-
QUU I   4 CCCV⌉ CCCIIII M   4 BESTIIS⌉ BESTEIS M   5 CCCVI⌉ CCCV M   6 CCCVII⌉ CCCVI
M   6 PUELLA⌉ PUELLAE M   6 XVI⌉ XVI ma I   7 CCCVIII⌉ CCCVII M   8 CCCVIIII⌉ CCCVIII
M   9 CCCX⌉ CCCVIIII M   9 MONACHATO⌉ MONACHO M   10 CCCXI⌉ *deest* M   10 DE
SERUITUTE FILII⌉ *deest* M   11 CCCXII⌉ CCCX M   12 CCCXIII⌉ CCCXI M   13 CCCXIIII⌉
CCCXII M   14 CCCXV⌉ CCCXIII M   14 ANCILLA⌉ ANCELLA* I   15 CCCXVI⌉ CCCXIIII M
15 MONASTERII⌉ MONASTERIO I   16 CCCXVII⌉ CCCXV M   16 DEI⌉ *deest* M   17 CCCXVIII⌉
CCCXVI M   18 CCCXVIIII⌉ CCCXVII M   19 CCCXX⌉ CCCXVIII M   20 CCCXXI⌉ CCCXVIIII M
21 CCCXXII⌉ CCCXX M   22 CCCXXIII⌉ CCCXXI M   23 CCCXXIIII⌉ CCCXXII M   24 CCCXXV⌉
CCCXXIII M   25 CCCXXVI⌉ CCCXXIIII M   26 CCCXXVII⌉ CCCXXV M

12 — Collectio CCCC capitulorum

	CCCXXVIII	DE PAENITENTIA IURAMENTI
	CCCXXVIIII	DE FURTU ET PENITENTIA FURI
	CCCXXX	DE HOMICIDIIS
	CCCXXXI	SI CLERICUS HOMICIDIUM FACIT
5	CCCXXXII	QUI OCCIDERIT HOMINEM
	CCCXXXIII	SI PRO ULTIONE OCCIDITUR
	CCCXXXIIII	QUI IN PUBLICO BELLO OCCIDIT
	CCCXXXV	QUI NON CONPOSUIT FURTUM AUT HOMICIDIUM
	CCCXXXVI	SI ALITER PERCUSSERIT
10	CCCXXXVII	SI QUIS BENEFICIUM FACIAT
	CCCXXXVIII	QUI MONACHUM OCCIDIT
	CCCXXXVIIII	QUI EPISCOPUM AUT PRESBITERUM OCCIDIT
	CCCXL	SI LAICUS LAICUM
	CCCXLI	DE PENITENTIA ADULTERII
15	CCCXLII	DE DIACONO ET PRESBITERO DATUM
	CCCXLIII	SI PRESBITERO CONMENDATUS INFANS INFIRMUS
	CCCXLIIII	DE NEGLEGENTIA PARENTUM
	CCCXLV	DE POLLUTIONE SACERDOTUM
	CCCXLVI	DE OSCULI POLLUTIONE
20	CCCXLVII	DE COGITATIONIS POLLUTIONE
	CCCXLVIII	DE GRADU PERDITO
	CCCXLVIIII	DE UIOLENTIA COGITATIONIS
	CCCL	DE EBRIETATIS UOMITU
	CCCLI	DE EBRIETATE SACERDOTUM
25	CCCLII	PRESBITER NON PRODENDUS PECCAT
	CCCLIII	DE POLLUTIONE PUERORUM
	CCCLIIII	SI MONACHUS FORNICAT
	CCCLV	DE UOTO PUERI
	CCCLVI	DE COMMUTATIONE
30	CCCLVII	DE TERRA RAPTA A REGE

I 122r

---

1 CCCXXVIII] CCCXXVI M **1** IURAMENTI] IURANTI M **2** CCCXXVIIII] CCCXXVII M
2 PENITENTIA] PAENITENTIA M **3** CCCXXX] CCCXXVIII M **4** CCCXXXI] CCCXXVIIII
M **5** CCCXXXII] CCCXXX M **6** CCCXXXIII] CCCXXXI M **7** CCCXXXIIII] CCCXXXII M
8 CCCXXXV] CCCXXXIII M **9** CCCXXXVI] CCCXXXIIII M **10** CCCXXXVII] *capitula* CCCXXX-
VIII…CCCXCVII *lacuna* M **14** ADULTERII] ADULTERIOS I **29** COMMUTATIONE] COMMOTATIONE
I

Collectio CCCC capitulorum   13

	CCCLVIII	De inuentione in uia
	CCCLVIIII	De tributu aecclesiae
	CCCLX	Non tollendum a seruo pecunia
	CCCLXI	De falsitate commissa
I 122v	CCCLXII	De ieiuniis legitimis
	CCCLXIII	Utrumque in baptismum accipiat
	CCCLXIIII	De reuerentia aecclesiae
	CCCLXV	De mutata aecclesia
	CCCLXVI	In uno altare duas missas
	CCCLXVII	Post pentecostam reuerentia septimana
	CCCLXVIII	De furata ecclesiae pecunia
	CCCLXVIIII	De missa offerenda
	CCCLXX	Missas pro infantibus
	CCCLXXI	De baptismo clericorum in infirmitate
	CCCLXXII	De indicto ieiunio
	CCCLXXIII	Si in quadragisima
	CCCLXXIIII	De fugientibus reis ad aecclesiam
	CCCLXXV	De raptoribus
	CCCLXXVI	De captiuantibus homines
	CCCLXXVII	De incensoribus domus
	CCCLXXVIII	De percussione in rixu
	CCCLXXVIIII	De gustu sanguinis
	CCCLXXX	De raptore fugiente ad aecclesiam
	CCCLXXXI	De culpa abbatis
	CCCLXXXII	Seruus fugiens ad aecclesiam
I 123r	CCCLXXXIII	Non uertendum terram aecclesiae
	CCCLXXXIIII	Cum consensu mutat terram
	CCCLXXXV	Monasterii commutatio
	CCCLXXXVI	Non cogendum abbatem ad synodum
	CCCLXXXVII	De electione alterius abbatis
	CCCLXXXVIII	De non retinendo abbato in loco suo
	CCCLXXXVIIII	De congregationis electione abbatis
	CCCXC	De monacho digno episcopatus

---

8 MUTATA AECCLESIA⌉ MUTATAE AECCLESIAE I   **16** QUADRAGISIMA⌉ XL ma I   **27** MUTAT⌉
MOTAT* I   **28** COMMUTATIO⌉ COMMOTATIO* I

Collectio CCCC capitulorum

CCCXCI	DE ORDINATIS NON ADUNATIS	
CCCXCII	DE CONFIRMATIONE AECCLESIA	
CCCXCIII	DE NON DANDO CHRISMA NON ADUNATIS	
CCCXCIIII	DE INMUNDO LIQUORE	
CCCXCV	DE NON CONFIRMATIS AB EPISCOPO	
CCCXCVI	DE CONSECRATIONE ABBATIS	*M 161r*
CCCXCVII	ET ABBATISSAE	
CCCXCVIII	DE BIGAMI	
CCCXCVIIII	ET TRIGAMI	
CCCC	DE BAPTISMO HERETICORUM	
CCCCI	DE SIMONE ET SAULO	
CCCCII	DE AQUA ECCLESIAE	
CCCCIII	DE LIBERTATE A REGE TERRENO	
CCCCIIII	DE TERMINIS ANTIQUIS	*I 123v*

EXPLICIUNT KAPITULA ISTIUS PARTIS

---

1 ADUNATIS] A UNATIS I   **3** NON DANDO] NUDANDO *corr.* NODANDO I   **7** CCCXCVII] CCCXCV M   **7** ET] DE CONSECRATIONE M   **8** CCCXCVIII] CCCXCVI M   **8** DE BIGAMI] DE BIGAMI *corr.* DE TRIGAMI M   **9** CCCXCVIIII] *deest* M   **9** ET TRIGAMI] *deest* M   **10** CCCC] CCCXCVII M   **11** CCCCI] CCCXCVIII M   **11** SIMONE] SYMONE M   **11** SAULO] SAULE M   **12** CCCCII] CCCXCVIIII M   **13** CCCCIII] CCC M   **14** CCCCIIII] CCC M   **15** EXPLICIUNT KAPITULA ISTIUS PARTIS] *deest* M

Collectio CCCC capitulorum   15

L 84r   Excerptio synodum

Domine et sancte pater patrum. Si quis condempnet excerpentem aut contem-
L 84v net cribrantem et limantem stantem in loco sancto: qui legit intellegat dominicam sermocinationem et canones sanctorum apostolorum; et sanctos uniuer-
sales quinque synodus; et eadem in sancto sexto synodo inuenit Niceam cccx   5
et viii episcopis; et Siluestrum romanae ecclesiae cum cclxxxiiii; Constanti-
nopolitano cum cl; et Calcidonensium cum cccxxx; et Effeseum cum cc; An-
quiritanensium; Cesariensium; Gangrentium; Cartaginensium; Sardicensium;
Antiocensium; Arelatensium cum dc episcopis; Reiensium; Arausicum; Ua-
M 161v; lentineam; et Uasentium apud Auspitium episcopum; Araladentium; et Aga- 10
I 124r tentium; Aurelianentium; et sanctorum episcoporum urbis Romae Innocentii,
Sergii, Caelestini, Leonis, Gregorii, et Syricii; Augustini episcopi Yppoliti.
Omnes causas utilitatis et nostrae necessitatis carpsimus; quos susceperunt
suscipimus secundum iussionem summi sacerdotis.

Praefatiuncula   15
Haec sunt uerba atque iuditia quae praecepit Dominus Mosi et filiis Israhel:

16–16.2 cf. Deut 6:6-8

---

1 Excerptio synodum] Haec sunt precepta quod Dominus precepit Moyse capitula xxxviii L Incipit excerptio synodum M   2 Domine] domne IL   2 sancte] sanctae L
2 condempnet] contemnet L condemnet M   2–3 contemnet] contempnet L condemnet
M   3 cribrantem] cribantem IM   3 sancto] suo L   4 sanctos] sanctas L   5 synodus]
sinodus L   5 synodo] sinodo L   5–6 cccx et viii] cum cccxviii LM   6 romanae] romane L   6 cum cclxxxiiii] cclxxxiiii L cclxxxiiiior M   6–7 Constantinopolitano] Constantinopoli L Constantinopolim M   7 Calcidonensium] Calchedonensium M   7 cccxxx]
cccccccxxx L dcxxx M   7 Effeseum] Effesium L Epheseum M   8 Cesariensium] Cae-
sariensium LM   8 Gangrentium] Gangentium L Gangrensium M   8 Cartaginensium]
Cartaginenstium *corr.* Cartaginentium L Carthaginensium M   8 Sardicensium] Sadir-
centium L   9 Antiocensium] Anteocentium L Anthiocensium M   9 Arelatensium]
Aratensium I Aratentium L Aralatensium M   9 Arausicum] Arausium *corr.* Arausicum I   9–10 Ualentineam] Ualtentinam L   10 Auspitium] hospitium L Auspicium
M   10 episcopum] episcoporum L   10 Araladentium] Araladencium L Aralatensium M
10–11 Agatentium] Agatensium M   11 Aurelianentium] Aurilianensium L Aurelianensium M   11 Romae] Rome L   11 Innocentii] Innocenti LM   12 Caelestini] Celestini
M   12 Syricii] Siric L   12 Yppoliti] Ippoliti L   13 nostrae] nostre L   13 carpsimus]
carpauimus IM   14 suscipimus] suscepimus*I   14 iussionem] iusione L   14 sacerdotis]
sacerdotis finit M   15 Praefatiuncula] Praefaciunculia L Incipit praefatiuncula M
16 iuditia] iudicia LM   16 quae] que L   16 praecepit] precepit M   16 Mosi] Moysi
LM

16 Collectio CCCC capitulorum

in corde et in domo meditare et in itinere quasi signum ligare in manu et inter oculos pendere in liminem cunctis uiuentibus.

In euangelio: quae littera occidit spiritus uiuificat.

Idem ipse qui euangelio Mosi anteposuit: quae Moses in mortem euangelia in poenitentia. Ergo ambis seruantibus seruemur in caelis, quia unus Deus unitatem seruantibus, quod canones euangelistarum et apostulorum sanctorum episcoporum et beatorum patriarcharum subsequentibus Deum timentium mosaica ratio in primis docet Deum diligere.

I De confirmatione caritatis Dei

Moses: Diliges Dominum Deum tuum ex toto corde tuo et ex tota anima tua et ex tota fortitudine tua. Hoc est maximum et primum mandatum Dominus in euangelio confirmauit secundum aut simile est huic.

II De amore confirmata proximi per deum

Moses: Diliges proximum tuum sicut te ipsum.

Et in alio loco: nec decipiat unusquisque proximum suum nec loqueris contra proximum tuum falsum testimonium, nec concupisces uxorem proximi tui, non domum, non agrum, non seruum, non ancillam, non bouem, non asinum, et uniuersa quae illius sunt.

Quia in his duobus mandatis, dixit Ihesus, universa lex pendet et prophete.

---

3 cf. 2 Cor 3:6   10–11 Deut 6:5; cf. Mt 22:37   11–12 Mt 22:38-9; cf. Mc 12:30; Lc 10:27   14 Mt 22:39; 19:19   15 Lev 19:11   15–18 Deut 5:20-21; cf. Ex 20:16-17   19 Mt 22:40

---

1 meditare⟧ meditari M   1 in itinere⟧ intimare M   2 liminem⟧ limine LM   3 quae⟧ quae *corr.* qua I que L quoque M   4 euangelio⟧ in euangelio LM   4 Mosi⟧ Moysi LM   4 quae⟧ que L quod M   4 Moses⟧ Moyses LM   4 mortem⟧ morte L   4 euangelia⟧ euangelica M   5 poenitentia⟧ penitentia L paenitentia M   5 seruemur⟧ seruemus I   5 quia⟧ quae IL   6 canones⟧ cannes L   8 mosaica ratio⟧ mosai curatio L moysiaca ratio *corr.* moysiac ratio M   8 diligere⟧ dilegere M   9 De confirmatione caritatis Dei⟧ *deest* IL   10 Moses⟧ *deest* L Moyses ait M   10 Diliges⟧ diligis LM   10 Dominum⟧ *deest* L   12 aut⟧ autem L   13 De amore confirmata proximi per deum⟧ De amore proximi confirmata per deum M *deest* IL   14 Moses⟧ *deest* L Moyses dicit M   14 Diliges⟧ diligis L   16 concupisces⟧ concupiscis L   19 prophete⟧ prophetae LM

Collectio CCCC capitulorum

III De Deo quod non est personarum acceptor

Moses: Nec consideres personam pauperis nec honores uultum potentis. Iuste iudica proximo tuo.

Dominus discipulis: Nolite inquid iudicare ut non iudicemini. In quo enim iuditio iudicaueritis iudicabimini et in qua mensura mensi fueritis remetietur uobis.

Et Petrus apostolus: In ueritate conperi quoniam non est personarum acceptor Deus.

Et Iacobus: Si autem personas accipitis peccatum operamini redarguti a lege quasi transgressores quicumque enim totam legem seruauerit offendat aut in uno factus est omnium reus.

Et in Deuteronomio: Quod iustum est iudicate siue ciues sit ille siue peregrinus. Nulla erit distantia personarum quia Dei iuditium est.

IIII De publica increpatione et de fratre lucrare

Moses: Non oderis fratrem tuum in corde tuo sed publice argues eum nec habeas super illum peccatum.

Idem Dominus in euangelio ait: Si autem peccauerit in te frater tuus uade et corripe eum inter te et ipsum solum. Si te audierit lucratus eris fratrem tuum. Si autem te non audierit adhibe tecum adhuc unum uel duos ut in ore duorum testium uel trium stet omne uerbum. Quae si non audierit eos dic aecclesiae si autem et aecclesiam non audierit sit tibi sicut ethnicus et publicanus.

2–3 Lev 19:15   **4–6** Mt 7:1-2   **7–8** Act 10:34   **9–11** Iac 2:9-10   **12–13** Deut 1:16-17   **15–16** Lev 19:17   **17–21** Mt 18:15-17

---

1 De Deo quod non est personarum acceptor] De Deo quod non est personarum acceptor M *deest* IL   **2** Moses] *deest* L Moyses dicit M   **2** Nec] non M   **4** discipulis] discipulus L discipulis suis dicit M   **4** inquid] inquit M   **4–5** In quo enim iuditio iudicaueritis iudicabimini] *deest* L   **5** remetietur] metietur* I medietur L   **7** apostolus] apostolus ait M   **7** conperi] conperii IL   **9** Iacobus] Iacobus dicit M   **9** accipitis] accipistis L   **10** aut] autem LM   **12** Deuteronomio] uteronomio* I   **12** ciues sit ille] ciuem et illae L   **13** iuditium] iudicium LM   **14** De publica increpatione et de fratre lucrare] *deest* IL   **14** fratre] fratres M   **15** Moses] *deest* L Moyses dicit M   **15** oderis] hoderis L   **15** nec] ne M   **17** ait] *deest* L   **18** eris] fueris L   **20** Quae] *deest* M   **20** si non audierit eos] si eos non audierit M   **20** aecclesiae] ecclesiae LM   **21** aecclesiam] aecclesia I ecclesiae L ecclesiam M   **21** ethnicus] etnicus L hethnicus M   **21** et] *deest* L

Collectio CCCC capitulorum

V De obliuione ultionis pro Deo dimittendum
Moses: Non sequeris ultionem non memor eris iniuriae ciuium tuorum.

Dominus discipulis: Si enim dimiseritis hominibus peccata eorum dimittet e⟨t⟩ uobis pater uester caelestis delicta uestra. Si autem non dimiseritis hominibu⟨s⟩
5 nec pater uester dimittet peccata uestra.

VI De cicatrice criminatoris a Deo eiecto
Moses: Non eris criminator et susurro in populis. Memento quod criminato⟨r⟩ fratrum deiectus est e gloria patris.

Dixit Iohannis in apocalipsi et Dominus per Salomonem: Susurro et bilingui⟨s⟩
10 maledictus: multos enim turbabit pacem habentes.

Tam durum iudicium est ut anima Domini detestatur eum qui seminat inte⟨r⟩ fratres discordias.

Si Dominus dicat: Omne uerbum otiosum quod locuti fuerint homines redden⟨t⟩ de eo rationem in die iuditii multo magis damnantur noxia uerba, quia otiosum
15 quippe uerbum est quod aut utilitate rectitudinis aut ratione iuste necessitati⟨s⟩ caret et tamen in die iuditii damnatur.

VII De mercede ad Deum clamantium
Moses: Non demoretur merces mercennarii tui apud te usque in mane.

Et in Sapientia: Quia inscius est uitae tuae.

---

2 Lev 19:18 **3–5** Mt 6:14–15 **7** Lev 19:16 **9–10** Ecclus 28:15 **11–12** Pro⟨v⟩ 6:19 **13–14** Mt 12:36 **18** cf. Tob 4:15 **19** cf. Sap 14:21-4

---

1 De obliuione ultionis pro Deo dimittendum] *deest* IL **2** Moses] *deest* L Moyses ai⟨t⟩ M **2** non] nec L **3** discipulis] discipulus L discipulis dicit M **5** nec] *superscriptum* M **6** De cicatrice criminatoris a Deo eiecto] *deest* IL **7** Moses] *deest* L Moyses dici⟨t⟩ M **7** susurro] susurrio I **8** e] de L **9** Salomonem] Salomonem ait M **9** Susurro⟨⟩ Susurrio ILM **9** bilinguis] in linguis L **10** turbabit] turbauit L **13** otiosum] ociosum L **13** homines] omines L **14** die] diem L **14** iuditii] iudicii LM **14** quia⟨⟩ que L **14** otiosum] ociosum L **15** quod] qui M **15** aut utilitate rectitudinis] *dees.* L **15** ratione] rationem L **16** et] ad L **16** iuditii] iudicii LM **16** damnatur] damnantur L **17** De mercede ad Deum clamantium] *deest* IL **18** Moses] Moyses dicit M **18** mercennarii] mercenarii L **19** Sapientia] Sapientia dicit M **19** Quia] qua* I que L

Collectio CCCC capitulorum

19

Et Iacobus apostolus: Ecce merces operariorum qui messuerunt regiones uestras qui fraudatus es a uobis clamat et clamor ipsorum in aures Domini Sabaoth introibit.

VIII De honore caeci et surdi

I 126v   Moses: Non maledices surdo nec coram caeco pones offendiculum sed timebis   5
Dominum Deum tuum.

L 86r   Sicut et in Exodo Dominus ad Mosen: Quis fabricatus est mutum et surdum
uidentem et caecum? Nonne ego? Quia qui maledicit eis creatori inproperat.

M 163v   De quo in Euangelio: Bene omnia fecit et surdos fecit audire et mutos loqui et
intellectu caecos uidere ergo maledictus qui errare facit caecum in itinere et   10
dicit omnis populus amen.

VIIII Non furandum nec mentiendum

Moses: Non facies furtum non mentiemini quia mors et uita in manu linguae.

Et Dominus in Euangelio: Ex uerbis tuis iustificaueris et ex uerbis tuis condemnaueris.   15

Et Paulus apostolus dicit: Quod furi regnum Dei non possiderint.

I 127r   Et Saluator: Non facies furtum non falsum testimonium dices. Haec sunt quae
coinquinant hominem.

Et Sapientia dicit: Os qui mentitur occidit animam.

1–3 Iac 5:4   **5–6** Lev 19:14   **7–8** Ex 4:11   **9** Mc 7:37   **10–11** Deut 27:18   **13** Lev 19:11   **13** Prov 18:21   **14–15** Mt 12:37   **16** cf. 1 Cor 6:10   **17** cf. Mt 19:18   **17–18** cf. Mt 15:20   **19** cf. Sap 1:11

---

1 apostolus] apostolus ait M   **2** aures] auribus   **2–3** Sabaoth] Saba L   **4** De honore caeci et surdi] *deest* IL   **5** Moses] *deest* L Moyses ait M   **7** et in Exodo] exaudo L   **7** Mosen] Moysen L Moysen dicit M   **7** fabricatus] frabricatus* L   **7** est] es L   **8** Quia] *deest* M   **8** maledicit] ledicit L   **9** Euangelio] Euangelio dicit M   **9** surdos] surdus L   **10** intellectu] intellectos L   **10** facit] fecit L   **12** Non furandum nec mentiendum] *deest* IL   **13** Moses] *deest* L Moyses ait M   **13** facies] facias L   **13** manu] manibus M   **14** Euangelio] Euangelio ait M   **14** Ex] aut ex M   **14–15** uerbis tuis iustificaueris…condemnaueris] uer inscius te condamnaueris iustificaueris L   **14** et] aut M   **16** dicit] *deest* L   **16** possiderint] possidebunt M   **17** Saluator] Saluator ait M   **17** facies] facias L   **17** Haec] Hec L   **18** coinquinant] quoinquinant L   **19** qui] qui non L

20   Collectio CCCC capitulorum

Et Moses: Non suscipies uocem mendatii nec iniungas manum tuam ut pro impio dicas falsum testimonium.

X   NON OCCIDENDUM NEQUE MOECHANDUM
Non occides non moechaueris.

5 Et Iacobus: Qui enim dixit non moechaueris dixit et non occides. Si non moechaueris occides autem factus es transgressor legis.

In lege scriptum est: Insontem et iustum non occides

Et: moechatus qui fuerit cum uxore alterius morte moriatur moechus et adultera.

10 Et Saluator: Audistis quia dictum est antiquis non moechaueris. Ego autem dico uobis quoniam omnis qui uiderit mulierem ad concupiscendum eam iam   *M 164r*
moechatus est eam in corde suo.

Et iterum: Audistis quia dictum est antiquis non occides. Qui autem occiderit   *I 127v*
reus erit iuditio. Ego autem dico uobis quia omnis qui irascitur fratri suo reus
15 erit iuditio. Qui autem dixerit fratri suo racha reus erit concilio. Qui autem
dixerit fatuae reus erit gehenne ignis. Si ergo offeres munus tuum ad altare   *L 86v*
et ibi recordatus fueris quia frater tuus habet aliquid aduersum te; relinque
ibi munus tuum ad altare et uade prius reconciliari fratri tuo et tunc ueniens
offeres munus tuum.

1–2 Ex 23:1   4 Ex 20:13-14; Deut 5:17-18   5–6 Iac 2:11   7 Ex 23:7   8–9 cf.
Lev 20:10   10–12 Mt 5:27-8   13–19 Mt 5:21-4

---

1 Moses] Moyses L Moyses dicit M   1 mendatii] mendacii LM   1 iniungas] iniun-
ges L   3 NON OCCIDENDUM NEQUE MOECHANDUM] deest IL   4 Non] Moyses dicit non M
4 moechaueris] mechaberis L moechaberis M   5 Iacobus] Iacobus ait M   5 dixit non
moechaueris] deest L   5 moechaueris] moechaberis M   6 moechaueris] mechaberis L
moechaberis M   7 Insontem] Infantem L   8 moechatus] mechatus L   8 qui] quis M
8 moriatur] morietur L   8 moechus] mechatus L moechatus M   10 Saluator] Saluator ait M   10 moechaueris] mechaberis L moechaberis M   11 quoniam] quoniam autem
L   11 concupiscendum] concupiscendam L   12 moechatus] mechatus L   13 dictum]
dictam L   14 iuditio] iudicio LM   15 iuditio] iudicio LM   16 gehenne] gehennae M
16 offeres] offeris L offers M   18 ad] ante M   18 ueniens] uenies LM   19 offeres]
offers I

Collectio CCCC capitulorum

21

XI Non periurare inaniter

Moses: Non periurabis in nomine meo nec pollues nomen Dei tui.

Et: nec adsumes nomen Domini Dei tui in uanum neque insontem habebit Dominus eum qui adsumpserit nomen Domini Dei sui frustra.

Et Saluator discipulis: Audistis quia dictum est antiquis: Non periurabis: reddes autem Domino iuramenta tua. Ego autem dico uobis: non iurare omnino neque per caelum quia thronus Dei est, neque per terram quia scabellum pedum eius, neque per Hierosolimam quia ciuitas est magni regis, neque per caput tuum iuraueris quia non potes unum capillum album facere aut nigrum. Sit autem sermo uester est est non non quod autem his habundantius est a malo est.

Et Iacobus: Facite fratres ut non sub iuditio decidatis.

XII De dilectione amici et odio inimici

Moses: Diliges amicum tuum tamquam te ipsum et odio habebis inimicum tuum.

Et in euangelio: Ego autem dico uobis: diligite inimicos uestros et benefacite his qui oderunt uos et orate pro persequentibus et calumniantibus uobis: ut sitis filii patris uestri qui in caelis est. Si enim diligatis eos qui uos diligunt quam mercedem habebitis? Nonne et publicani hoc faciunt? Et si salutaueritis fratres uestros tantum quid amplius facitis? Nonne ethnici hoc faciunt? Estote ergo uos perfecti sicut et pater uester caelestis perfectus est.

---

2 Lev 19:12   3–4 Ex 20:7   5–11 Mt 5:33-7   12 cf. Iac 5:12   14 cf. Lev 19:18; cf. Mt 5:43   14–15 cf. Mt 5:43   16–21 cf. Mt 5:44-8

---

1 Non periurare inaniter] *deest* IL   2 Moses] *deest* L Moyses ait M   2 pollues] pullues L   3 adsumes] adsummes L   3 Domini] *deest* M   3 habebit] habeat L   4 eum] cum L   4 adsumpserit] sumpserit L   5 discipulis] discipulis suis ait M   5 quia] que L   5 antiquis] *deest* L   7 thronus] trono L   7 scabellum] scabillum est L scapillum M   8 eius] eius est M   8 Hierosolimam] Hierusolimam L Hierosolymam M   9 caput] capud L   9 potes] potest L   10 Sit] Si L   10 habundantius] abundantius LM   12 Iacobus] Iacobus dicit M   13 De dilectione amici et odio inimici] *deest* IL   14 Moses] *deest* L Moyses dicit M   14 Diliges] Diligis L   14 odio] hodio L   16 euangelio] euangelio Dominus ait M   17 oderunt uos] uos hoderint L   17 uobis] uos L   18 diligatis] diligitis L   19 quam] quia L   20 uestros] uestris L   20 Nonne] nonne L nonne et M   20 ethnici] hetnici L   21 caelestis] celestis L

22   Collectio CCCC capitulorum

XIII   De oculis et dentibus eruentis
Moses: Oculum pro oculo et dentem pro dente etcetera.

Et Saluator contra his omnia: Ego autem dico uobis non resistere malo sed   *L 87r*
si quis te percusserit in dexteram maxillam tuam prebe illi et alteram. Et ille
5 qui uult tecum iuditio contendere et tunicam tuam tollere remitte et pallium.
Et quicumque te angariauerit mille passus uade cum illo alia duo.

XIIII   Ultionem septies dimittendum
Moses: Non sequeris ultionem.

Idem et Saluator discipulis: Adtendite uobis. Si peccauerit in te frater tuus in-   *M 165r*
10 crepa illum et si paenitentiam egerit dimitte illi. Et si septies in die peccauerit
in te et si septies in die conuersus fuerit ad te dicens paenitet me dimitte illi.   *I 129r*

De istis supradictis Saluator caelebrem uerbum esse contrarium nostris cor-
poribus insinuans esto consentiens aduersario tuo cito dum es in uia cum eo:
ne forte tradat te aduersarius iudici et iudex tradat te ministro et in carcerem
15 mittaris. Amen dico tibi non exies inde donec reddas nouissimum quadrantem.

XV   De muliere repudiata
Moses: Quicumque dimiserit uxorem suam det illi libellum repudii.

Dicunt pharisaei ad Ihesum: Si licet homini dimittere uxorem suam quacumque ex causa? Respondit et dixit: Quod ergo Deus coniunxit homo non se-
20 paret. Itaque iam non sunt duo sed una caro. Dico autem quia quicumque

---

2 Ex 21:24; Lev 24:20; Deut 19:21   **3–6** Mt 5:39-41   **8** Lev 19:18   **9–11** Lc 17:3-4
13–15 Mt 5:25-6   **17** Mt 5:31   **18–19** Mt 19:3   **19–20** cf. Mt 19:6; changed word
order   **20–23.2** Mt 19:9

---

1 De oculis et dentibus eruentis⌉ *deest* IL   **2** Moses⌉ *deest* L Moyses ait M   **4** ille⌉
illi IL   **5** iuditio⌉ in iudicio LM   **5** tunicam⌉ tonicam L   **5** remitte⌉ remitte ei M
6 mille⌉ in ille L   **7** Ultionem septies dimittendum⌉ *deest* I   **8** Moses⌉ *deest* L Moyses dicit M   **9** Idem⌉ Id est L   **9** discipulis⌉ discipulus L discipulis dicit M   **10** paenitentiam⌉
penitentiam L   **10** dimitte⌉ demitte M   **11** paenitet⌉ poenitetus L   **11** me⌉ *deest* L
12 nostris⌉ nostri M   **12–13** corporibus⌉ corporis M   **13** insinuans⌉ insunuam* I in-
sinuae M   **13** es⌉ eas M   **14** te⌉ *deest* L   **14** carcerem⌉ cercere L   **15** mittaris⌉ rem-
mittaris L   **16** De muliere repudiata⌉ *deest* IL   **17** Moses⌉ *deest* L Moyses ait M   **17** det⌉
debet L   **17** illi⌉ ille* L   **18** pharisaei⌉ pharisei LM   **19** Respondit⌉ respondit Dominus M   **19** dixit⌉ dicit M   **19** coniunxit⌉ coniunxix *corr.* coniuncix L   **19–20** separet⌉
seperet L   **20** non⌉ *deest* L

Collectio CCCC capitulorum

23

I 129v
dimiserit uxorem suam nisi ob fornicationem et aliam duxerit moechatur; et qui dimissam duxerit moechatur.

Cuius rei apostolus Paulus meminit dicens: Mulier uiuente uiro sui corporis potestatem non habet sed uir. Similiter sui corporis uir potestatem non habet sed mulier.

M 165v
L 87v
Idem: Si nec illi nubere conceditur uiuo uiro a quo recesserat nec huic alteram ducere uiua uxore quam dimisit, an peccet uir si cum adultera uiuat? Non peccat quamdiu non cognouerit deprehensa penitentiam egerit et si dimissa fuerit. Si ad maritum suum reuerti uoluerit recipietur ne paenitentiae occasionem mulieri auferat. Si recepta non fuerit peccat maritus grande in se delictum.

Quia apostolus dicit: Non ego mando sed Dominus mulierem a uiro non discedere sed si discesserit manere innuptam aut uiro suo reconciliare et uir uxorem
I 130r
non dimittat. Nolite fraudare inuicem nisi ex consensu ad tempus ut uacetis orationi et iterum in id ipsum reuertimini.

XVI De marito fidele
Moses: Si quis baptizatus uxorem habet infidelem aut mulier uirum infidelem non relinquat.

Sanctificatus est uir infidelis per mulierem fidelem.

3–5 1 Cor 7:4   **6–7** cf. Augustinus, *De sermone Domini in monte,* I.14 §39   **7–11** cf. *Hermas Pastor, mandatum* IV.1   **12–14** cf. 1 Cor 7:10-11   **14–15** 1 Cor 7:5   **17–18** cf. 1 Cor 7:12   **19** cf. 1 Cor 7:14

---

1 fornicationem] fornicatione L fornicationem suam M   **1** moechatur] mechatur L   **1–2** et qui dimissam...moechatur] *deest* M   **2** moechatur] mechatur L   **3** uiuente] uiuenti L   **4** habet] habeat I   **4** uir] et uir L ur* M   **4** sui corporis uir] sui corporis L uir sui corporis M   **6** illi] illa L   **6** conceditur] concidetur L   **7** peccet uir] peccetur M   **7** uiuat] uiuit M   **8** deprehensa] si deprehensa L   **8** penitentiam] paenitentiam M   **8** egerit] aegerit M   **8** si] *deest* M   **9** fuerit] fuerat I   **9** paenitentiae] penitentia L   **10** mulieri] muliere L   **11** delictum] delectum* L   **12** apostolus] postolus* L   **13** reconciliare] reconciliarei L   **14** dimittat] dimittet L   **14** fraudare] fraudere L   **15** id ipsum] ipdispum L   **16** De marito fidele] *deest* IL   **17** Moses] *deest* L Moyses dicit M   **17** baptizatus] baptizatos L   **19** Sanctificatus] Petrus ait: Sanctificatus M

24 Collectio CCCC capitulorum

Quia si infidelis discedit <discedat> non est seruituti deditus frater aut soror in eiusmodi.

XVII DE HONORE PARENTUM
Moses: Honora patrem tuum et matrem tuam ut sis longeuus super terram.

5 Idem et Paulus: Filii, oboedite parentibus uestris. Hoc enim iustum est.

Et Dominus in Euangelio honorem patris et matris confirmauit. *M 166r*

XVIII DE DIIS ALIENIS
Moses: Non habebis deos alienos coram me.

Idem: Non facies tibi sculptile neque omnem similitudinem qui est in caelo de
10 super et qui in terra deorsum neque eorum qui sunt in aquis sub terra. Non *I 130v*
adorabis ea neque coles. Ego sum Dominus Deus tuus fortis et zelotis.

XVIIII DE MUNERIBUS CECATIS
Moses: Non accipies munera quae excecant etiam prudentes et subuertunt uerba iustorum.

15 Imitemur Danihelem et munera et dona regis contempnentem qui absque pretio proferens ueritatem dicens: Munera tua sint tibi et dona domus tuae alteri *L 88r*
da: scripturam hanc legam tibi rex.

Quia semel dona spiritalia, si merces media sit uiliora fiunt. Auaritiae con-
demnatio: Gratis accepistis gratis date.

1–2 1 Cor 7:15 **4** Ex 20:12 **5** cf. Eph 6:1 **6** cf. Mc 7:10; Mc 10:19; Lc 18:20 **8** Ex 20:3 **9–11** Ex 20:4–5 **13–14** Ex 23:8 **16–17** Dan 5:17 **18–19** Hier., *In Matt.* 1.10 **19** Mt 10:8

---

1 Quia⌉ Que L Paulus dicit: Quod M **1** est⌉ *deest* L **1** soror⌉ sorori M **3** DE HONORE PARENTUM⌉ *deest* IL **4** Moses⌉ *deest* L Moyses dicit M **5** Idem⌉ Id est L **5** Paulus⌉ Paulus ait M **5** oboedite⌉ oboeditae L **6** honorem⌉ honora L **7** DE DIIS ALIENIS⌉ *deest* IL **8** Moses⌉ *deest* L Moyses ait M **9** Idem⌉ Id est L **9** caelo⌉ celo L **9** de⌉ *superscriptum* I **10** neque eorum⌉ *deest* L **10** terra⌉ terra deorsum M **11** adorabis⌉ adhorabis L **11** sum⌉ *deest* L **12** DE MUNERIBUS CECATIS⌉ DE MUNERIBUS CAECATIS M *deest* IL **13** Moses⌉ *deest* L Moyses dicit M **13** quae⌉ que L **13** excecant⌉ exceca sunt L excaecant M **15** Danihelem⌉ Danielem L **15** contempnentem⌉ conctempnentem* L contemnnentem M **15** qui⌉ quia L **15–16** pretio⌉ precio L praetio M **16** proferens⌉ preferens L **17** hanc⌉ aut I **18** merces⌉ mercis L **18** Auaritiae⌉ Auariciae L **18–19** condemnatio⌉ condempna L **19** accepistis⌉ accipistis L

Collectio CCCC capitulorum   25

Recolite Iudam pro amore pecuniae xxx argenteis Dominum damnantem et
Petrum non accipientem sed dicentem: Pecunia tua tecum sit in perditione.

XX   NON ERIS ONEROSUS PEREGRINO

I 131r Moses: Peregrino molestus non eris scitis enim aduenarum animas quia et ipsi
fuistis peregrini in terra Aegypti.   5

M 166v Et in Leuitico: Si habitauerit aduena in terra uestra et moratus fuerit inter uos
ne exprobratis ei sed sit inter uos quasi indigena et diligitis eum quasi uosmet
ipsos.

XXI   NON COMEDENDUM CARNEM PREGUSTATAM

Moses: Carnem quae a bestiis fuerit pregustata non comedetis sed proiecetis   10
canibus.

Et Iacobus in Actibus Apostulorum: Sustinete uos ab omni suffocato.

Adipem cadaueris morticini et eius animalis quod a bestia captum est habebitis
in usus uarios.

XXII   DEOS NON DETRAHERE NEC PRINCIPES   15
Moses: Diis non detrahes principes populi tui non maledices. Non auguria-
mini non obseruabitis somnia.

Et in Deuteronomio: Qui ariolos sciscitetur et obseruet somnia aut qui auguria
ne sit maleficus.

---

2 Act 8:20   **4–5** Ex 23:9   **6–8** Lev 19:33-4   **10–11** Ex 22:31   **12** cf. Act 21:25
13–14 Lev 7:24   **16** Ex 22:28   **16–17** Lev 19:26   **18–19** Deut 18:10

---

1 Recolite⌉ Recolitae L   **1** amore⌉ amorem L   **1** xxx⌉ triginta M   **1** Dominum⌉
Deum L   **2** Petrum⌉ precium L   **2** accipientem⌉ accipientes* L   **3** NON ERIS ONEROSUS
PEREGRINO⌉ *deest* IL   **4** Moses⌉ *deest* L Moyses dicit M   **5** in terra⌉ inter L   **5** Aegypti⌉
Egypti LM   **6** moratus⌉ mortuus M   **7** exprobratis⌉ exploratis L exprobretis M   **7** sit⌉
si L   **7** quasi⌉ quia si L   **7** diligitis⌉ diligentes M   **9** NON COMEDENDUM CARNEM PREGUSTA-
TAM⌉ NON COMEDENDUM CARNEM PRAEGUSTATAM M *deest* IL   **10** Moses⌉ *deest* L Moyses ait
M   **10** quae⌉ que L   **10** a⌉ *deest* M   **10** bestiis⌉ besteis L   **10** pregustata⌉ praegustata
M   **10** comedetis⌉ commeditis L   **10** proiecetis⌉ proicitis L proicietis M   **12** Iacobus⌉
deest M   **12** Sustinete⌉ Sustinate I Abstinete M   **13** animalis⌉ animalibus L   **15** DEOS
NON DETRAHERE NEC PRINCIPES⌉ *deest* IL   **16** Moses⌉ *deest* L Moyses dicit M   **16** detrahes⌉
trabes L   **17** somnia⌉ omnia LM   **18** ariolos⌉ ariolus L   **18** sciscitetur⌉ sciscitatur M
18 obseruet⌉ obseruat M   **19** ne⌉ *del.* I   **19** maleficus⌉ meleficus M

26   Collectio CCCC capitulorum

XXIII Nec cantatores sciscitare
Moses: Ne incantatur ne pithones consulatur quam uir siue mulier in quibus   *I 131v*
pithonicus uel diuinationis fuerit spiritus morte moriatur. Lapidibus obruent
eos. Sanguis eorum sit super eos.

5 **XXIIII** De decimis et primitiis
Moses: Decimas tuas et primitias non tardabis offerre: boues et oues et ca-
preae quae sub pastoris uirga transeunt quicquid decimum uenerit Domino
sanctificabitur. Non elegitur nec bonum nec malum nec altero commutabitur.   *L 88v*

XXV De segete et uinea
10 Moses: Si intraueris in segetem amici tui frange spicas et manu contere falce   *M 167r*
autem non metas hoc.

Et discipuli Saluatoris in euangelio: Spicas manibus fricantes et manducan-
tes sabbatis. Seu ingressus uineam proximi tui comedes uuas quantum tibi
placuerit foras aut ne feras tecum.

15 **XXVI** De seruis empticiis
Si emeris seruum hebreum sex annis seruiet tibi, in septimo egredietur liber   *I 132r*
gratis. Cum quali ueste intrauerit cum tali exeat. Si habet uxorem et uxor
egredietur simul. Si autem dominus eius dederit ei uxorem et peperit filios et
filias mulier et liberi erunt domini sui ipse uero exibit cum uestimento suo.

---

2 cf. Deut 18:11   **2–4** Lev 20:27   6   Ex 22:29   **6–8** Lev 27:32-3   **10–11** Deut
23:25   **12–13** cf. Lc 6:1   **13–14** Deut 23:24   **16–19** Ex 21:2-4

---

1 Nec cantatores sciscitare] *deest* IL   2 Moses] *deest* L Moyses ait M   2 incantatur]
sis incantator L incantator M   2 pithones] phitonis L phytones M   2 consulatur] con-
solator L consulator M   2 quam] que L quia M   3 pithonicus] phitonicus L phytonicus
M   3 moriatur] moriantur M   5 De decimis et primitiis] *deest* IL   5 primitiis] primitiuis M   6 Moses] *deest* L Moyses dicit M   6 primitias] primicias tuas L   6 offerre]
offeret L   6–7 capreae] capre L caprae M   7 quae] que L qui M   7 pastoris] pastore L   8 elegitur] elegatur M   8 altero] alterum L   8 commutabitur] commotabitur*
I   9 De segete et uinea] *deest* IL   10 Moses] *deest* L Moyses ait M   10 segetem]
segitem L   10 falce] falcem L   12 discipuli] discipulus L   14 aut] *deest* L autem M
14 ne] non M   15 De seruis empticiis] De empticiis I *deest* L   15 empticiis] empticis
M   16 Si] Moyses dicit: Si M   16 seruiet] seruiat L   17 Cum] Cumque L   17 quali]
quale L   17 ueste] uestitum L   17 cum tali] tale L   18 ei] *deest* M   19 ipse] ipsi L
19 exibit] exhibit L

Collectio CCCC capitulorum   27

XXVII   De filia famulata

Moses: Si quis uendiderit filiam suam in famulam non egredietur sicut ancillae exire consuerunt. Si displicuerit in oculis domini sui cui tradita fuerit dimittat eam. Populo autem alieno uendendi non habebit potestatem si spreuerit eam. Si autem filio suo disponderit eam iuxta morem filiarum faciet illi. Si alteram ei acceperit prouidebit puellae nuptias et uestimenta et pretium pudicitiae non negabit. Si tria ista non fecerit egredietur gratis absque pecunia.

XXVIII   De uirgine seducta

I 132v;
M 167v

Moses: Si seduxerit quis uirginem necdum desponsatam uiro et dormierit cum ea dotauit eam et habebit eam. Ita quando res ad iudicium uenerit: dabit puellae patri qui dormierit cum ea L siclos argenti et habebit eam uxorem quam humiliauit illam: non potest dimittere eam omnibus diebus uitae suae. Si pater uirginis dare noluerit reddat pecuniam iuxta modum dotis quam accipere consueuerunt.

XXVIIII   De lusco seruo uel ancilla

L 89r

Moses: Si percusserit quispiam oculum serui sui aut ancillae et luscos eos fecerit dimittat eos liberos pro oculo quem eruit. Dentem uero si excusserit seruo uel ancillae suae similiter dimittat eos liberos.

XXX   De percussione mancipiorum

Moses: Qui percusserit seruum suum uel ancillam uirga et mortui fuerint

---

2–7 Ex 21:7-11   **9–10** Ex 22:16   **10–12** Deut 22:28-9   **12–14** Ex 22:17   **16–18** Ex 21:26-7   **20–28.2** Ex 21:20-1

---

1 De filia famulata⏋ *deest* IL   **2** Moses⏋ *deest* L Moyses ait M   **2** uendiderit⏋ uinderit L   **3** cui tradita⏋ contradita L   **3** fuerit⏋ fuerat M   **3** dimittat⏋ dimittit L   **4** uendendi⏋ uindendii L   **4** habebit⏋ habeat LM   **5** morem⏋ mortem L   **5** filiarum⏋ filiorum L   **6** acceperit⏋ acceperit M   **6** et pretium⏋ et precium L *superscriptum* M   **6** pudicitiae⏋ pudiciciae L   **8** De uirgine seducta⏋ *deest* IL   **9** Moses⏋ *deest* L Moyses dicit M   **9** seduxerit⏋ ducerit L   **9** necdum⏋ nec L   **9** desponsatam⏋ disponsatam M   **10** dotauit⏋ dotabit L   **10–11** puellae patri⏋ patri puelle L patri puellae M   **11** L⏋ quinquaginta M   **11** quam⏋ que L qui M   **12** illam⏋ eam M   **12** uitae⏋ uite L   **13** noluerit⏋ uoluerit L   **14** consueuerunt⏋ consuerunt L   **15** De lusco seruo uel ancilla⏋ *deest* IL   **16** Moses⏋ *deest* L Moyses dicit M   **16** oculum⏋ oculi L   **16** ancillae⏋ ancillae suae M   **16** luscos⏋ luscus L   **16** eos⏋ eas L   **17–18** pro oculo…liberos⏋ *deest* L   **19** De percussione mancipiorum⏋ *deest* IL   **20** Moses⏋ *deest* L Moyses dicit M

28   Collectio CCCC capitulorum

in manibus eius criminis erit reus. Sin autem uno die superuixerint uel duobus
non subiacebit poene quia pecunia eius est.   *I 133r*

XXXI   DE PUGNO ET LAPIDE

Moses: Si rixati fuerint uiri et percusserit alter proximum suum lapide uel
pugno et ille mortuus non fuerit et iacuerit in lectulo si surrexerit et ambu-
lauerit foris super baculum suum; innocens erit qui percusserit ita tamen ut
opera eius et inpensa in medicos restituet.

XXXII   DE PREGNANTE PERCUSSA

Moses: Si rixati fuerint uiri et percusserit quis mulierem pregnantem et abortiuum fecerit sed ipsa uixerit: subiacebit damno quantum expetierit maritus
mulieris et arbitrii iudicauerint. Sin autem mors fuerit subsecuta reddat animam pro anima.

XXXIII   DE ADPREHENSA UERECUNDA

Moses: Si habuerint inter se uiri iurgium et unus contra alterum rixare coeperint uolensque uxor alterius eruere uirum suum de manu fortioris miserit
manum suam et adprehenderit uerecunda eius abscides manum illius nec flec-   *I 133v*
teris super eam ulla misericordia.

XXXIIII   DE CORNUPETO PECODE

Moses: Si bos cornupetierit uirum aut mulierem et mortui fuerint lapidibus
obruetur et non comedentur carnes eius. Dominus aut bouis innocens erit.
Quod si bos cornupeta fuerit ab heri et nudiustertius et contestati sunt domino eius nec recluserit illum occideritque uirum aut mulierem et bos lapidibus

---

4–7 Ex 21:18-19   **9–12** Ex 21:22-3   **14–17** Deut 25:11   **19–29.2** Ex 21:28-30

---

1 erit reus⌉ reus erit M   1 Sin⌉ Si M   2 quia⌉ que L   3 DE PUGNO ET LAPIDE⌉ *deest*
IL   4 Moses⌉ *deest* L Moyses ait M   4 percusserit⌉ percussit L   5 surrexerit⌉ sure-
xerit L surrexit M   6 foris⌉ fors L   6–30.7 innocens...II Auus enim⌉ *lacuna* M   6 ut⌉
deest L   8 DE PREGNANTE PERCUSSA⌉ *deest* IL   9 Moses⌉ *deest* L   9 pregnantem⌉ prignantem L   9–10 abortiuum⌉ abortiuam L   10 expetierit⌉ expeterint L   11 arbitrii⌉
ad arbrii L   11 subsecuta⌉ subiecta L   11–12 animam⌉ anima L   13 DE ADPREHENSA
UERECUNDA⌉ *deest* IL   14 Moses⌉ *deest* L   14 inter se⌉ in te L   14 uiri⌉ *superscriptum*
I   14–15 coeperint⌉ ceperint* I coeprint L   16 uerecunda⌉ uereconda* I uiracundia L
18 DE CORNUPETO PECODE⌉ *deest* IL   19 Moses⌉ *deest* L   20 comedentur⌉ comedantur L
20 carnes⌉ carnis L   20 aut⌉ autem L   21 nudiustertius⌉ nudustertius I nudiustercius
L   21 contestati⌉ non testati L   22 recluserit⌉ cluserit L

Collectio CCCC capitulorum

29

obruetur et dominum illius occident. Quod si pretium ei fuerit inpositum dabit pro anima sua quicquid fuerit postulatus.

XXXV Sɪ ᴄᴏʀɴᴜᴘᴇᴛɪᴇʀɪᴛ ꜰɪʟɪᴜᴍ

L 89v Moses: Filium quoque aut filiam si cornu percusserit simili sententia subiacebit. Si seruum aut ancillam inuaserit xxx siclos argenti dabit domino bos uero lapidibus obruetur.

XXXVI Dᴇ ᴜᴜʟɴᴇʀᴀᴛᴏ ʙᴏᴜᴇ

I 134r Moses: Si bos alienus bouem uulnerabit alterius et ille mortuus fuerit uendent bouem uiuum et diuident inter se pretium eius cadauer aut mortui inter se dispertient.

XXXVII Sɪ ᴀɴᴛᴇ ᴇʀɪᴛ ᴄᴏʀɴᴜᴘᴇᴛᴜs

Moses: Si autem sciebat quia bos cornupetus esset ab heri et nudiustertius et non custodiuit eum dominus suus reddet bouem pro boue et cadauer integrum accipiet.

XXXVIII Dᴇ ᴄɪsᴛᴇʀɴᴀ ᴀᴘᴇʀᴛᴀ

Moses: Si quis aperuerit cisternam et foderit et non operuerit eam cecideritque bos uel asinus in eam dominus cisternae reddet pretium iumentorum quod autem est mortuum ipsius erit.

4–6 Ex 21:31-2   **8–10** Ex 21:35   **12–14** Ex 21:36   **16–18** Ex 21:33-4

---

1 Quod] Quae L   1 pretium] precium L   2 postulatus] postolatus L   3 Sɪ ᴄᴏʀɴᴜᴘᴇᴛɪᴇ-ʀɪᴛ ꜰɪʟɪᴜᴍ] *deest* IL   4 Moses] *deest* L   4 simili] simile L   4–5 subiacebit] subiaceat L   5 xxx] triginta L   5 domino] dominus L   7 Dᴇ ᴜᴜʟɴᴇʀᴀᴛᴏ ʙᴏᴜᴇ] *deest* IL *sequitur cap.* XXXVI *post cap.* XXXVII L   8 Moses] *deest* L   8 uulnerabit] uulnerauerit L   8 uendent] uindent L   9 se] se se L   9 pretium] precium L   9 aut] autem L   9 mortui] *deest* L   10 dispertient] dispicient L   11 Sɪ ᴀɴᴛᴇ ᴇʀɪᴛ ᴄᴏʀɴᴜᴘᴇᴛᴜs] *deest* IL *praecedit cap.* XXXVII *ante cap.* XXXVI L   12 Moses] *deest* L   12 quia] que L   12 cornupetus] cornupeta L   12 nudiustertius] nudustertius I   13 bouem] et bouem L   13 boue] bouem L   13 et cadauer] cadauer autem L   15 Dᴇ ᴄɪsᴛᴇʀɴᴀ ᴀᴘᴇʀᴛᴀ] *deest* IL   16 Moses] *deest* L   17 uel] et L   17 asinus] asynus L   17 cisternae] cisterne L   17 pretium] precium L   17 quod] que L

30 Collectio CCCC capitulorum

XXXVIIII Moses turpitudinem multiplicius consanguinitatis quam leges Theodosi et Romanorum

i Primo gradu continentur pater mater. Haec personae sequentibus quoque gradibus pro substantia earum, ipso ordine duplicantur: duo aui paternus et maternus aui, patruus, id est patris frater, et soror pater, amita, auunculus et matertera matris frater et soror.

ii Auus enim et auia ex patre quam ex matre; nepus, neptis tam ex filio quam ex filia; frater, soror tam ex patre quam ex matre accipiuntur.

iii Tertio gradu ueniunt proauus, proauia, infra pronepus nepos, proneptis; et oblico fratris sororisque filius, filia.

iv Quarto gradu ueniunt supra abauus, abauia, infra abnepus, abneptis; patruelis soror, patruelis id est patrui filius filia, consobrinus consobrina, id est auunculi et materterae filius filia. Itemque consobrini, qui ex duobus sororibus nascuntur, quibus adcrescit patruus magnus, amita magna, id est aui paterni frater et soror quam mater frater et soror.

v Quinto gradu ueniunt supra quidem adauus et adauia, infra adnepus, adneptis; ex oblico fratris et sororis pronepus, proneptis; fratres patrueles, amitini amitinae, consobrinus consobrinae, filius filia; proprius sobrinus, sobrina, id est patrui magni, amitae magnae, auunculi magni, materterae magnae filius, filia. His adcrescunt propatruus, proamita, hi sunt patrui materni frater et

margin: I 134v · M 168r · L 90r · I 135r

3–31.16 *Brev. Pauli* IV.10

1–2 Moses turpitudinem multiplicius consanguinitatis quam leges Theodosi et Romanorum] Moses tupitudinis multiplicus consanguinitatis quam legis Theodosio et Romanorum L 3 continentur] continentiae L 3 Haec] Hec L 4 substantia earum, ipso] substantiarium L 4 duplicantur] duplicanter L 4 aui] autem L 4 paternus] pater unus L 5 aui] auii L 5 patruus] pateruus L 5 frater] fratris L 5–6 pater, amita, auunculus et matertera matris frater et soror] *deest* L 7 Auus] Auius L 8 tam] quam L 8 patre] patrem L 9 iii] *deest* M 9 ueniunt] uenius sit M 9 proauus] proauius L 9 pronepus] *deest* L 9 proneptis] proneptiis L 9 et] ex M 10 oblico] obliquo M 11 iv] *deest* M 12 consobrinus] consubrinus L 12 consobrina] consubrina L 13 auunculi] auunculus L 13 materterae] matertera L 13 filius filia] *deest* L 13 consobrini] consubrini L 13 qui] que L 16 v] *deest* M 16 ueniunt] ueniuntur L 17 oblico] obliqo *corr.* obliquo M 17 fratris] fratres L 17 pronepus] prooepus M 17 patrueles] patruelis M 18 consobrinus] consubrinus L 18 consobrinae] et consubrinae L 18 sobrinus] subrinus L 18 sobrina] subrina L 19 patrui] patruii L 19 amitae magnae, auunculi magni] *deest* L 19 materterae magnae] materterae magne L 20 filia] et filia L 20 propatruus] propatriuis L 20 hi] hii L 20 patrui] patriui L proaui M 20 materni] maternie L

Collectio CCCC capitulorum   31

M 168v

I 135v

soror; proauunculus, promatertera, hi sunt proaui et paterni et materni, quia frater et soror, proauique materni.

vi Sexto gradu ueniunt supra tritauus, tritauia, infra trinepus, trineptis; ex oblico fratres sorores abnepus, abneptis; fratres patrueles, sorores patrueles, amitini, amitinae, consobrini, consobrinae, patrui magni, amitae magnae, auunculi magni, materterae magnae, nepus, neptis, proprii subrini filius, filia, qui consobrini appellantur, quibus ex latere succrescunt proamitae, patrui, proauunculi, promaterterae filius, filia; abpatruus, abamita, hi sunt abaui paterni frater et soror; abauunculus, abmatertera, hi sunt abauiae paternae materneque frater et soror; abauique materni. Hoc quoque explanare amplius non potest quia auctor ipse adseruit.

vii Septimo gradu qui sunt cognati, recta linia supra infraque propriis nominibus non appellantur: sed ex transuersa linea continentur fratres sororesque abnepus, abneptis; consobrini filieque. Successiones inter his septem gradibus omnia propinquitatum nomina continentur, ultra quos nec ad finitas inueniri nec successio amplius propagari potest.

I 136r

L 90v

Explicit de propinquitate

XL De matrimoniis

Non omnes personas ducere licet, quia nec patri filiam nec filio matrem nec

---

19–32.15 cf. *Epitome Gai* I.4

---

1 promatertera⟧ matertera L   1 hi⟧ hii L   1 quia⟧ que L   2 proauique⟧ et proauique L   3 vi⟧ *deest* M   3 tritauus⟧ triauus L   3 tritauia⟧ triauia L   3 trineptis⟧ trinepus L   3 ex⟧ et L   4 oblico⟧ obliquo M   4 abnepus⟧ anepus M   4 abneptis⟧ aneptis M   4 patrueles⟧ patruelis L   4–5 sorores patrueles⟧ *deest* L   5 amitini⟧ *superscriptum* M   5 amitinae⟧ amitae M   5 consobrini⟧ *deest* L   5 consobrinae⟧ consubrine L   5 patrui⟧ patru L   5 amitae magnae⟧ amite magne L   6 auunculi⟧ abunculi L   6 materterae magnae⟧ matertere magne L   6 subrini⟧ sobrini M   7 consobrini⟧ cansubrini I consobrini L   7 proamitae⟧ proamite L   8 proauunculi⟧ proabunculi L   8 promaterterae⟧ promaterterа L   8 abpatruus⟧ apatruus L   8 hi⟧ hii L   9 abauunculus⟧ abauunculis L   9 hi⟧ hii L   9 abauiae⟧ abauihe I   9 paternae⟧ *deest* L   10 materneque frater et soror; abauique materni⟧ *deest* L   10 materneque⟧ maternaeque M   10 Hoc⟧ Hic L   10 explanare⟧ explanari LM   11 quia⟧ quod M   12 vii⟧ *deest* M   12 qui⟧ que L   12 recta⟧ recte L   13 transuersa⟧ trans uerba M   13 linea⟧ linia LM   13 sororesque⟧ sororesue I sorores L   14 abnepus⟧ anepus M   14 abneptis⟧ aneptis M   14 consobrini⟧ consubrini L   14 filieque⟧ filiaeque LM   14 his⟧ bis L   16 nec⟧ *deest* L   17 Explicit de propinquitate⟧ *deest* M   17 propinquitate⟧ propinqui L   18 XL⟧ XLI M   18 De matrimoniis⟧ De matrimonio caput xl L

32 Collectio CCCC capitulorum

auo neptim nec nepoti auiam. Fratris quoque sororis filiam uxorem ducere *M 169r*
non licet. Sororem quoque patris ac matris uxorem accipere non licet. Gene-
ro quoque socrum suam uxorem accipere non licet nec uitrico priuignam nec
priuigno nouercam. Fratres etiam amittenos et consobrinos in matrimonio
5 iungi nulla ratione permittitur. Sed nec uir unus duas uxores habere nec uni
mulieri duobus fratribus iungi permittitur. Quod non solum de personis, quae
nobis coniunctae sunt et propinquis, sed etiam uel adoptiuis, hoc est adfilia-
tis dissoluatur, iussum est obseruare; nam etsi per emancipationem adobtio *I 136v*
dissoluatur nuptias tamen inter has personas semper constat inlicitas. Inter
10 fratrem quoque et sororem siue patre eodem ac matre nati fuerint siue diuer-
sis patribus ac matribus matrimonia esse non possunt. Inter adoptiuos etiam
fratres inlicita sunt coniugia ne forte adoptio emancipatione fuerit dissoluta,
nam si emancipatio interuenerit nuptiae inter huiusmodi licito contrahuntur,
quia si quis incestas uel nefarias, id est quae sunt superius nec nuptias nec filios
15 habere uidetur sed spuri pueri appellantur, hoc est sine patre.

XLI De propinquitate Gregorius respondit
De Mose Gregorius in interrogationibus Augustini respondit: Quaedam ter- *M 169v*
rena lex in romana republica permittit ut siue frater et soror seu duorum fratrum germanorum uel duarum sororum filius et filia misceantur. Sed experi- *I 137r*
20 mento didicimus ex tali coniugio sobolem non posse succrescere et sacra lex
mosaica prohibet cognationis turpitudinem reuelare. Unde necesse est ut iam *L 91r*

17–33.12 Greg. I, *Lib. resp.*, 6

---

1 neptim] nepotum L   1 nepoti] nepti M   1 Fratris] Fratri L   1 sororis] et sorores L et sororis M   2 Sororem quoque patris ac matris uxorem accipere non licet] *deest*
L   3 uxorem] nec socere non uestrum suam uxorem L   3 non] *deest* L   4 Fratres]
patris M   4 amittenos] amittenus L amitenus M   4 consobrinos] consobrinos L consobrinus M   5 uir unus] unus uir LM   6 quae] que L qui M   7 propinquis] propinque L
7–8 adfiliatis] adfiliatus L   8 dissoluatur] *deest* LM   8 emancipationem] mancipationem
L   8 adobtio] adoptilio L adoptio M   9 dissoluatur] dissoluantur* I   9 nuptias] neptias
L   10 matre] matri M   12 inlicita sunt] inlicitas L   12 adoptio emancipatione] adop-
tione L   12 dissoluta] desolata I desoluta LM   13 nam] non L   13 emancipatio] man-
cipatione I mancipatio L   13 contrahuntur] contrauntur L   14 quia] que L   15 spuri]
spueri L   15 patre] patris L patre sine matre M   16 XLI] XLII M   16 De propinquitate
Gregorius respondit] *deest* IL   17 De Mose] Moyse L *deest* M   17 Quaedam] quidam
L   18 et] aut L   19 filius] filios L   19–20 experimento] exprimento L   20 sobolem]
subolem LM   21 mosaica] moysiaca LM   21 prohibet] proibet* M

Collectio CCCC capitulorum

33

tertia uel quarta generatio fidelium licenter sibi iungi debeat. Nam secunda, quam prediximus, a se omnimodo abstinere debet. Graue est facinus, qui turpitudinem nouercae, quae una caro cum patre fuit reuelare presumpserit profecto patris turpitudinem reuelabit. Cum cognata quoque miscere prohibitum est, quia per conpunctionem priorem caro fratris fuerat facta. Pro qua re etiam Iohannis Baptista capite truncatus est et sancto martyrio consummatus. Cui non est dictum ut Christum negaret et pro Christi confessione occisus est; sed quia isdem Dominus noster Ihesus Christus dixerat: 'Ego sum ueritas', quia pro ueritate Iohannis occisus est.

I 137v
M 170r
Omnes autem qui ad fidem ueniunt admonendi sunt ne tale aliquid audeant perpetrare. Si quid autem perpetrauerint corporis et sanguinis Domini commonione priuandi sunt.

XLII   De furtu bouis et ouis

Moses: Si quis furatus fuerit bouem aut ouem et occiderit uel uendiderit: v boues pro uno boue et iiii oues pro una oue restituet. Si non habuerit quod pro furtu reddat uenundabitur. Si inuentum fuerit apud eum quod furatus est uiuens siue bos siue asinus siue ouis sit duplum restituet.

XLIII   De fure effringente domum

Moses: Si effringens fur domum siue suffodiens fuerit inuentus et accepto uulnere mortuus fuerit: percussor non erit reus sanguinis. Quod si orto sole hoc

---

14–15 Ex 22:1   **15–16** cf. Ex 22:3   **16–17** Ex 22:4   **19–34.1** Ex 22:2-3

---

1 licenter] *deest* L   1 iungi] inungi L   1 debeat] debeant L   3 turpitudinem] rpitudinem* M   3 quae una] quina L   4 profecto] profacio L   4 reuelabit] reuelauit L   4 cognata] cognita L   4 miscere] *deest* M   4–5 prohibitum] proibitum L   5 conpunctionem] coniunctionem LM   5 fuerat] fuerit L   6 Baptista] Baptiste L   6 consummatus] consumatus LM   7 negaret] necaret* M   7 confessione] confessio M   7 occisus] occissus L   8 isdem] hisdem L   8 dixerat] dixerit L   9 quia] que L   9 pro] per L   9 occisus] occissus L   10 ne tale] natale L   11–12 commonione] communione LM   13 XLII] XLIII M   13 De furtu bouis et ouis] *deest* IL   14 Moses] Moyses L Moyses dicit M   14 uendiderit] uindiderit LM   14 v] quinque M   15 iiii] quartuor L quattuor M   15 una] uno L   16 furtu] furto L   16 uenundabitur] uenudabitur L   16–17 furatus est uiuens] inuentus est L   17 ouis sit] oues L   18 XLIII] XLIIII M   18 De fure effringente domum] *deest* IL   19 Moses] Moyses L Moyses ait M   19 effringens] es fringens L   19 suffodiens] effodiens M   19 fuerit] domum fuerit M   20 fuerit] erit L   20 orto] orte L

34   Collectio CCCC capitulorum

fecerit homicidium perpetrauerit et ipse morietur.

XLIIII DE COMMENDATA PECUNIA
Moses: Si quis commendauerit amico suo pecuniam aut uas in custodiam et ab
eo qui susciperat furtu oblatum fuerit: si inuenitur duplum reddet.

⁵ XLV DE DIIS ADIURANTIBUS
Moses: Si latet dominus domus applicabitur ad deos adiurauit quod non ex-   *I 138r; *
tenderit manum suam in rem proximi sui ad perpetrandam fraudem tam in   *91v*
boue quam in asino ac uestimento et quicquid damnum inferre potest ad deos
utriusque causa perueniet et si illi iudicauerint duplum restituet proximo suo. *M 170v*

¹⁰ XLVI DE ASINO COMMENDATO
Moses: Si quis commendauerit proximo suo asinum bouem ouemque et omne iumentum ad custodiam et mortuum fuerit aut debilitatum uel captum ab
hostibus et nullus hoc uiderit: iusiurandum erit in medio quod non extenderit
manum suam in rem proximi sui. Et suscipiet dominus iuramentum et ille
¹⁵ reddere non cogetur.

XLVII QUOD NON SOLUM FUR IN MAGNIS
Fur non solum in maioribus sed in minoribus iudicatur. Non enim id quod
furtu ablatum est sed mens furantis adtenditur. Quomodo in fornicatione ita
et in furtu quantumque seruus abstulerit furtu crimen incurrerit. Unde et   *I 139r*
²⁰ Mosi lege: Fures nonnumquam septuplum nonnumquam quadruplum reddere
conpelluntur et interdum obtruncatur interdum uenditur fur ipse pro furtu.

3–4 Ex 22:7 **6–9** Ex 22:8-9 **11–15** Ex 22:10-11 **17–21** Hier., *In ep. ad Titum,*
II.9-10

---

1 perpetrauerit⌉ perpetrauit M **2** XLIIII⌉ XLV M **2** DE COMMENDATA PECUNIA⌉ *deest* IL
3 Moses⌉ Moyses L Moyses dicit M **3** commendauerit⌉ conmendauerit L **4** oblatum⌉
ablatum LM **4** si inuenitur⌉ sibi uenitur L **4** duplum⌉ dupplum L **4** reddet⌉ reddat
L **5** XLV⌉ XLVI M **5** DE DIIS ADIURANTIBUS⌉ *deest* IL **6** Moses⌉ Moyses L Moyses
ait M **6** Si⌉ Si autem M **6** ad⌉ a ILM **6** adiurauit⌉ adiurabit LM **8** damnum⌉
damno L **8** ad⌉ a ILM **10** XLVI⌉ XLVII M **10** DE ASINO COMMENDATO⌉ *deest* IL
11 Moses⌉ Moyses L Moyses ait M **11** commendauerit⌉ conmendauerit L **11** ouemque⌉
quae L **12** debilitatum⌉ debilitatem* L **14** suam⌉ *deest* L **14** iuramentum⌉ iu-
ramentem* L **16** *XLVII*⌉ XLVIII M **16** QUOD NON SOLUM FUR IN MAGNIS⌉ *deest* IL
18 ablatum⌉ oblatum IL **18** furantis⌉ furatus L **19** seruus⌉ seruis L **19** furtu⌉ in furtu M **19** incurrerit⌉ incurrit LM **20** Mosi⌉ Moysi LM **20** nonnumquam septuplum⌉
deest L **21** interdum⌉ et interdum L **21** furtu⌉ furto M

Collectio CCCC capitulorum   35

XLVIII   De pecunia ecclesiastica Gregorius

Gregorius in responsionibus: Quia ea quae furtu de ecclesiis abstulerint reddere debeant attamen ex persona furis pensare potest qualiter ualeat corrigi. Sunt enim quidam qui habentes subsidia furtum perpetrant et sunt aliqui hac in re ex inopia delinquunt. Unde necesse est ut quidam damnis quidam uero uerberibus et quidam districtus quidam autem lenius corrigatur ex caritate agendum est ita ut mens extra rationis regulam omnino nihil faciat.

XLVIIII   De lesione agri et uineae

Moses: Si leserit quispiam agrum uel uineam et dimiserit iumentum suum ut depascatur alienum: quicquid optimum habuerit in agro suo uel in uinea pro damni aestimatione restituet.

L   De foco uago

Si egressus ignis inuenerit spicas et incenderit aream aut segetem aut uineas aut campum uel conprehenderit aceruos frugum siue stantes segetes in agris reddet damnum qui ignem incenderit.

LI   De mutuo populo dei

Moses: Si pecuniam dederis mutuam populo meo pauperi qui habitat tecum non urgues eum quasi exactor nec usuris opprimes.

Et Saluator in euangelio: Qui petit a te da ei et uolenti mutuare a te ne auertaris.

2–7 Greg. I, *Lib. resp.*, 4   **9–11** Ex 22:5   **13–15** cf. Ex 22:6   **17–18** Ex 22:25   **19** Mt 5:42

---

1 XLVIII⌉ XLVIIII M   1 De pecunia ecclesiastica Gregorius⌉ *deest* IL   2 Gregorius⌉ Augustinus* I   2 Quia⌉ qua* I Que L   2 furtu⌉ pro furtu L   2 abstulerint⌉ substulerit L   3 attamen⌉ adtamen L   3 corrigi⌉ corregi* I corregi L   4 quidam⌉ quidem L   4 hac⌉ qui hac L   5 ut⌉ *deest* L   5 quidam⌉ quidem L quid M   5–6 uero⌉ *deest* M   6 quidam⌉ quidem L   6 districtus⌉ disctrictius M   7 rationis⌉ rationes L   7 faciat⌉ fiat L   8 XLVIIII⌉ L M   8 De lesione agri et uineae⌉ De lesione agri et uineae M *deest* IL   9 Moses⌉ Moyses L Moyses ait M   9 dimiserit⌉ dimiserit L   9 ut⌉ aut L   11 aestimatione⌉ stimatione L   12 L⌉ LI M   12 De foco uago⌉ *deest* IL   13 Si⌉ Moyses: Si L Moyses dicit: Si M   13–14 aut segetem aut uineas aut campum⌉ aut campum L   14 aceruos⌉ aceruus L   14 frugum⌉ fruguum* I frugrum L fruguum M   14 segetes⌉ segites L   16 LI⌉ LII M   16 De mutuo populo dei⌉ *deest* IL   17 Moses⌉ Moyses L Moyses ait M   18 opprimes⌉ obprimes L   19 a⌉ ad L   19 mutuare⌉ mutuari LM   19 a⌉ ad L

36 Collectio CCCC capitulorum

Et in Deuteronomio: Pecuniam tuam non dabis fratri tuo ad usuram et frugum habundantiam non exiges.

Et in alio: Qui pecuniam non dedit ad usuram in caelis habitat. Equum iudicium sit inter uos siue ciues sit siue peregrinus. Id est ne iniquum aliquit in iuditio in regula in pondere in mensura. Statera iusta et aequa sint pondera. Iustus modius et aequus sextarius. Et si occurreris boui inimici tui aut asino *M 171v* erranti reduces ad illum. Si uideris asinum odientis te iacere sub onere non pertransibis sed leuabis cum eo.

LII   DE PIGNO ACCEPTO ET MOLA REDDENDA

Moses: Si pignus acceperis a proximo uestimentum ante solis occasum reddes. Ipsum enim est solum quo operitur indumentum carnis eius nec habet aliud *I 140v* in quo dormiat si clamauerit ad me exaudiam eum quia misericors sum nec molam pugnaueris.

LIII   DE DUABUS UEL TRIBUS TESTIBUS

Moses: In ore duorum aut trium testium peribit qui interficietur. Nemo occidatur uno contra se dicente testimonium.

In alio loco: Manus testium prima interficiet eum et manus reliqui populi *L 92v* extrema mittetur in eum.

1–2 cf. Lev 25:37   3 cf. Ps 14:5   3–4 cf. Lev 24:22   4–6 cf. Lev 19:35-6   6–8 Ex 23:4-5   10–12 cf. Ex 22:26-7   15–16 Deut 17:6   17–18 Deut 17:7

---

2 habundantiam] abundantiam LM   2 exiges] exies L   3 alio] alio loco M   3 usuram] usuram et frugum habundatiam L   3 habitat] habitet L   3 Equum] Aequum L   4 uos] oues L   4 siue ciues sit] *deest* L   4 Id est] idem M   4 aliquit] aliquid LM   5 iuditio] iudicio LM   5 Statera] in statera L   5 aequa] equa L   5 pondera] pondere L   6 Iustus] iustos* I   6 modius] modus* I   6 aequus] equis L equus M   6 sextarius] sistarius L   7 onere] onore L   8 sed] uel L   9 LII] LIIII M   9 DE PIGNO ACCEPTO ET MOLA REDDENDA] DE PIGNO ACCEPTO M *deest* IL   10 Moses] Moyses L Moyses dicit M   10 acceperis] acciperis LM   11 quo] qui L   13 molam] malam L   13 pugnaueris] pignaueris L pignoraueris M   14 LIII] LIIII M   14 DE DUABUS UEL TRIBUS TESTIBUS] DE DUOBUS UEL TRIBUS TESTIBUS M *deest* IL   15 Moses] Moyses L Moyses dicit M   16 se] *deest* M   17 In] Et in LM   17 interficiet] interficiat LM

Collectio CCCC capitulorum

37

LIIII De mendacis testibus

Moses: Si steterit testis mendax contra hominem accusans eum preuaricationis, stabunt ambo quorum causa est ante Dominum in conspectu sacerdotum et iudicum qui fuerit in diebus illis, cumque diligentissime perscrutantes quam per odium quis hominem inpulerit uel iecerit quippiam in eum per insidias inuenerint falsum testem dixisse contra fratrem suum mendatium, reddent ei sicut fratri suo facere cogitauit et auferes malum de medio tui. Non declinabis in iudicio pauperis mendatium fugies.

Recolite Iob dicentem: Seruum meum et ancillam meam in iuditio non dispexi et causam quam nesciebam diligentissime inuestigabam.

Et Dominus: Nec in iuditio plurimorum adquiescas sententiae ut a uero deuies. Quia testis falsus non erit inpunitus et qui mendatia loquitur peribit.

LV Si quid fortuitu acciderit

Moses: Quod si fortuitu et absque odio et inimicitia quicquid horum fuerit et hoc audiente populo fuerit conprobatum atque inter percussorem et propinquum sanguinis quaestio uentilata: liberabitur innocens de ultoris manu.

Et Iacobus: Sic loquimini et sic facite sicut per legem libertatis incipientes iudicari. Iudicium sine misericordia illi qui non fecerit misericordiam. Superexaltat misericordia iuditio.

2–7 cf. Deut 19:16-19   4–5 Num 35:20   7–8 Ex 23:6-7   10 Iob 29:16   11 Ex 23:2   12 Prov 19:9   14–16 Num 35:22-5   17–19 Iac 2:12-13

---

1 LIIII] LV M   1 De mendacis testibus] *deest* IL   2 Moses] Moyses L Moyses ait M   3 stabunt] istabunt L   4 iudicum] iudicium L   4 quam] que L quia M   5 odium] hodium L   5 iecerit] eiecerit M   5 quippiam] quispiam L   5 in eum per insidias] per insidias in eum M   6 mendatium] mendacium LM   7 auferes] auferas L   8 iudicio] iuditio L   8 mendatium] mendacium LM   9 dicentem] dicentum L   9 iuditio] iudicio LM   9 non dispexi] *deest* I   10 diligentissime] diligentissimae* I   11 iuditio] iudicio LM   11 deuies] debies* I debeas L   12 mendatia] mendacia M   13 LV] LVI M   13 Si quid fortuitu acciderit] *deest* IL   14 Moses] Moyses L Moyses dicit M   14 fortuitu] furtuitu L   14 odio] hodio L   14 quicquid] quiaquid* L   16 sanguinis] sanguis M   16 quaestio] questio L   16 ultoris] adulteris L   17 Iacobus] Iacobus ait M   17 libertatis] liberatis L   18 iudicari] iudicare L   18 misericordia] misericordia erit M   19 iuditio] iudicio L iudicium M

38 Collectio CCCC capitulorum

LVI Si fuerit aliqua causa apud iudices
Si fuerit causa aliqua inter aliquos et interpellauerint iudices quem iustum esse
perspexerint illi iustitiae palmam dabunt quem impium condemnabunt impietatis. Sin autem qui peccat dignum uiderint plagas prosternent et coram se   *L 93r*
5 facient uerberari pro mensura peccati erit plagarum modus ne foede laceratur
ante oculos tuos habeatur frater tuus.   *M 172v*

Ut apostolus: Superexaltat misericordia iuditio.

LVII Moses de nocturna pullutione
Si fuerit inter uos homo qui nocturno pullutus sit somno et nisi lotum aqua ei   *I 142r*
10 usque ad uesperum intrare ecclesiam non concedit.

Gregorius in responsione Augustini: Populus spiritalis intellegens sub eodem
intellectu accipiet. Quia quasi per somnium inludetur qui temptatus inmun-
ditia ueris imaginibus in cogitatione inquinatur. Sed lauandus est aqua ut
culpas cogitationis lacrimis abluat et nisi prius ignis temptationis recedent
15 reum se quasi usque ad uesperum cognoscat. Sed est in eadem inlusione ualde
necessaria discretio, quae subtiliter pensare debeat, ex qua re accedat men-   *I 142v*
ti dormientis; aliquando enim ex crapula aliquando ex naturae superfluitate
uel infirmitate, aliquando ex cogitatione contingit. Et quidem cum ex naturae uel superfluitate uel infirmitate euenerit, omnimodo haec inlusio non est
20 ei timenda, quia hanc animus nesciens pertulisse magis dolendum est quam

---

2–6 Deut 25:1-3   **7** Iac 2:13   **9–10** cf. Deut 23:10-11   **11–39.15** Greg. I, *Lib. resp.*,
9

---

1 LVI] LVII M   **1** Si fuerit aliqua causa apud iudices] *deest* IL   **2** Si] Moyses ait:
Si M   **2** interpellauerint] interpellauerunt L   **3** quem impium condemnabunt] *deest*
M   **3** condemnabunt] condempnabunt L   **3–4** impietatis] impiaetatis L   **4** Sin] Si L
5 facient] faciant L   **5** foede] fide L   **5** laceratur] leceratur L laceratus M   **7** apostolus]
post L apostolus dicit M   **7** iuditio] iudicio M   **8** LVII] LVIII M   **8** Moses de nocturna
pullutione] De nocturna pollutione laicorum seu sacerdotum M   **9** Si] Moyses dicit: Si
M   **9** nocturno] nocturna L   **9** pullutus] pollutus LM   **9** aqua] aque L   **10** uesperum]
uaesperam L   **10** ecclesiam] in ecclesiam M   **11** responsione] responsiones L responsionibus M   **11** Augustini] Agustini I   **12** Quia] Et quia L   **12** inludetur] illud uidetur
M   **12–13** inmunditia] inmundicia L   **13** ueris] uiris L   **13** imaginibus] inmagini-
bus L   **14** cogitationis] cogitationibus L   **14** recedent] recederit LM   **15** cognoscat]
cognuscat L   **16** quae] qui L   **17** dormientis] dormienti dormientis *corr.* dormienti
L   **17** ex] *superscriptum* I   **17** naturae] nature L natura M   **18** contingit] contigit
M   **19** superfluitate] fluitate L   **20** pertulisse] pertullisse L

Collectio CCCC capitulorum

39

fecisse. Cum uero ultra modum appetitus gulae insumendis alimentis rapitur
atque idcirco humorum receptacula grauantur, habet exinde animus aliquem
reatum; non tamen usque ad prohibitionem percipiendi sancti misterii uel missarum solemnia celebrandi, cum fortasse aut festus dies exigit aut exhiberi
mysterium pro eo quod sacerdos alius in loco deest ipsa necessitas conpellit. 5
Nam si adsunt alii qui implere ministerium ualeant, inlusio pro crapula facta a
perceptione sacri mysterii prohiberi non debet, sed ab immolatione sacri mysterii abstinere ut arbitror humiliter debet si tamen dormientis animum turpi
imaginatione non concusserit. Nam sunt quibus ita plerumque inlusio nasci-
tur ut eorum animus etiam in somno corporis positus turpis imaginationibus 10
non foedetur. Qua in re unum ubi ostenditur ipsa mens rea, non tamen uel
suo iuditio libera cum se etsi dormienti corpore meminit nihil uidisse tamen
in uigiliis corporis meminit ingluuiem cicidisse. Sin uero ex turpi cogitatione
uigilantis oritur inlusio dormientis patet animo suus reatus; uidet enim a qua
radice inquinatio illa processerit quia quod cogitauit hoc pertulit nesciens. 15

LVIII   De uotu uirorum et uiduarum et mulierum
Moses: Si quis uirorum uotum Domino uouerit et se constrinxerit iuramento:
non faciat irritum uerbum suum sed omne quod promisit implebit, quia requi-
ret illum Dominus Deus tuus et si mortuus fuerit reputauit tibi in peccatum.
Si nolueris polliceri absque peccato eris. 20

17–18 Num 30:3   **18–20** Deut 23:21-2

---

2 humorum] honorum L   **3** misterii] mysterii LM   **3** uel] *superscriptum* I
3–4 missarum] myserum L   **4** solemnia] solempnia L   **4** celebrandi] caelebranda L
caelebrandi M   **4** cum] con L   **5** mysterium] ministerium L   **5** quod] pro L   **5** alius]
alios LM   **6** alii] ali *corr.* alii I   **6** implere] inplere L   **6** ministerium] mysterium M
7 mysterii] misterii L   **7** prohiberi] prohibere L   **7** ab] ad L   **8** abstinere] abstineri
L   **10** etiam] aetiam L   **10** imaginationibus] imaginibus M   **11** foedetur] fodetur L
11 ubi] ibi M   **11** mens rea] mensura M   **12** iuditio] iudicio M   **12** corpore meminit
nihil] *deest* L   **12** meminit nihil] nihil meminit M   **13** meminit] meminit corpore nihil
meminit L   **13** cicidisse] caecidisse L cecidisse M   **13** Sin] Si* M   **14** animo suus rea-
tus] animos suos reatos L   **15** quia quod] quiaque L   **15** cogitauit] cogitauit sciens M
15 pertulit] pertullit* L   **16** LVIII] LVII I LVIIII M   **16** De uotu uirorum et uiduarum
et mulierum] De uoto uirorum et uiduarum et mulierum M *deest* IL   **17** Moses] Moyses L Moyses ait M   **17** constrinxerit] constrixerit L   **18** irritum] inritum* I inritum L
in irritum M   **18** omne] ex omne L   **19** illum] illud M   **19** mortuus] moratus LM
19 reputauit] reputabit LM   **19** in peccatum] impeccatum M   **20** polliceri] polliceris
M

40 Collectio CCCC capitulorum

Hoc ita apud Salamonem et in Sapientia similiter.

Moses: Uidua et repudiata quicquid uouerint reddent. Uxor in domo uiri uoto se constrinxit. Si autem audierit uir et tacuerit nec contradixerit sponsioni
reddet quodcumque promiserat. Sin autem contradixerit exemplo maritus uo- *L 94r*
5 tis innocens. Similiter et puella in domo patris uotum uouerit. Sin autem pater
statim ut audierit contradixerit innocens uotis. Sin in alteram diem distulerit *I 144r*
sententiam reddat uotum.

LVIIII DE SOLUTIONE UOTIS AB EPISCOPO
Canones nouae: Licitum est episcopo uotum soluere si uult, quia scriptum est:
10 uota stulta et inportabilia frangenda sunt.

LX DE ABBATE
Qui uouerit uotum sine permissu abbatis commotetur ab abbate et uideat abbas.
In alio loco: Monacho non licere uotum uouere sine consensu abbatis sui. Sin
15 minus frangendum est, si iusserit abbas.

LXI QUI SE UOUERIT ET ITERAUERIT
Si quis postquam se uouerit Domino saecularem habitum acciperit, iterum ad *M 174r*
aliquem gradum accedere omnino non debet.

2–5 Num 30:10-12 **5–6** cf. Num 30:4-5 **6–7** cf. Num 30:14 **9–10** cf. *Iud. Theod.*
C 201-2 **12–13** cf. *Hibernensis* 17.9 (p. 99, ln. 11-12) **14–15** *Iud. Theod. C* 199-200; *D*
167; *U* II.6.9; *G*44 **17–18** *Iud. Theod. U,* I.9.2

---

1 Salamonem⌉ Salomonem M **2** Moses⌉ Moyses LVIIII L Item Moyses M **3** constrinxit⌉
constrinxerint L constrinxerit M **3** sponsioni⌉ responsioni L **4** quodcumque⌉ quocum-
que* I quecumquae L **4** exemplo⌉ extimplo I **5** puella⌉ puelle L **5** Sin⌉ SiM **6** Sin⌉
Si LM **6** distulerit⌉ distullerit L **7** sententiam⌉ sententia L **8** LVIIII⌉ LX LM **8** DE
SOLUTIONE UOTIS AB EPISCOPO⌉ *deest* IL **8** SOLUTIONE⌉ DESOLUTIONE M **9** Canones⌉ Canonum L **9** nouae⌉ *deest* LM **11** LX⌉ LXI LM **11** DE ABBATE⌉ DE MONACHORUM UOTIS
AB ABBATO M **12** uouerit⌉ nouerit L **12** commotetur⌉ commotetus* I **12** ab⌉ *deest* L
14–15 Sin minus⌉ Si in missus L Si minus M **16** LXI⌉ LXII LM **16** QUI SE UOUERIT ET
ITERAUERIT⌉ *deest* IL **17** saecularem⌉ saeculare LM **17** acciperit⌉ acceperit M

Collectio CCCC capitulorum 41

LXII DE MENSTRUATA

Ad mulierem quae patitur menstrua non accedes; sin aperuerit fontem sanguinis sui moriantur.

Gregorius: Audistis ut morte lex sacra feriat, si quis uir ad menstruatam mulierem accedat. Nuncque tamen mulier, dum consuetudinem menstruam patitur, prohibere ecclesiam intrare non debet, quae ei naturae superfluitas in culpam non uolet reputari, et per hoc quod inuita patitur iustum non est ut ingressus ecclesiae priuetur. Nouimus namque quod mulier, quae fluxum patiebatur sanguinis, post tergum Domini humiliter ueniens uestimenti eius fimbriam tetigit, atque ab ea statim sua infirmitas recessit. Si ergo in fluxu sanguinis posita laudabiliter potuit Domini uestimentum tangere, cur quae menstruam sanguinis patitur non liceat domini ecclesiam intrare? Si dicis illam infirmitas conpulit, medicamentum quidem contra egritudines explorare. Feminae itaque et menstruus sui sanguinis fluxus egritudo est. Si illa sanguinaria conceditur sanitas, cur non concedatur cunctis mulieribus, que naturae suae uitio infirmantur? Sanctae communionis mysterium in eisdem diebus percipere non debet prohiberi.

LXIII DE LAUACRO UIRORUM

Moses: Si mixtus uir mulieri et lauari aqua debeat et ante solis occasum ecclesiam non intrare. Lex autem ueteri populo precepit. Quod autem intellegi

---

2 Lev 18:19 **2–3** Lev 20:18 **4–17** cf. Greg. I, *Lib. resp.*, 8 **19–42.9** cf. Greg. I, *Lib. resp.*, 8

---

1 LXII⌉ LXIII M **1** DE MENSTRUATA⌉ DE MENSTRUATAM L DE MENSTRUATA ECLESIAE INTRARE M **2** Ad⌉ Moyses dicit: Ad M **2** quae⌉ que L qui M **2** accedes⌉ accedis L **2** sin⌉ si L **4** Gregorius⌉ Gregorius ait M **4–5** menstruatam mulierem⌉ mulierem menstruatam M **5** dum⌉ de L **6** ecclesiam⌉ aecclesiam L **6** quae⌉ que L **6** superfluitas⌉ superfluetas L **7** uolet⌉ ualet L **8** ingressus⌉ ingressu L **8** ecclesiae⌉ aecclesie L eclesiae M **8** quae⌉ que L **9** patiebatur⌉ paciebatur L **9** post tergum⌉ postergum I postergum L **10** fimbriam⌉ frimbriam I **10** fluxu⌉ fluxus L **11** sanguinis⌉ in sanguinis I **11** quae⌉ quam I qui L **12** ecclesiam⌉ aecclesiam L **13** conpulit⌉ compulit M **13** egritudines⌉ egritudinis I aegritudinis LM **14** menstruus sui⌉ menstruis suis L **14** egritudo⌉ aegritudo LM **14–15** sanguinaria⌉ sanguinarea M **15** conceditur⌉ concedit I **15** que⌉ qui LM **16** communionis⌉ communis L commonionis M **16** eisdem⌉ eiusdem M **18** LXIII⌉ LXIIII M **18** DE LAUACRO UIRORUM⌉ *deest* IL **19** Moses⌉ Moyses L Gregorius M **19** Si mixtus⌉ Si mixtus est M **19** aqua⌉ aquia* L **20** autem⌉ in L **20** Quod⌉ Quae LM **20** intellegi⌉ intellegis* I

42 Collectio CCCC capitulorum

spiritaliter potest. Nunc autem uir cum propria coniuge dormiens nisi lotus aqua intrare ecclesiam non debet; sed neque lotus intrare statim debet. Romanorum tamen semper ab antiquioribus usus fuit post ammixtionem proprie coniugis et lauacri purificationem quaerere et ab ingressu ecclesiae paululum
5 reuerenter abstinere. Quia ipsa licita ammixtio coniugis sine uoluntate carnis fieri non potest a sacri loci ingressu abstinendum est, quia uoluntas ipsa esse *I 145v* sine culpa nullatenus potest. Uigilanti uero mente pensandum est, quia in Syna monte Dominus ad populum locuturus prius eundem populum abstinere a mulieribus precepit.

10 LXIIII De creandis liberis

Gregorius: Si quis uero suam coniugem non cupidine uoluntatis raptus, sed solummodo creandorum liberorum gratia utitur, iste profecto siue de ingressu ecclesiae seu de sumendo dominici corporis sanguinisque misterio sui est re- *M 175r* linquendus iuditio, quia a nobis prohibere non debet, cum ei iuxta prefinitam
15 sententiam etiam ecclesiam licuerit intrare. Hinc de pueris Dauid dicitur ut si a mulieribus mundi essent panes propositionis acciperent; quos omnino non ac- *I 146r;* ciperent, nisi prius mundos eos David a mulieribus fateretur. Tunc autem uir *L 95r* qui post ammixtionem coniugis lotus aqua fuerit etiam sacrae communionis misterium ualet accipere.

11–19 Greg. I, *Lib. resp.*, 8

---

1 uir⌉ cur L   1 dormiens⌉ dorminens L   2 ecclesiam non debet; sed neque lotus intrare⌉ *deest* L (*homeoteleuton*)   3 tamen⌉ *deest* M   3 ammixtionem⌉ amaxionem L ammixtione M   3 proprie⌉ propriae LM   4 coniugis⌉ coniuges L   4 lauacri⌉ lauari I   4 quaerere⌉ querere LM   4 paululum⌉ paulum* I paulum L paulolum M   5 ammixtio⌉ amixtio L   5 coniugis⌉ coniungis* L   7 quia⌉ quae L   7–8 Syna⌉ sina L   8 monte⌉ mortem L   8 ad⌉ quod L   8 locuturus⌉ locutus est L   8 populum⌉ populus *corr.* populu L   10 LXIIII⌉ LXV M   10 De creandis liberis⌉ *deest* IL   11 cupidine⌉ conpidine M   11 uoluntatis⌉ uoluntates L   12 iste⌉ istae L   13 ecclesiae seu de sumendo⌉ mendo L (*homoeteleuton*)   13 ecclesiae⌉ eclesiae M   13 dominici⌉ domini* I   13 misterio⌉ ministerium L mysterio M   13 sui⌉ siui* L   14 iuditio⌉ iudicio M   14 quia a⌉ qui a L   14 ei⌉ ea L   14 prefinitam⌉ praefinita M   16 propositionis⌉ propositiones* I propositiones L   16 acciperent⌉ acciperunt L   17 mundos⌉ mundis L   17 fateretur⌉ fateratur L   18 ammixtionem⌉ amixtionem L   18 sacrae⌉ sacre L   19 misterium⌉ mysterium LM

Collectio CCCC capitulorum

43

LXV Postquam dies purificationis

Cum uero enixa fuerit mulier, quot dies debeat ecclesiam intrare, testamenti ueteris preceptione didicisti ut pro masculo diebus xxxiii, pro femina autem lxvi diebus debeat abstinere. Quod tamen sciendum est, quia in misterio accipitur. Nam si hora eadem qua genuerit actura gratias intret ecclesiam, nullo peccati pondere grauatur, uoluptas etenim carnis non dolor in culpa est. In carnis commixtione uoluptas est: nam in prolis prolatione gemitus. Unde et ipsi primae matri omnium dicitur: 'in doloribus paries.' Si itaque enixam mulierem prohibemus ecclesiam intrare ipsam ei paenam suam in culpam deputamus.

I 146v

5

10

M 175v

LXVI De pregnante baptizate

Baptizare autem pregnantem uel enixam mulierem uel hoc quod genuerit si mortis periculo urguetur uel ipsa hora eadem qua gignit uel hoc quod gignetur eadem qua natum est, nullo modo prohibetur.

LXVII De purificatione post partum

Ad eius concubitum uir suus accedere non debet, quoadusque qui gignitur ablactatur. Praua autem consuetudo in coniugatorum moribus surrexit, ut mulieres filios quos gignunt nutrire contemnant, eos aliis mulieribus ad nutriendum tradant, quod uidelicet ex sola causa incontinentiae uidetur. At tamen nisi purgationis tempus transierit, uiris suis non debent misceri.

I 147r

15

20

2–10 Greg. I., *Lib. resp.*, 8   **12–14** Greg. I., *Lib. resp.*, 8   **16–20** Greg. I, *Lib. resp.*, 8

---

1 LXV] LXVI M   1 Postquam dies purificationis] Post quae dies purificationis L De ingressu mulieris ecclaesie M   2 Cum] Gregorius: Cum M   2 enixa] enixta M   2 quot] quod IM que L   2 debeat] debet L   3 preceptione] preceptionem I   3 didicisti] dediscisti* L   3 xxxiii] xxxiiii M   4 debeat] *deest* L   4 Quod] Que L Quae M   4 tamen] amen* I   4 quia] qua* I que L quod M   4 misterio] ministerio L mysterio M   5 hora] ore L   5 intret] intrat L   5 ecclesiam] eclesiam M   7 gemitus] gemitos M   8 primae] prime L   8 matri omnium] matrimonio M   8 dicitur] dierunt L   8–9 enixam] enixa M   9 paenam] poenam LM   11 LXVI] XLVII M   11 De pregnante baptizate] Ad pregnato baptizando L De pregnante baptizanda M   12 Baptizare] Gregorius: Baptizare M   13 urguetur] urguent L   13 ipsa hora] ipsa ora L ipsam horam M   13 qua] que L   15 LXVII] XLVIII M   15 De purificatione post partum] Gregorius de purificatione post partum L De ablutione infantis M   16 Ad] Gregorius: Ad M   16 eius] mulieris M   16 suus] suis L   16 quoadusque] quiadusque M   18 filios] filios suos M   18 contemnant] contempnant LM

44 Collectio CCCC capitulorum

LXVIII De abstinentia ante partum et communione
Apud Romanos: Mulier tres menses debet se abstinere a uiro quando concepit   *L 95v*
antequam pariat. Mulieri quoque per omnia licet ante communicare quando
debet peperire.

5 LXVIIII De duobus germanis fratribus
Interrogat Augustinus: Si debeant duo germani fratres singulas sorores accipere, quia sunt ab illis longa progenie generati? Respondit Gregorius: Hoc
fieri modis omnibus licet; nequaquam enim in sacris eloquiis inuenitur, quod
huic capitulo contradicere uideatur.   *M 176r*

10 Et in alio loco: Duo fratres duas sorores in coniugio possunt habere, quidam
pater et filius matrem et filiam.   *I 147v*

LXX De propinquitate
In quarta propinquitate carnis secundum Grecos licet nubere sicut in lege
scriptum est. In quinta secundum Romanos. Tamen in tertia non soluunt
15 coniugium postquam factum fuerit. In tertia tamen propinquitate non licet
uxorem alterius accipere post obitum eius.

LXXI De amborum licencia seruitutis dei
Legitimum coniugium non licet separari sine consensu amborum, potest autem alter alteri licentiam dare accedere ad seruitutem dei.

2–4 *Iud. Theod.* U II.12.3-4; *G* 80-1   **6–9** Greg. I, *Lib. resp.*, 4   **10–11** *Iud. Theod.*
U II.12.29; *G* 71; *D* 110; *C* 81   **13–16** *Iud. Theod. G* 78; cf. *C* 82; U II.12.26-7; *D* 29-30
18–19 *Iud. Theod.* U II.12.7-8; *B* 32; *C* 79-80; cf. *Statuta Bonifatii*, §35

---

1 LXVIII] XLVIIII M   **1** De abstinentia ante partum et communione] *deest* IL
3 antequam] antequando L   **3** pariat] pariet L   **3** Mulieri] mulier M   **5** LXVIIII]
LXX M   **5** De duobus germanis fratribus] *deest* IL   **6** Interrogat] Interrogatio L
6 sorores] sororis L   **7** quia] qui L quae M   **7** progenie] progeniae* I progenia L progeniae M   **7** generati] generatae M   **7** Respondit] responsio M   **7** Gregorius] Gregorii
M   **10** coniugio] congio* M   **12** LXX] LXXI M   **12** De propinquitate] De propinquitate carnis M   **14** tertia] tercia L quarta M   **15** tertia] tercia L   **17** LXXI] LXXII
M   **17** De amborum licencia seruitutis dei] De amborum licentia seruitutis dei M *deest*
IL   **18** separari] separare L   **18** consensu] consen L   **18** potest] post L

Collectio CCCC capitulorum

45

LXXII Moses prohibeat Dominus licebit
Gregorius: Nam cum multa lex uelut inmunda manducare prohibeat, in euangelium tamen Dominus dicit: 'Non quod intrat in os coinquinat hominem sed
quod exeunt de ore illa sunt quae coinquinant hominem'; atque paulo post
subiecit exponens: 'Ex corde exeunt cogitationes malae.' Ubi ubertim indica- 5
tum est, quia illud omnipotenti deo pollutum esse in opere ostenditur, quod ex
pollutae cogitationis radice generatur. Unde Paulus apostolus quoque dixit:
'Omnia munda mundis coinquinatis autem et infidelibus nihil mundum'. Atque mox eiusdem causam coinquinationis adnuntians subiungit: 'Coinquinata
sunt enim et mens eorum et conscientia.' Si ergo ei cybus inmundus non est 10
cui mens inmunda non fuerit.

LXXIII De heredibus mosaice rationis
Moses: Homo cum mortuus fuerit absque filio ad filiam eius transibit hereditas. Si filiam non habuerit habebit successores fratres suos. Quod si et fratres
non habuerit dabitis hereditatem fratribus patris eius. Si autem nec patruos 15
habuerit dabitur hereditas his qui ei proximi sunt.

LXXIIII Leo ancillarum filios de hereditate abeiecit
Leonis pape: Non omnis mulier uiro iuncta uxor est uiri, quia nec omnis filius
heres est patris. Nuptiarum autem foedera inter ingenuos sunt legitima et in-

---

2–11 Greg. I, *Lib. resp.*, 8 **3–4** Mt 15:11* **13–16** cf. Num 27:8-11 **18–46.5** Leo
I, *ep. 167, ad Rusticum*, §4

---

1 LXXII] LXXIII M 1 Moses prohibeat Dominus licebit] Quod lex multa prohibet M 1 Moses] Moyses L 2 Gregorius] *deest* LM 2 uelut] uelud L 2 in]
Gregorius in L 2–3 euangelium] euangelio M 3 tamen] *deest* M 4 quae] que L
4 coinquinant] quoinquinat L 5 malae] male L 5 Ubi] Ube* L 5–6 indicatum]
iudicatum L 6 quia] que L quod M 6 illud] illi L 6 omnipotenti] ab omnipotenti LM 7 pollutae] pollute L 7 Paulus apostolus quoque] quoque Paulus apostolus
M 8 coinquinatis] coinquinationis L 8–9 autem et infidelibus...coinquinationis] *om.*
L *(homoeteleuton)* 8 nihil] nihil est M 9 mox] in M 9 adnuntians] adnuncians L
9 subiungit] subiiungit L 9 Coinquinata] Quoinquinata L 10 conscientia] constientia
L 10 ei] *deest* M 10 cybus] cibus M 11 inmunda] munda M 12 LXXIII] LXXIIII
M 12 De heredibus mosaice rationis] *deest* IL De heredibus M 13 Moses] Moyses L
Moyses ait M 15 Si] sin M 15 autem] *del.* L 15 patruos] patruus L 16 dabitur]
debitur I 16 hereditas] hereditatem L 17 LXXIIII] LXXV M 17 Leo ancillarum
filios de hereditate abeiecit] Leo ancillarum filios de hereditate eiecit M 18 Leonis
pape] Leo papa dicit M 18 pape] papae L 18 omnis] omnes L 19 heres] heris LM
19 ingenuos] ingenuis L genuos M

46 Collectio CCCC capitulorum

ter aequales, multo prius hoc ipsud Domino constituente quam initium Romani iuris existeret. Itaque aliud est uxor aliud concubina, sicut aliud est ancilla aliud libera. Propter quod etiam apostolus ad manifestandam harum personarum discretionem testimonium ponit in Genesi, ubi dicitur: 'Eice ancillam et filium eius; non enim erit heres filius ancillae cum filio meo Isaac'.

LXXV Leo ancillam a thoro abiecit
Interogatio Leonis: Ancillam a thoro abiecere et uxorem certe ingenuitatis accipere, non duplicatio coniugii, sed profectus est honestatis.

I 149r

M 177r

LXXVI Leonis ut supra de puellis quae concubinas habentibus nupserint
Paterno arbitrio uiris iunctae carent culpas si mulieres quae a uiris habebantur in matrimonio non fuerint, quia aliud est nupta aliud concubina.

LXXVII Apostolus matrimonio licentiam dedit
Apostolus et Gregorius: 'Melius est nubere quam uri'. Sine culpa scilicet ad coniugium ueniunt si tamen necdum meliora deuouerint.

LXXVIII Non conmiscearis cum masculo
Cum masculo non commisceris coitu feminaeo, et subditur ambo moriantur.

L 96v

4–5 Gen 21:10 Gal 4:30 7–8 cf. Leo I, *ep. 167, ad Rusticum*, §6 10–11 cf. Leo I, *ep. 167, ad Rusticum*, §§5-6 13–14 Greg. I, *Reg. past.*, III.27 13 1 Cor 7:9 16 Lev 18:22

---

1 aequales] equales L 1 Domino] Dominum M 1 initium] inicium L 2 aliud] aliut L 3 harum] arum L 4 Eice] gece L 5 heres] heris LM 5 filius] filios *corr.* filius L 6 LXXV] LXXVI M 6 Leo ancillam a thoro abiecit] *deest* IL 7 Interogatio Leonis] Iterum Leo L *deest* M 7 Ancillam] ancellam* I 7 thoro] toro L 7 abiecere] eicere L abiere *corr.* abigere M 8 duplicatio] dupplicatio L 9 LXXVI] LXXVII M 9 Leonis] Leonis papa M 9 quae] que* M 9 concubinas] concubinis L 9 nupserint] nupserunt LM 10 culpas] culpa LM 10 mulieres] mulieris LM 10 quae] que L 10 a uiris] auris L 11 est] *deest* M 12 LXXVII] LXXVIII M 12 Apostolus matrimonio licentiam dedit] *deest* IL 13 et Gregorius] dicit M 13 est] *superscriptum* M 13 uri] uiri L 13 Sine] Gregorius ait: Sine M 14 ueniunt] ueniunt *corr.* uenirunt L 14 deuouerint] deuouerunt L 15 LXXVIII] LXXVIIII M 15 conmiscearis] conmiscendum L coire M 15 masculo] omni pecode *corr.* masculo M 16 commisceris] commiscearis M 16 feminaeo] femineo L feminino M 16 subditur] subdito L 16 moriantur] *add.* In canone nunc autem si masculus cum masculo fornicat annis x paenitet M (*cf. Iud. Theod. U* II.1.5)

Collectio CCCC capitulorum 47

LXXVIIII Non coire cum omni pecode

Similiter: Cum omni pecore non coibis nec maculaueris cum eo, quia qui iumento et pecore coierit moriatur, pecus quoque occidetur.

I 149v In canone: Nunc autem si masculus cum masculo fornicat, annis x peniteat.

LXXX De penitentia amborum abundanter

Qui cum pecoribus coierit, xi annis. Qui sepe cum pecode aut cum masculo x annis ut peniteret iudicauit.

Alii ita: Si quis fornicatur sicut sodomitae fecerunt, x annis penitet tribus integris.

Alii: Sodomitae vii annis et molles sicut mulier adultera vii annis peniteat.

Qui semen aut sanguinem biberit, iii annis peniteat.

M 177v Qui sepe fecerit fornicationem, primus canon iudicauit x annis peniteat, secundus canon vii annis, sed pro infirmitate hominis et per consilium dixerunt iii annos penitentia eius.

Mulier quae subcubuerit cuilibet iumento simul interfitiatur cum eo.

I 150r In nouo: Illa sicut ille qui cum pecoribus coierit xv alii xi annis peniteat.

---

2 Lev 18:23 **2–3** Lev 20:15 **4** *Iud. Theod. U* II.1.5 **6** cf. *Iud. Theod. U* I.2.3; *G* 93 **6–7** *Iud. Theod. U* I.2.2; cf. *G* 93 **8–9** *Paen. Columbani*, §3 **10** cf. *Iud. Theod. U* I.2.6 **11** cf. *Iud. Theod. U* I.7.3 **12–14** *Iud. Theod. U* I.2.18; *G* 92 **15** cf. Lev 20:16 **16** cf. *Iud. Theod. U* I.2.3

---

1 LXXVIIII] LXXX M **1** Non coire cum omni pecode] *deest* IL **2** Similiter] *deest* LM **2** pecore] pecora L **2** quia] *deest* M **2** qui] qui cum M **3** pecore] pecora L **3** coierit] iecerit L **3** occidetur] occidatur M **4** annis] annus L **5** LXXX] LXXXI M **5** De penitentia amborum abundanter] *deest* IL **5** penitentia] paenitentia M **6** annis] annis penetiit L annis paeniteat M **6** sepe] saepe M **7** annis] annus L **7** peniteret] peneteret L paeniteret M **8** fecerunt] fecerit I **8** annis] annus L **8** penitet] penitiit L **10** annis] annus L **10** vii] *deest* L **10** annis] annus L **10** peniteat] penetiit L paeniteat M **11** annis] annus L **11** peniteat] *deest* L **12** sepe] saepe M **12** peniteat] paeniteat M **12–13** secundus] secunda* M **13** annis] annus L **13** et] *deest* LM **13** iii] tres L **14** annos] annus L **15** quae] qui L que M **15** interfitiatur] interficiatus L interfitiatus M **16** ille] illae L **16** annis] annos M **16** peniteat] paeniteat M

48 Collectio CCCC capitulorum

LXXXI DE COINQUINATIS ANIMALIBUS
Animalia talia coitu hominum polluta occidantur carnesque canibus proiciantur, sed coria adsumantur. Ubi autem dubium est, non occidantur.

LXXXII MOSES DE PREDA
Omnem predam exercitui diuides et comedes de spoliis hostium tuorum, quae Dominus Deus tuus dederit tibi.

LXXXIII HOC DAVID DE PREDA IN I LIBER REGUM
Aequa enim erit pars descendentis ad proelium et remanentis ad sarcinas et *L 97r* similiter diuident. Et factum est hoc ex die illa et deinceps constitutum et prefinitum et quasi lex in Israhel usque ad diem hanc.

LXXXIIII NON MORIATUR PATER PRO FILIO
Moses in Deuteronomio et in IIII Regum: Non moriuntur patres pro filiis, neque filii morientur pro patribus, sed unusquisque in peccato suo morietur. *I 150v*

LXXXV DE PECUNIA ALIENA
De pecunia quae in aliena prouintia ab hoste alterum superantium rapta fuerit: tertia pars ad ecclesiam tribuatur uel pauperibus et XL diebus penitentia, quia *M 178r* iussio regis erat.

2–3 cf. *Iud. Theod. G* 139; *C* 123; *U* II.11.9; *D* 54   **5–6** Deut 20:14   **8–10** 1 Sam 30:24–5   **12–13** 2 Reg 14:6; cf. Deut 24:16   **15–17** *Iud. Theod. B* 74; *G* 154; cf. *U* I.7.2; *C* 133

---

1 LXXXI] LXXXII M   **1** DE COINQUINATIS ANIMALIBUS] *deest* IL   **2** talia] ad alia L *deest* M   **2** polluta] pulluta* I   **2** carnesque] carnuque* I carnisque L   **4** LXXXII] LXXXIII M   **4** MOSES DE PREDA] DE PRAEDA DIUIDENDA M   **4** MOSES] MOYSES L   **5** Omnem] Moyses dicit: Omnem M   **5** predam] praedam M   **5** diuides] diues *corr.* diuides I diues L   **5** de spoliis] populus L   **5** quae] que L   **7** LXXXIII] LXXXIIII M   **7** HOC DAVID DE PREDA IN I LIBER REGUM] DE QUALE PARTE PREDAE M   **8** Aequa] aequae L equa M   **8** pars] pras L   **8** descendentis] discentes L descendentibus M   **8** proelium] prehelium L prohelium M   **8** remanentis] remanentes L remanentibus M   **9** est] *deest* M   **9** et deinceps] deinceps M   **11** LXXXIIII] LXXXV M   **11** NON MORIATUR PATER PRO FILIO] *deest* IL   **12** Moses] Moyses L Moyses dicit M   **12** Deuteronomio] deutero L   **12** in IIII Regum] regnum* L regum quartum M   **12** IIII] IIII L   **12** moriuntur] moriantur M   **13** morientur pro patribus] pro patribus morientur L   **14** LXXXV] LXXXVI M   **14** DE PECUNIA ALIENA] DE ALIENA PECUNIA M   **15** quae] qui L que M   **15** prouintia] prouincia M   **15** superantium] seperantum L   **16** pars] pras L   **16** XL] CXL L quadraginta M   **16** penitentia] paeniteant M

Collectio CCCC capitulorum   49

LXXXVI De uidua liberos habentes
Dominus Mose precepit honorare uiduas et pupillos et eadem nobis per pro-
phetas precepit multipliciter.

Hieronimus: Si qua autem habet uidua liberos et maxime si nobilis familiae,
egentes filios non dimittat, sed aequalitate ut meminerit primum animae suae
et ipsum putat esse de filiis ut patiatur potius cum liberis quam omnia filiis
relinquat, immo Christum liberorum suorum coheredem faciat. Respondit:
'Difficile, durum, contra naturam'. Sed Dominum tibi respondentem audies:
'Qui potest capere capiat.'

LXXXVII Hieronimus de uidua quae sine liberis est
Quomodo perfectus esse quis possit et quomodo uiuere debeat uidua, quae sine
liberis derelicta est? Hoc idem in Euangelio legis doctor interrogat: 'Magister, quid faciens uitam aeternam possidebo?' Cui Dominus respondit: 'Man-
data nosti?' Et illo dicente: 'Haec omnia feci', Dominus intulit: 'Unum deest
tibi: si uis perfectus esse uade et uende omnia' et reliqua.
Itaque et ego tibi Domini nostri respondebo: 'Si uis esse perfectus et tollere
crucem tuam' et reliqua; 'Uade et uende omnia tua quae habes et da pauperibus' et reliqua. Non dixit: 'Da filiis, da fratribus, da propinquis', quos etiam si
haberes, iure his Dominus preferetur, sed 'da pauperibus' immo Christo.

2–3 cf. Isa 10:2; Mal 3:5   4–9 Hier., *ep. 120, ad Hebidiam*, §1   11–19 cf. Hier., *ep. 120,
ad Hebidiam*, §1

---

1 LXXXVI⸃ LXXXVII M   1 De uidua liberos habentes⸃ De honore uiduae M
2 Mose⸃ Moyse L Moysi M   2 uiduas⸃ uiduis* I uiduis LM   2 pupillos⸃ puppil-
lis* I pupillis LM   3 precepit multipliciter⸃ multipliciter precepit M   4 autem⸃ *del.* L
4 maxime⸃ maximae LM   5 egentes⸃ aegentes M   5 animae⸃ anime L   7 faciat⸃ facit
LM   7 Respondit⸃ Responsio M   8 audies⸃ audiens M   10 LXXXVII⸃ LXXXVIII
M   10 Hieronimus de uidua quae sine liberis est⸃ Hieronimus de uidua qui sine liberis
L De uidua sine liberis M   11 Quomodo⸃ Hieronimus ait: Quomodo M   11 quae⸃ que
L   12 idem⸃ diem L   12 Euangelio⸃ euagelio M   15 si uis⸃ suus L   15 esse⸃ est
L   15 uende⸃ uinde L   16 respondebo⸃ respondebo sermone M   17 uende⸃ uinde L
17 tua⸃ *deest* LM   17 quae⸃ que L   19 haberes⸃ habueris L habere M   19 iure⸃ iurae
L   19 preferetur⸃ preferretur L

50 Collectio CCCC capitulorum

LXXXVIII De diuersitate morum aecclesiarum
Interrogatio Augustini: Cum una sit fides, sunt ecclesiarum diuerse consue-
tudines? Alter consuetudo missarum in sancta Romana ecclesia atque aliter
in Galliarum?
5 Gregorius respondit: Nouit fraternitas tua Romane ecclesiae consuetudinem
in qua se meminit nutritam. Sed mihi placet ut siue in Romana siue in Galliarum siue in qualibet ecclesia aliquid inuenisti, quod plus omnipotenti Deo
possit placere, sollicite elegas et in Anglorum ecclesias, quae adhuc ad fidem
noua est, institutionem precipua, quam de multis ecclesiis collegere potuisti,
10 infundas. Non enim pro locis res, sed pro bonis rebus loca amanda sunt. Ex   I 152r
singulis ergo quibusque ecclesias quae pia, quae religiosa, quae recta sunt elege
et haec quasi in fasciculum collecta apud Anglorum mentes in consuetudinem
depone.

LXXXVIIII De electione episcoporum et examinatione
15 Haec Noui Testamenti canones subsequentes apostolorum Clementi canones:
Qui ordinandus est ante examinetur ut nec post baptismum secundis fuerit
nuptiis copulatus aut concubinam habuerit aut uiduam iectam uel meretricem   M 179r
aut ancillam uel duas sorores acceperit in coniugium aut filiam fratris.

2–13 Greg. I, *Lib. resp.*, 6   16 cf. *Stat. eccl. ant.* prol.   16–17 *Can. apost.* §17

---

1 LXXXVIII] LXXXVIIII M   1 De diuersitate morum aecclesiarum] *deest* IL
1 aecclesiarum] ecclesiarum M   2 sunt] cur sunt M   2 ecclesiarum] eclesiarum
M   2 diuerse] diuersae M   3 consuetudo] consuetudo est M   3 Romana] Romam L
3 ecclesia] ecclesiam L eclesia M   3 aliter] alter M   4 Galliarum] Galiarum L Gallia M
5 Gregorius respondit] respondit Gregorius L responsio Gregorii papae M   5 Romane]
romanae M   6 meminit] miminit L   6 ut] et L   7 ecclesia] eclesiae M   8 placere]
superscriptum M   8 sollicite] sollicitate* L   8 Anglorum] angelorum* L   8 ecclesias]
ecclesiae L eclesia M   8 quae] que L   9 institutionem] institutione LM   9 collegere]
colere M   10 amanda] emenda L manda* M   10 Ex] et L   11 ecclesias] ecclesies L
ecclesiis M   11 quae] que L   11 quae] que L   11 religiosa] relegiosa* I relegiosa LM
11 quae] que L   11 elege] elegere L   12 quasi] quas I   12 Anglorum] angelorum*
L   13 depone] *deest* M   14 LXXXVIIII] XC M   14 De electione episcoporum et exa-
minatione] *deest* IL   15 apostolorum] pro apostolorum L   15 Clementi] Clemens ILM
15 canones] canonum L   17 iectam] eiectam LM   18 acceperit] acciperit LM

Collectio CCCC capitulorum

51

L 98r   Et Paulus nouissimus eorum meminit unius uxoris uirum esse et non neophitum ne forte elatus in iuditium incidat et laqueum diaboli.

I 152v   Nec sibi amputauerit uirilia, quia qui fecerit suus homicida est, et Dei conditionis inimicus. Si per insidias hominum factus uel in persecutionem, si eius sunt amputanda uirilia si quidem in egritudinem uel a medicis uel si ita natus   5
est et est dignus gradu effitiatur. Uel si aliquam de his quae publicis spectaculis mancipantur, non potest esse episcopus aut presbyter uel diaconus nec ex eorum numero qui ministerio sacro deseruiunt.

Oportet episcopum esse sine crimine ut epistulae beati Pauli ad Timotheum in quibus eum erudi restuduit qualiter in domo Dei conuersare debuisset et ante   10
I 153r   omnia fidei documenta sanctae trinitatis deitatem coessentialem et consubstantialem et coaeternalem et coomnipotentem uerbum predicans. Cum ergo in his omnibus inuentus fuerit plene instructus tunc cum consensu clericorum et totius
M 179v   prouintiae episcoporum maximaeque metropolitani uel auctoritate uel presentia ordinatur.   15

XC   De ordinatione episcopi
Nicena: Episcopus a duobus aut tribus episcopis ordinetur.

Et in Nicena: Episcopum oportet ab omnibus, si fieri potest, qui sunt in prouintiae episcopis ordinari, si uero hoc dificile fuerit uel urgente necessitate uel itineris longitudine certe omnimodo tres episcopi debent in unum esse con-   20

1–2 cf. 1 Tim 3:6; *Nicaea* §2   **3–4** cf. *Can. apost.* §22   **4–6** *Can. apost.* §21   **6–8** *Can. apost.* §18   **10** cf. 1 Tim 3:15   **11–15** cf. *Stat. eccl. ant.* prol.   **17** *Can. apost.* §1   **18–52.2** *Nicaea* §4

---

1 meminit] miminit L   **1–2** neophitum] neophytum L   **2** iuditium] iudicium LM   **2** diaboli] diabuli M   **4** uel] in uel* L   **4** persecutionem] persecutione LM   **5** amputanda] amputata M   **5** egritudinem] egritudine LM   **5–6** natus est] est natus M   **5** natus] netus I   **6** effitiatur] efficiatur LM   **6** quae] que L qui M   **8** ministerio] in ministerio L   **9** episcopum esse] esse episcopum L   **9** epistulae] epistule L   **9** ad] a L   **9** Timotheum] thimotheum L   **10** restuduit] restudiuit L   **10** conuersare] *deest* M   **11** sanctae] sanctam L   **11** deitatem] dei tamen L   **12** coaeternalem] coeternalem L   **12** uerbum] uerbis L uerbi M   **13** consensu] sensu L   **13** et] e L   **13** totius] totus L   **14** prouintiae] prouinciae LM   **14** maximaeque] maximeque M   **16** XC] XCI M   **16** De ordinatione episcopi] *deest* IL De ordinatione presbiteri et episcopi M   **17–52.2** Nicena...ordinationem] *deest* L   **17** Nicena] *deest* M   **18–19** prouintiae] prouincia M   **19** dificile] difficile M   **19** urgente] urguente M   **20** longitudine] longitudinem M

52 Collectio CCCC capitulorum

gregati. Ita ut etiam ceterorum qui absentes sunt consensum litteris teneant et ita faciant ordinationem.

Carthaginis: Similiter Cartaginensis synodus.

Et Gregorius pater: Episcoporum ordinatio sine adgregatis tribus uel IIII epi- *I 153v*
scopis fieri non debet. Nam in ipsis rebus ut sapienter et mature disponantur exemplum trahere a rebus etiam carnalibus possimus. Certe enim dum coniugia in mundo celebrantur, coniugati quique conuocantur, ut qui in uia iam coniugii precesserit in subsequentis quoque copulae gaudio misceantur. Cur non ergo et in hac spiritali ordinationem, qua per sacrum ministerium homo Deo coniungitur tales conueniant, qui uel in profecto ordinati episcopi gaudeant *L 98v*
uel pro eius custodia omnipotenti Deo preces pariter fundant? *M 180r*

XCI De ordinatione presbyteri et ceterorum
Apostolus: Presbiter ab uno episcopo ordinetur et diaconus et reliqui clerici.

XCII Quo temporum pascha celebratur
Apostolus: Si quis episcopus aut presbyter aut diaconus sanctum paschae diem ante uernale aequinoctium cum Iudaeis celebrauerit, deponatur.

XCIII Non inuadendum aliena parrochia
Episcopo non licere alienam parrochiam, propria relicta, peruadere, licet co- *I 154r*
gatur a plurimis, nisi forte quis eum rationabiliter causa conpellat, tamquam

---

4–11 Greg. I, *Lib. resp.*, 6   13 *Can. apost.* §2   15–16 *Can. apost.* §8   18–53.3 *Can. apost.* §14

---

3 Carthaginis] Cartaginensis L   3 synodus] sinodus L   4 Episcoporum] Baptismam episcoporum ILM   4 ordinatio] ordinatione M   4 IIII] quattuor M   5 debet] debeant L   5 mature] muturae L maturae M   6 etiam] aetiam L   6 possimus] posumus L possumus M   7 celebrantur] caelebrantur L   8 precesserit] precesserunt M   8 subsequentis] subsequentes L   9 ordinationem] ordinatione L ordinatione M   9 qua] quae M   10 profecto] profectu M   12 XCI] XCII M   12 De ordinatione presbyteri et ceterorum] *deest* IL Quo tempore pascha celebratur M   13–53.4 Apostolus...Et in Arelatense] *deest* L   13 Apostolus] *deest* M   13 Presbiter] prebiter M   14 XCII] XCIII M   14 Quo temporum pascha celebratur] *deest* I *illegible* M   15 Apostolus] *deest* M   15 paschae] pasche M   16 aequinoctium] equinoctium M   16 Iudaeis] iudeis M   16 celebrauerit] caelebrauerit M   17 XCIII] XCIIII M   17 Non inuadendum aliena parrochia] *deest* I   18 Episcopo] Episcopum M   18 licere] licet M   18 parrochiam] parochiam M

Collectio CCCC capitulorum

53

qui possit ibidem constitutus plus lucri conferre et in causa religionis aliquod profectu proficere. Et hoc non a semetipso presumat, sed multorum episcoporum iuditio et maximae supplicatione perficiat.

Et in Arelatense DCCCC episcoporum synodo: Nullus episcopus alium episcopum conculcet.

Quia scriptum est in lege: Per alienam messem transiens falcem mittere non debet, sed manu spicas conterere et manducare. Non potes in ea segete, quia alteri uidetur esse commissa, sed per affectum boni operis frumenta dominica uitiorum suorum paleis expolia et in ecclesiae corpore monendo et persuadendo quasi mandendo conuerte. Quicquid uero ex auctoritate agendum est, nec pretermitti possit hoc quod antiqua patrum institutio inuenit.

Hoc dixit Gregorius ad Augustinum de messe Galliarum alienum esse nisi per affectum sed propriam Brittaniorum episcopos.

XCIIII   Episcopus precipitur res aecclesia

Responsio Apostolorum: Episcopus, ut habeat, precipimus in potestate sua res ecclesiae. Si enim animae hominum pretiosae sunt illi creditae multo magis oportet eum curam de pecuniis agere, ita ut potestate eius indigentibus omnia dispensentur per presbiteros et diacones cum timore omnique reuerentia ministrentur.

4–5 Arelat. §17   **6–11** Greg. I, *Lib. resp.*, 7   **6–7** cf. Deut 23:25   **15–19** *Can. apost.* §41 (fragm., see ch. 95)

---

1 plus lucri⟧ pluri M   **1** religionis⟧ relegionis* I relegionis M   **1** aliquod⟧ aliquid* I aliquid M   **2** profectu⟧ profecto* I profecto M   **3** iuditio⟧ iudicio M   **4** Arelatense⟧ aratense I aretense* M   **4** DCCCC⟧ Gregorius DCCCCrum I Gregorius L tricentorum M **4** episcoporum synodo⟧ *deest* L   **6** alienam⟧ aliam M   **6** falcem⟧ transiens falcem I **7** conterere⟧ contere M   **7** segete⟧ segitae L   **7** quia⟧ qui M   **8** alteri⟧ alter L **9** ecclesiae⟧ eclesiae M   **9** monendo⟧ memento L   **10** quasi mandendo⟧ quasi manendo *superscriptum* M   **10** mandendo⟧ madendo* I madendo L   **10** conuerte⟧ conuertere L   **10** auctoritate⟧ auctore L   **11** pretermitti⟧ permitti L pertemitti M   **11** antiqua⟧ antiqui L   **11** patrum⟧ patruum L   **11** institutio⟧ institutione M   **12** Augustinum⟧ Agustinae L   **12–13** per affectum⟧ perfectum L   **14** XCIIII⟧ XCV M   **14** Episcopus precipitur res aecclesia⟧ *deest* IL Episcopi precipitur res ecclesiae M   **15** Responsio Apostolorum⟧ Respondit apostolus L *deest* M   **16** animae⟧ anime L   **16** pretiosae⟧ preciose L   **16** creditae⟧ credite L   **18** dispensentur⟧ dispensator *corr.* dispensatur L   **18** per⟧ *deest* L   **18** diacones⟧ diaconus L   **19** ministrentur⟧ ministrat L

54 Collectio CCCC capitulorum

Gregorius: Mos autem sedis apostolicae est ordinatis episcopis precepta tradere ut omni stipendio quod accedit iiii^{or} debeant fieri portiones: una uidelicet   *I 155r*
episcopo et familiae propter hospitalitatem atque susceptionem, alia clero, tertia pauperibus, quarta ecclesiis reparandis.

5 Nouimus scriptum quod diuidebatur singulis, prout cuique opus erat. De eorum quoque stipendio cogitandum atque prouidendum est et sub ecclesiastica regula sunt tenendi ut bonis moribus uiuant et canendis psalmis inuigilent et ab omnibus inlicitis et cor et linguam et corpus, Deo auctore, conseruent.   *L 99r; I*
181r

XCV   DE HIS QUAE INDIGET AECLESIA

10 Apostolus: Ex his autem quae indiget sit tamen indiget ad suas necessitates et ad peregrinorum fratrum usum ipse percipiat ut nihil his omnino possit deesse. Lex enim Dei precepit ut qui altario deseruiunt de altario pascantur. Nec miles stipendiis propriis arma contra hostes adsumit.

XCVI   DE USURIS EXIGENDIS   *I 155v*

15 Apostolus: Episcopus aut presbyter aut diaconus usuras a debitoribus exigens aut emendet aut certe damnetur.

Saluator. De quibus Saluator in Euangelio: Qui deuorant domus uiduarum sub obtentu prolixe orationis, hi accipient prolixius iuditium.

Et Lucas: Simulantes longam orationem, hi accipient damnationem maiorem.

1–8 Greg. I, *Lib. resp.*, 1   **10–13** *Can. apost.* §41   **15–16** *Can. apost.* §44   **17–18** Mc 12:40   **19** Lc 20:47

---

1 Gregorius⸥ Gregorius dicit M   **1** Mos⸥ omnes si L   **2** iiii^{or}⸥ quattuor LM   **2** debeant fieri⸥ fieri debeant L   **3** hospitalitatem⸥ hospitatem L   **3** atque⸥ ad M   **5** Nouimus⸥ nouismus* L   **5** quod⸥ *del.* L   **5** diuidebatur⸥ deuidebatur L   **7** sunt⸥ *del.* L *deest* M   **7** tenendi⸥ tenendi sunt I   **9** XCV⸥ XCIII L XCVI M   **9** DE HIS QUAE INDIGET AECLESIA⸥ *deest* IL DE HIS QUAE INDIGET ECCLESIA M   **10** Apostolus⸥ *deest* L Apostolus ait M   **10** his⸥ *deest* L   **10** autem quae⸥ autemque L   **10** sit⸥ si L episcopus si M   **11** usum⸥ usu ILM   **12** altario⸥ alterio L   **12** altario⸥ alterio L   **13** miles⸥ milis IL   **13** propriis⸥ proprius L   **13** adsumit⸥ adsumsit L   **14** XCVI⸥ XCIIII L XCVII M   **14** DE USURIS EXIGENDIS⸥ *deest* IL   **15** Apostolus⸥ Apostolus dicit M   **15** a debitoribus⸥ addiditoribus L   **15** exigens⸥ exiens L   **16** emendet⸥ emendentur L   **17** Saluator⸥ XCV Saluator L *deest* M   **17** Euangelio⸥ Euangelio ait M   **17** domus⸥ domos LM   **18** prolixe⸥ prolixae LM   **18** hi⸥ hii L   **18** prolixius⸥ prolixus L   **18** iuditium⸥ iudicium LM   **19** Lucas⸥ Lucas dicit M   **19** hi⸥ hii L

Collectio CCCC capitulorum

55

Nicena: Hoc sanctum concilium quem multi clerici auaritia causa turpia lu-
cra ad usuras sectantes, omnis qui tale aliquid commentus fuerit ad quaestum
deiecitur ex clero et alienus ab ecclesiastico habebitur gradu.

Augustinus: Noli thesauris uanis, thesauris caducis. Noli sub imagine pietatis
augere pecuniam. Dicens: Filiis meis seruo, magnas res; quare non potius illi
serues qui te fecit ex nihilo? Et ei qui te pascit ex his qui fecit, ipse qui pascit
et filios tuos? Neque melius commendare filio tuo, quam creatori tuo, qui
dicit: thesaurizate uobis thesauros in caelo; hic tenetur ubi periit thesaurus,
illic permanet ubi Christus custas est.'

XCVII   Ut cura rerum aecclesiae episcopis
Uerba Apostoli: Omnium negotiorum ecclesiasticarum curam episcopus habeat et ea uelut Deo contemplante dispenset. Nec ei liceat ex his aliquid omnino presumere aut parentibus propriis quae Dei sunt condonare. Quod si pauperes sunt tamquam pauperibus subministret, nec eorum occasione ecclesiae
negotia depredentur.

XCVIII   De cura uiduarum episcopis
Unica, et in unica ecclesia: Episcopus gubernationem uiduarum et pupillo-
rum et peregrinorum non per semetipsum, sed per archipresbyterum uel per
archidiaconum agat.

1–3 cf. *Nicaea* §17   **4–9** cf. Aug., *Serm.* 9   **11–15** *Can. apost.* §39   **17–19** *Stat. eccl. ant.* §7

---

1 Nicena⌉ *deest* L   1 auaritia⌉ auaricia L   1 turpia⌉ turpi M   **2** sectantes⌉ sectentes
L   **2** quaestum⌉ questum LM   **3** alienus⌉ alienis L   **3** ab ecclesiastico⌉ ecclesiestico L
3 habebitur⌉ habitur M   **4** Augustinus⌉ *deest* LM   **4** Noli⌉ Nolite L   **4** uanis⌉ uanus
L   **4** thesauris⌉ theauris L   **4** Noli⌉ Nolite L   **4** imagine⌉ magine* M   **5** pecuniam⌉
M   **6** serues⌉ seruas M   **6** ex his qui fecit, ipse qui pascit⌉ *deest* L   **6** qui⌉ quae M
7 commendare⌉ cummodare *corr.* commodare M   **8** dicit⌉ dixit LM   **8** thesauros⌉ thesaurus L   **8** caelo⌉ celo L   **8–9** hic tenetur ubi periit thesaurus, illic⌉ *deest* M   **9** custas⌉
custus L custos M   **10** XCVII⌉ XCVI L XCVIII M   **10** Ut cura rerum aecclesiae epi-
scopis⌉ *deest* IL Ut cura rerum eclesiarum episcopus haberet M   **11** Uerba Apostoli⌉
deest L Apostolus M   **11** negotiorum⌉ negotium M   **12** uelut⌉ uelud L   **13** quae⌉ que
L   **13** Quod si⌉ Quasi L   **15** negotia⌉ negotiae L   **16** XCVIII⌉ XCVII L XCVIIII M
16 De cura uiduarum episcopis⌉ *deest* IL De cura uiduarum episcopi M   **17** Unica⌉ *deest*
LM   **17** et in unica ecclesia⌉ unica ecclaesia M   **18** archipresbyterum⌉ arcipresbyterum
L   **18–19** per archidiaconum⌉ diaconorium L

56 Collectio CCCC capitulorum

XCVIIII Nᴇ ᴀᴍᴀɴᴛ sᴀᴇᴄᴜʟᴀʀᴇs ʀᴇs
Apostolus: Episcopus, aut presbyter uel diaconus nequaquam seculares curas adsumat, sin aliter deponatur.

Et in unica ecclesia: Ut episcopus nullam rei familiaris curam ad se reuocet,
5 sed ut lectioni et orationi et uerbi Dei predicationi tantum uacet et uilem sub-pellectilem ac uictum pauperem habeat et dignitatis suae auctoritatem fide et uitae meritis quaerat.

Cum apostolis: Penuriam pati.

C Nᴏɴ sᴜᴍᴇɴᴅᴜᴍ ᴘᴇʀ ᴘᴇᴄᴜɴɪᴀᴍ ᴅɪɢɴɪᴛᴀᴛᴇᴍ
10 Apostolus: Si quis episcopus aut presbyter aut diaconus per pecunias hanc ob- *M 182r*
tinuerit dignitatem, deiciatur et ipse et ordinator eius et a communione modis omnibus abscidatur, sicut Symon magus a Petro.

CI Nᴇ sᴜᴍᴀᴛ ᴘᴇʀ ᴘᴏᴛᴇsᴛᴀᴛᴇᴍ ᴀᴇᴄᴄʟᴇsɪᴀᴇ
Apostolus: Si quis episcopus saeculi potestatibus usus aecclesiam per ipsos
15 obtineat, deponatur et segregentur omnesque qui illi communicant. *I 157r*

CII Nᴏɴ ᴀᴜᴅᴇɴᴅᴜᴍ ᴇxᴛʀᴀ ᴛᴇʀᴍɪɴᴏs ᴘʀᴏᴘʀɪᴏs
Apostolus: Episcopum non audere extra terminos proprios ordinationes fa-cere in ciuitatibus et uillis, que illi nullo iure subiectae sunt. Si uero conuic-tus fuerit hoc fecisse preter eorum conscientiam qui ciuitates ipsas et uillas
20 detinent et ipse et qui ab illo ordinati sunt deponantur.

2–3 *Can. apost.* §7   **4–7** cf. *Stat. eccl. ant.* §3-4   **8** cf. Phil 4:12   **10–12** *Can. apost.* §30
14–15 *Can. apost.* §31   **17–20** *Can. apost.* §36

---

1 XCVIIII] XCVIII L C M   1 Nᴇ ᴀᴍᴀɴᴛ sᴀᴇᴄᴜʟᴀʀᴇs ʀᴇs] *deest* IL   2 Apostolus]
deest LM   2 nequaquam] *deest* M   2 seculares] saeculares M   4 unica] unia
M   4 familiaris] famularis L   5–6 subpellectilem] sepelectilem L suppellectilem M
7 quaerat] querat L   8 apostolis] apostoli L   8 Penuriam] Sunt L   9 C] XCVIIII
L CI M   9 Nᴏɴ sᴜᴍᴇɴᴅᴜᴍ ᴘᴇʀ ᴘᴇᴄᴜɴɪᴀᴍ ᴅɪɢɴɪᴛᴀᴛᴇᴍ] *deest* IL   10 aut] au L   10 hanc]
hoc L   10–11 obtinuerit] obtenuerit M   12 Symon] Simon LM   12 a] *deest* * L
13 CI] C L CII M   13 Nᴇ sᴜᴍᴀᴛ ᴘᴇʀ ᴘᴏᴛᴇsᴛᴀᴛᴇᴍ ᴀᴇᴄᴄʟᴇsɪᴀᴇ] *deest* IL Nᴏɴ sᴜᴍᴀᴛ ᴘᴇʀ
ᴘᴏᴛᴇsᴛᴀᴛᴇᴍ ᴇᴄᴄʟᴇsɪɪs M   14 aecclesiam] ecclesiam LM   15 obtineat] obteneat* I obteneat LM   15 omnesque] omnes M   15 communicant] communicant L   16 CII] CI
L CIII M   16 Nᴏɴ ᴀᴜᴅᴇɴᴅᴜᴍ ᴇxᴛʀᴀ ᴛᴇʀᴍɪɴᴏs ᴘʀᴏᴘʀɪᴏs] *deest* IL   18 que illi] *deest* L
18 que] qui M   18 iure] iurae* I iurae L   18 subiectae] subiecte L   19 qui] que L
20 detinent] detenent* I detenent L

Collectio CCCC capitulorum

57

CIII Q<small>UIS PRIMUS EPISCOPUS IN GENTE</small>
Apostolus: Episcopus gentium singularum scire conuenit, quis inter eos primus habeatur, quem uelud caput existiment et nihil amplius preter eius conscientiam gerant, quam sola illa singulae, que parochiae propriae et uillis, quae sub ea sunt, conpetunt; sed nec ille preter omnium conscientiam faciat aliquid; sic enim unanimitas erit et glorificabitur Deus per Christum in spiritu sancto.

Et Nicena: Potestas sane uel confirmatio pertinebit per singulas prouintias ad metropolitanum.

CIIII D<small>E SACRIFICANTE ET NON MANENTE</small>
Apostolus: Episcopus si quis aut presbiter aut diaconus aut quilibet ex sacerdotale catalogo facta oblatione non communicauerit, aut causam dicat, et si rationabilis fuerit ueniam consequatur, aut si non dixerit communione priuetur tamquam qui populo causae lesionis extiterit, suspitionem faciens de eo qui sacrificauerit, quod recte non obtulerit.

CV Q<small>UIA NON DEBEANT SACERDOTES PERCUTERE</small>
Apostolus: Episcopum aut presbiterum aut diaconum percutientem fideles delinquentes aut infideles inique agentes et per huiusmodi uolentes timeri, deieci ab offitio suo precipimus, quia nusquam Dominus hoc nos docuit. E contrario uero ipse, dum percuteretur, non percuciebat; cum malediceretur, non remalecebat; cum pateretur, non comminabatur.

2–6 *Can. apost.* §35; Iohannes VIII   **7–8** *Nicaea* §4   **10–14** *Can. apost.* §9   **16–20** *Can. apost.* §28

---

1 CIII] *deest* L CIIII M   **1** Q<small>UIS PRIMUS EPISCOPUS IN GENTE</small>] *deest* IL   **2** Apostolus] *deest* L   **2–3** primus] primos* I   **3** uelud] uelut M   **3** caput] capud L   **3** existiment] exestiment L   **3–4** conscientiam] constientiam L   **4** que] quae LM   **4** propriae] ᴹ   **4** uillis] uillas L   **4** quae] que L   **5** ille] illae L   **5** conscientiam] constientiam L   **5** aliquid] aliquis* L   **6** unanimitas] unianimitas I unianimitas L   **7** sane] sine L   **7** prouintias] prouincias LM   **9** CIIII] CIII L CV M   **9** D<small>E SACRIFICANTE ET NON MANENTE</small>] *deest* IL   **10** si quis] *deest* M si quis episcopus* L   **11** catalogo] cathalogo L   **11** oblatione] oblationem L   **13** causae] causa IM   **13** lesionis] lesiones I   **13** suspitionem] suspitione L   **15** CV] CIIII L CVI M   **15** Q<small>UIA NON DEBEANT SACERDOTES PERCUTERE</small>] *deest* IL Q<small>UIA NON DEBENT SACERDOTES PERCUTERE</small> M   **16** Episcopum] Episcopus L   **16** presbiterum] presbiter L   **16** diaconum] diaconus L   **17** inique] iniquae L   **17–18** deieci] deiecti I   **18** offitio] officio LM   **18** precipimus] praecipimus M   **18** E] Et L   **19** percutiebat] percuciebat L   **20** remaledicebat] remaledicetur L maledicebat M

58 Collectio CCCC capitulorum

CVI Q<small>UIA DAMNATI NON DEBEANT USURPARI</small>
Apostolus: Episcopus aut presbiter aut diaconus depositus iuste super certis
criminibus, ausus fuerit adtractare ministerium dudum sibi commissum, hic
ab ecclesia omnimodo abscidatur.

CVII U<small>T BIS IN ANNO CONCILIA EPISCOPORUM</small>
Apostolus, Nicena, et omnes posteriores: Episcoporum bis in anno conci- *M 183r*
lia celebrentur ut inter se inuicem dogmata pietatis explorent et emergentes
ecclesiasticas contentiones absoluant.

Et in Nicena: In singulis quibusque prouintiis bis in anno episcoporum concilia *L 100v*
fieri ante dies quadragesimae ut omnibus, si quae sunt, simultatibus amputa-
tis mundum solemnem Deo munus possit offerri. Secundum uero agatur IIII
kalendis octobris.

CVIII N<small>ULLUS EPISCOPUS</small> <UEL> P<small>RESBITER PEREGRINET SINE LITTERAM</small>
Episcoporum nullus peregrinorum aut presbiterorum aut diaconorum sine *I 158v*
conmendaticiis suscipiatur epistolis, et cum scripta detulerint, discutiantur
attentius et ita suscipiantur, et si precones pietatis extiterint, admittantur;
minus, ne quae sunt necessaria subministrentur eis, et ad communionem nullatenus admittantur, quia per subreptionem multa proueniunt.

2–4 *Can. apost.* §29 **6–8** *Can. apost.* §38 **9–12** *Nicaea* §5 **14–18** *Can. apost.* §34

---

1 CVI⟧ CV L CVII M **1** Q<small>UIA DAMNATI NON DEBEANT USURPARI</small>⟧ *deest* IL Q<small>UIA DAMNATI</small>
<small>OFFICIUM NON DEBEANT USURPARE</small> M **2** iuste⟧ iustae L **2** super⟧ sub L **3** ministerium⟧
misterium L **4** ecclesia⟧ ecclesiae* L **5** CVII⟧ CVI L CVIII M **5** U<small>T BIS IN ANNO</small>
<small>CONCILIA EPISCOPORUM</small>⟧ *deest* IL **6** Nicena⟧ Niceae I Niceni L **7** celebrentur⟧ caelebran-
tur L caelebrentur M **9** Nicena⟧ Nicene L **9** prouintiis⟧ prouinciis LM **9** anno⟧ an
etno* L **9** episcoporum⟧ episcopus L episcopi M **10** quadragesimae⟧ XLME L quadra-
gisimae M **10** quae⟧ que L **10** simultatibus⟧ simultantibus M **10–11** amputatis⟧
ambuitati L **11** solemnem⟧ solemnen L **11** offerri⟧ offeri M **11** Secundum⟧ Se-
con L **12** kalendis⟧ *deest* L **13** CVIII⟧ CVII L CVIII M **13** N<small>ULLUS EPISCOPUS</small>
<UEL> P<small>RESBITER PEREGRINET SINE LITTERAM</small>⟧ *deest* IL D<small>E PEREGRINIS EPISCOPIS ET PRESBITE</small>-
<small>RIS</small> M **14** Episcoporum⟧ Regula (?): Episcoporum I **15** conmendaticiis⟧ conmen-
datus L commendaticiis M **16** suscipiantur⟧ suscipiant L **16** precones⟧ preconiis L
17 quae⟧ que L **17** subministrentur⟧ subministrantur L subministrent M **18** per⟧ *deest*
L **18** proueniunt⟧ proueniant L

Collectio CCCC capitulorum

59

CVIIII De ebrietate sacerdotum

Apostolus: Episcopus aut presbiter aut diaconus aleae atque ebrietati deseruiens aut desinat aut certe damnetur. Subdiaconus aut lector aut cantator similia faciens aut desinat aut communione priuetur; similiter etiam laicus

M 183v Quia et Saluator discipulis: Adtendite ne grauentur corda uestra in crapula et ebrietate.

Et Paulus: Non in commessationibus et ebrietatibus

Et iterum: Neque ebriosi et cetera.

I 159r Et in sinodo Agatensi: Ebriosus ut ordo patitur xxx diebus a communione submouendus aut corporali subdendus supplitio est.

CX Qui cum hereticis orauerit damnetur

Apostolus: Episcopus, presbiter, aut diaconus qui cum hereticis orauerit tantummodo communione priuetur. Si uero tamquam clericos hortati eos fuerint agere uel orare, damnetur.

CXI De baptismo hereticorum

Apostolus: Episcopum uel presbiterum hereticorum suscipientem baptismum dampnari precipimus quae enim conuentio Christi ad Belial aut quae pars fideli cum infidele?

CXII Non iterum baptizandum

Apostolus: Episcopus aut presbiter si eum qui secundum ueritatem habuerit baptismum denuo baptizauerit, deponatur.

2–4 *Can. apost.* §42-3 **5–6** Lc 21:34 **7** Rom 13:13 **8** I Cor 6:10 **9–10** *Agath.* §41 **12–14** *Can. apost.* §45 **16–18** *Can. apost.* §46 **20–21** cf. *Can. apost.* §47

---

1 CVIIII] *capitula* cviiii-cxi *deest* L CX M   **1** De ebrietate sacerdotum] *deest* IL **2–18** Apostolus…infidele] *deest* L   **2** ebrietati] ebreitate* I ebreitate M   **3** cantator] cantor M   **4** etiam] et M   **5** discipulis] discipulis suis ait M   **7** Paulus] Paulus dicit M **7** commessationibus] commisationibus M   **9** sinodo] synodo M   **9** Agatensi] *underlined* M   **10** supplitio] supplicio M   **11** CX] CXI M   **11** Qui cum hereticis orauerit damnetur] *deest* I   **12** Episcopus] Episcopus aut M   **13** hortati] ortati M   **15** CXI] CXII M   **15** De baptismo hereticorum] *deest* I   **16** Apostolus] *deest* M   **17** dampnari] damnari M   **17** precipimus] praecipimus M   **19** CXII] CVIII L CXIII M   **19** Non iterum baptizandum] *deest* IL

60 Collectio CCCC capitulorum

CXIII De hereditate episcopi in obitum eius
Apostolus: Episcopi autem sint manifestae res propriae (si tamen habet pro-
prias) et manifeste dominicae ut potestatem habeat de propriis moriens episcopus si cum uoluerit et quibus uoluerit derelinquere. Nec occasione eccle- *I 159v*
5 siasticarum rerum quae episcopi esse probantur, intercidant. Fortassis enim
aut uxorem habet aut filios aut propinquos aut seruos. Et iustum est hoc *M 184r*
apud Deum et homines, ut nec ecclesia detrimentum patiatur, ignorantiae rerum pontificis, nec episcopus uel propinqui eius sub obtentu ecclesiae pro-
scribantur, et in causas incidant, qui ad eum pertinent morsque eius iniuriis
10 infametur.

CXIIII De damnatione graduum
Apostolus: Episcopus aut presbiter aut diaconus qui in fornicatione aut periu-
rio aut furto captus est, deponatur. Non tamen communione priuetur. Dicit
enim Scriptura: 'Non uindicabit Dominus bis in idipsum.' Similiter et reliqui
15 clerici huic conditioni subiaceant.

CXV Non ordinandum sine consilio
In unica ecclesia: Episcopus, ut absque consilio conpresbiterorum suorum
clericos non ordinet, ita ut et ciuium testimonium quaerat. *I 160r*

CXVI Non uagandum per loca sacerdotibus
20 Unica: Episcopus uel clericus de loco ignobili per ambitionem ad nobilio-
rem non transeat et ut clerici sine consilio episcoporum suorum ad alias non

---

2–9 cf. *Can. apost.* §40 **12–15** *Can. apost.* §25-6 **14** Referring to Nah. 1:9 **17–18**
Stat. eccl. ant. §10 **20–61.1** cf. *Stat. eccl. ant.* §11

---

1 CXIII] *deest* L CXIIII M **1** De hereditate episcopi in obitum eius] *deest* IL De
hereditate episcopis M **2–10** Apostolus…infametur] *deest* L **2** Apostolus] *deest*
M **2** manifestae] manifeste M **4** si cum] sicut M **4** occasione] occansione M
5 intercidant] interdicant M **8** ecclesiae] eclesiae M **9** incidant] incedant* I incedant
M **9** qui] quae I **11** CXIIII] CVIIII L CXV M **11** De damnatione graduum] De damnatione gradu L De damnatione graduum ecclesiae M **13** furto] furtu M **14** uindicabit]
iudicabit L **14** bis] *deest* L **15** conditioni] conditione L **16** CXV] CX L CXVI M
16 Non ordinandum sine consilio] *deest* IL **17** ut] *deest* M **17** conpresbiterorum] con-
presbiter I presbiterum L conpresbiterorum *corr.* presbiterorum M **18** clericos] clericus
L **18** quaerat] queret L **19** CXVI] CXI L CXVII M **19** Non uagandum per loca sacerdotibus] *deest* IL **20** Unica] Unica ecclesia M **20** ambitionem] ambitione L
20–21 nobiliorem] nouiliorem LM **21** ad alias] ab aliis L

Collectio CCCC capitulorum   61

transmigrent ecclesias.

CXVII Episcopus sedenti et presbiteri eadem
Unica: Episcopus ut quolibet loco sedens, stare presbiteros non patiatur.

CXVIII Episcopus numquam sine testibus iudicatur
Unica: Episcopus ut nullus causam audiat absque clericorum suorum presen-   5
tia, alioquin irrita erit sententia episcopi, nisi clericorum presentia firmetur.

CXVIIII Episcopus res aecclesia non utatur quasi sua
Unica: Episcopus ut rebus ecclesiae tamquam conmendatis, non tamquam
propriis utatur.

CXX Episcopus nullum prohibeat intrare aecclesia   10
Unica: Episcopus ut nullum prohibeat ingredi ecclesiam et audire uerbum Dei
siue gentilem siue hereticum siue iudaeum.

CXXI Episcopi desidentes reconciliet
Unica: Episcopos desidentes, si non timor Dei, synodus.

CXXII Episcopus discordantes per sinodus damnet   15
Unica: Episcopus discordantes clericos uel ratione uel potestate ad concor-
diam trahat; inoboedientes autem synodus per audientiam damnet.

L 101r;
M 184v

I 160v

---

3 *Stat. eccl. ant.* §12   **5–6** cf. *Stat. eccl. ant.* §14   **8–9** *Stat. eccl. ant.* §15   **11–12** cf.
Stat. eccl. ant. §16   **14** cf. *Stat. eccl. ant.* §47   **16–17** *Stat. eccl. ant.* §48

---

1 transmigrent⏋ trasmigrent* I transmigant L   2 CXVII⏋ CXII L CXVIII M
2 Episcopus sedenti et presbiteri eadem⏋ *deest* IL Episcopis sedendi et presbiteris eandem
M   3 Unica⏋ Unica ecclesia M   3 quolibet⏋ qulibet* I   3 presbiteros⏋ presbiterum
L   3 patiatur⏋ paciatur L   4 CXVIII⏋ *deest* L CXVIIII M   4 Episcopus numquam sine
testibus iudicatur⏋ *deest* IL   5 Unica⏋ Unica ecclesia M   5 ut⏋ *del.* L   7 CXVIIII⏋
deest L CXX M   7 Episcopus res aecclesia non utatur quasi sua⏋ *deest* IL Episcopus res ecclesiae non utetur quasi suas M   8 Unica⏋ Unica ecclesia M   8 ut⏋ *del.* L   8 ecclesiae⏋
eclesiae M   8 conmendatis⏋ conmendatos L commendatis M   9 propriis⏋ proprius L
10 CXX⏋ *deest* L CXXI M   10 Episcopus nullum prohibeat intrare aecclesia⏋ *deest* IL
Episcopus nullum prohibeat in ecclesia intrare M   11 Unica⏋ Unica ecclesia M   11 ut⏋
deest M   11 ingredi⏋ intrare M   13 CXXI⏋ *deest* L CXXII M   13 Episcopi desidentes reconciliet⏋ *deest* IL   14 Unica⏋ Unica ecclesia M   14 Episcopos⏋ Episcopus ILM
14 desidentes⏋ desidentes reconciliet M   14 synodus⏋ sinodus L   15 CXXII⏋ *deest* L
CXXIII M   15 Episcopus discordantes per sinodus damnet⏋ *deest* IL Episcopus discordantes per synodum damnet M   16 Unica⏋ Unica ecclesia M   17 synodus⏋ sinodus
L

62 Collectio CCCC capitulorum

CXXIII Episcopus fratres ad pacem hortetur
Unica: Episcopus studendum ut desidentes fratres ad pacem magis quam ad
iuditium cohortetur.

CXXIIII Nullum absentem damnare
Unica: Episcopus caueant et iudices ecclesiae ne absente eo, cuius causa uen-
tilatur, sententiam proferant, quia irrita erit, immo et causam in sinodo pro-
ferent.

CXXV De altera eclesia nullum elegatur si alteri non est
Innocentius Papa Caelestinus: Episcopus nullus inuitus detur, sed clerici ple-
bis ad ordinationis consensus requirantur. Tunc autem aliter de altera elegatur   *M 185r*
ecclesia, si de ciuitatis illius clericis cuius est episcopus ordinandus, nullus
dignus poterit reperiri.

Caelestinus: Habeat unusquisque suae fructum militiae in ecclesia in qua suam
per omnia offitia transegit aetatem.

CXXVI Nec alter alterius monachum ordinet
Episcopus nullus clericum sine consensu eius episcopi ordinet, qui suo episco-   *I 161r*
po relicto ad alium conuolat degradetur.

2–3 Stat. eccl. ant. §54 5–7 cf. Stat. eccl. ant. §53 9–12 Cael., ep. 4, §5 13–14 Cael.,
ep. 4, § 16–17 cf. Statuta Bonifatii §10

---

1 CXXIII] deest L CXXIIII M   1 Episcopus fratres ad pacem hortetur] deest IL
2 Unica] Unica ecclesia M   2 Episcopus] Episcopo M   2 studendum] stupendum* I
studendum est M   3 iuditium] iudicium LM   3 cohortetur] quo ortetur L   4 CXXIIII]
deest L CXXV M   4 Nullum absentem damnare] deest IL   5 Unica] Unica ecclesia M
5 Episcopus] Episcopi M   5 caueant] caneant L   6 sinodo] sydo corr. synodo L synodo
M   6–7 proferent] proferint L   8 CXXV] deest L CXXVI M   8 De altera eclesia nullum elegatur si alteri non est] deest IL   9 Innocentius] Innocenti I Innocentia
L   9 Papa Caelestinus] Pape Celestinis L deest M   9 Episcopus] deest M   9 clerici]
cleri L   10 ad] deest L   10 consensus] consensu L   10 requirantur] requirentur L
10 aliter] alter M   10 altera] alteri L   11 si de] sine L   11 ciuitatis] ciuitatibus L
11 est] deest L   13 Caelestinus] Caelestinus L Caelestinus papa M   13 militiae] miliciae
L   13 ecclesia] ecclesiam L   13 suam] sua L   14 offitia] officia LM   14 transegit]
transaegit M   15 CXXVI] deest L CXXVII M   15 Nec alter alterius monachum ordinet]
deest IL Ne alter alterius monachum ordinet M   16 nullus] nullum M

Collectio CCCC capitulorum   63

CXXVII Causae magnae ad sedem apostolicam
Si maiores causae fuerint exortae, ad sedem apostolicam referantur.

CXXVIII Nullus sacerdos canones ignorat
Caelestinus Papa: Nulli sacerdotum suos canones ignorare licet nec quicquam
facere quam patrum regulis possit obuiare.   5

CXXVIIII De confessione uera criminis et mendatii
L 101v Synodus Ualentina: Episcopi uel presbiteri uel diaconi siue ueraciter siue fallaciter dicentes se mortali crimine pollutos esse degradentur, rei scilicet uel
ueri confessione uel crimine mendatii. Neque enim absolui in his potest, si
in ipso se dixerint quod dictum in alios puniretur, cum omnis qui sibi fuerit   10
mortis causa maior homicida sit.

CXXX De ecclesia in morte episcopi
M 185v Synodus Regensis: Statuitur ut ne quis ad eam ecclesiam quae episcopum per-
I 161v didisset, nisi episcopus uicinae ecclesiae exequiarum tempore accedat, qui tam
statim ecclesiae ipsius curam distinctissime agat, ne quid ante ordinationem   15
discordantium in ciuitatibus clericorum subuersioni liceat. Id exequiarum
temporum usque diem defuncti septimam agat. Ut eidem ecclesiae mandatum

---

2 cf. Innocentius I, *ep. 2, ad Victricium*, §6   **4–5** Cael., *ep. 5*, §1   **7–11** cf. *Ualentinum* §4
13–64.3 Regense §5-6

---

1 CXXVII] *deest* L CXXVIII M   **1** Causae magnae ad sedem apostolicam] *deest* IL Causam magnam ad sedem apostolicam M   **2** causae] cause L causas M   **2** exortae] ex-
orte L   **3** CXXVIII] *deest* L CXXVIIII M   **3** Nullus sacerdos canones ignorat] *deest*
IL Nullus sacerdotes canones ignoret M   **4** Caelestinus Papa] Caelestini Papae I Celestinus Pape L Celestinus Papa M   **4** quicquam] quiquam L   **5** quam] quae L quod
M   **6** CXXVIIII] *deest* L CXXX M   **6** De confessione uera criminis et mendatii] *deest*
IL De crimine uera confessio et mendacii M   **7** Synodus] Sinodus L   **7** Ualentina]
Ualentiniam M   **7** Episcopi] Episcopus L   **7** presbiteri] presbiter L   **7** uel] *deest* L
7 ueraciter] ueracitem I   **7–8** siue fallaciter] sium fallaciter *in margine* L   **8** mortali]
mortale L   **8** crimine] criminae L   **9** confessione] confessio me* I   **9** mendatii] mendacii M   **10** ipso] ipse M   **10** fuerit] fuerint L   **11** sit] *deest* L   **12** CXXX] *deest* L
CXXXI M   **12** De ecclesia in morte episcopi] *deest* IL De ecclesiae in morte episcopi M
13 Synodus Regensis] Senodus Retnensis L   **13** episcopum] episcopus L   **14** uicinae]
uicine L   **14** exequiarum] exaequiarum L   **14** tempore] temporum I   **14** accedat] accidat* I accidat L   **15** ante] ante orte L   **16** exequiarum] exequarum *corr.* ex quarum L
17 temporum] tempore LM

64 Collectio CCCC capitulorum

referens metropolitani simul cum omnibus sanctis episcopis reperiatur. Nec
quisque ad ecclesiam quae suum perdidisset sacerdotem, nisi metropolitani
litteris inuitatus accedat.

CXXXI De territorio episcopi in alterius parrochia

Synodus Arausica: Episcopus siue alius aedificauerit ecclesiam in territorio
alterius episcopi, huius ecclesiae consecratio reseruetur ei, in cuius territorio
aedificata est, et eius gubernatio ad eundem pertinebit; si quis aliter fecerit,
excommunicetur.

CXXXII Episcopus non damnetur in repetendo propriae iuris

Synodus Aureliensis: Episcopus uel de ecclesiae uel de proprio iure dedide- *I 162r*
rit aliquid repetendum, et nihil conuicii aut contentionis aut criminationis
obiecerit, eum pro sola conuentione a communione non liceat submoueri.

CXXXIII De episcopo non faciente ministerium

Apostolus: Episcopus, si quis non susciperit officium sibi commissum, hic *L 102r;*
communione priuetur quoadusque oboedientiam commodans adquiescat; si- *M 186r*
militer autem et presbiteri et diaconi. Si uero perrexerit, nec receptus fuerit
non pro sua sententia, sed pro malitia populi; ipse quidem maneat episcopus.
Clerici uero ciuitatis communione priuentur, quod eruditores sic inoboedientis
populi non fuerunt.

5–8 cf. Araus. §9   10–12 Aurel. §6   14–19 *Can. apost.* §37

---

1 episcopis] *deest* L   1 reperiatur] repperiatur M   2 quae] que L   3 inuitatus] inuitus
M   3 accedat] accidat* I acedat M   4 CXXXI] *deest* L CXXXII M   4 De territorio
episcopi in alterius parrochia] *deest* IL De territorio episcopi in alterius parrochiae M
5 Synodus] Sinodus L   5 territorio] teriturio L   6 reseruetur] referetur L   6 ei]
deest L   6 territorio] teriturio L   7 aliter] alter L   9 CXXXII] *deest* L CXXXIII
M   9 Episcopus non damnetur in repetendo propriae iuris] *deest* IL   10 Synodus Aure-
liensis] Sinodus Aurelianensium L   10 uel de] ualde L   10–11 dediderit] crediderit LM
11 aliquid] aliquit I   11 conuicii] conuitia L conuitii M   11 contentionis] contentiones L
11 aut criminationis] *deest* L   12 obiecerit] abiecerit L   13 CXXXIII] *deest* L CXXXIIII
M   13 De episcopo non faciente ministerium] *deest* IL   14 commissum] commissam L
14 hic] hoc L   17 malitia] malicia L   17 episcopus] episcopi L   18 communione] com-
mune L   18 quod] que L   18 eruditores] eruditoris L   18 inoboedientis] inoboedientes
L   19 fuerunt] fuerint L

Collectio CCCC capitulorum

65

CXXXIIII De presbiteris et diaconis
Apostolus: Si quis presbiter aut diaconus aut quilibet de numero clericorum relinquit propriam parochiam, pergat ad alienam et omnino demigrans praeter episcopi sui conscientiam in alienam parochiam commoretur, hunc ulterius ministrare non patimur: precipue si uocatus ab episcopo redire contempserit in suam inquietudinem perseuerans. Uerum tamen tamquam laicus ibi communicet. Episcopus uero apud quem moratus esse constiterit si contra eos directam cessationem pro nihilo reputans tamquam clericos forte susciperit, uelut magister inquietudinis communionem priuetur.

CXXXV Segregato ab alio non recipi
Apostolus: Si quis presbiter aut diaconus ab episcopo suo segregetur, hunc non licere ab alio recipi, sed ab ipso qui eum segregauerat, nisi forsitan obierit episcopus ipse qui eum segregasse cognoscitur.

CXXXVI Alter alterius non ordinet
Nicena: Si quis autem ausus fuerit aliquem quia ad alterum pertinet ordinare in sua ecclesia, cum non habet consensum sui episcopi ipsius a quo recesserit clericus, qui in canone continentur, irrita sit huiusque modi ordinatio.

2–9 *Can. apost.* §15-16 **11–13** *Can. apost.* §33 **15–17** cf. *Antioch* §22

---

1 CXXXIIII] *deest* L CXXXV M **1** De presbiteris et diaconis] De presbiteris et episcopis L Propria parrochia relicta M **2** Apostolus] *deest* L **2** aut] au L **3** relinquit] relinquid L **3** parochiam] parrochiam LM **3** pergat] pergit M **3** ad] *deest* L 4 conscientiam] constientiam L **4** parochiam] parrochiam M **4** ulterius] alterius L *5* episcopo] eo L **6** suam] sua I sua L **6** inquietudinem] inquietudine LM **7** quem] quam L **7** moratus] commoratus M **7** constiterit] constituerit M **8** directam cessationem] directa cessatione M **8** directam] directas L **8** reputans] reputamus M **8** forte] formate L **8** susciperit] susceperit M **9** uelut] uelud L **9** communionem] communione LM **10** CXXXV] *deest* L CXXXVI M **10** Segregato ab alio non recipi] *deest* IL **11** Apostolus] Apostolos I **12** recipi] recepi L **12** segregauerat] segregauerit L **12** obierit] obierat L obiecerit M **14** CXXXVI] *deest* L CXXXVII M **14** Alter alterius non ordinet] *deest* IL **15** Nicena] Niceni L Synodus Nicena M **15** quia ad] qui ad LM **17** continentur] continetur LM **17** huiusque] uniusque L

66 · Collectio CCCC capitulorum

CXXXVII   Nemo episcopum contemnens
Apostolus: Si quis presbiter contemnens episcopum proprium extra collegerit
et altare aliud erexerit, nihil habens in quo reprehendat episcopum in causa
impietatis et iniustitiae, deponatur quasi principatus amator, existens est enim
⁵ tyrannus, et ceteri clerici quicumque tali consentiunt, laici uero segregentur.
Haec autem fieri post unam et secundam et tertiam obsecrationem episcopi
conuenit.

L 102v

CXXXVIII   Nemo in domo cum excommunicato
Apostolus: Si quis exommunicato, saltim in domo simul orauerit, et iste com-
¹⁰ munione priuetur.

CXXXVIIII   Nemo cum damnato clerico orauerit
Apostolus: Si quis cum damnato clerico, ueluti cum clerico, simul orauerit, et
iste damnetur.

CXL   Laicus excommonicatus non recipiatur
¹⁵ Apostolus: Si quis clericus aut laicus a communione suspensus, seu communi-
cans ad aliam properet ciuitatem, et suscipiatur preter conmendatitias litteras,
et qui susceperint, et qui susceptus est communione priuentur.

I 163v;
M 187r

CXLI   Excommonicato protelletur correctio
Excommunicato uero protelletur ipsa correctio, tamquam qui mentitus fuerit,
²⁰ et seduxerit ecclesiam Dei.

2–7 *Can. apost.* §32   **9–10** *Can. apost.* §11   **12–13** *Can. apost.* §12   **15–17** *Can. apost.*
§13   **19–20** *Can. apost.* §13

---

1 CXXXVII⌉ *deest* L CXXXVIII M   1 Nemo episcopum contemnens⌉ *deest* IL
2 contemnens⌉ contempnens L   3 aliud⌉ aliut* I   4 quasi⌉ quia si L   4 amator⌉ amor
L   5 ceteri⌉ caeteri L   5 tali⌉ talia L   6 post⌉ potest M   8 CXXXVIII⌉ *deest* L CXX-
XVIIII M   8 Nemo in domo cum excommunicato⌉ *deest* IL   11 CXXXVIIII⌉ *deest* L CXL
M   11 Nemo cum damnato clerico orauerit⌉ *deest* IL Nemo condemnato clerico orauerit
M   12–13 Apostolus...damnetur⌉ *deest* L   14 CXL⌉ *deest* L CXLI M   14 Laicus excom-
monicatus non recipiatur⌉ *deest* IL Laicus excommunicatus non recipiatur M   15 seu⌉
se L   16 ad⌉ et L   16 properet⌉ properans M   16 conmendatitias⌉ commendatus
L commendaticias M   17 susceperint⌉ susciperit L susciperint M   18 CXLI⌉ *deest* L
CXLII M   18 Excommonicato protelletur correctio⌉ *deest* IL De excommunicato M
19 Excommunicato⌉ Apostolus: Excommunicato L   19 uero⌉ *deest* M   19 protelletur⌉
protoletur L proteletur M   19 correctio⌉ correptio L   20 ecclesiam⌉ ecclesiae M

Collectio CCCC capitulorum · 67

CXLII Presbiteri preter episcopi licentiam nihil habentes
Apostolus: Presbiteri et diaconi, preter episcopum, nihil agere pertempnent,
nam Domini populus ipsi commissus est et pro animabus eorum hic redditurus
est rationem.

CXLIII Qui se ipsum castrauerit non potest esse clericus quia se ipsum
amputauit
Apostolus: Si quis abscidit semetipsum, id est, si quis amputauerit sibi uirilia,
non fiat clericus, quia suus homicida est et Dei conditionis inimicus.

CXLIIII De clerico damnato amputato
Apostolus: Si quis cum clericus fuerit abscidit semetipsum omnino damnetur,
quia suus homicida est.

CXLV De penitentia laici castrati
Apostolus: Laicus semetipsum abscidens, anni iii communione priuetur, quia
suae uitae insidiator existens extitit.

CXLVI De uxore repudiata
Apostolus: Si quis laicus uxorem propriam pellens, alteram uel duxerit ab alio
dimissam, communione priuetur.

CXLVII De ordinatis per ignorantiam
Nicena: Quicumque ex his qui lapsi sunt et per ignorantiam ordinati sunt uel
contemptu aut disimulatione ordinantium eorum qui eos ordinauerunt, hoc

---

2–4 *Can. apost.* §40 **7–8** *Can. apost.* §22 **10–11** *Can. apost.* §23 **13–14** *Can. apost.*
§24 **16–17** *Can. apost.* §48 **19–68.2** *Nicaea* §10

---

1 CXLII] *deest* L CXLIII M   1 Presbiteri preter episcopi licentiam nihil habentes]
deest IL   1 episcopi] episcopis M   2 Presbiteri] uel presbiteri M   2 pertempnent]
pertemptent LM   5 CXLIII] *deest* L CXLIIII M   5–6 Qui se ipsum castrauerit non potest
esse clericus quia se ipsum amputauit] *deest* IL   7 abscidit] abscedit* I   7 amputauerit]
amputauit* I ambutauit L amputauit M   9 CXLIIII] *deest* L CXLV M   9 De clerico
damnato amputato] *deest* IL   10 abscidit] abscedit* I   12 CXLV] *deest* L CXLVI M
12 De penitentia laici castrati] *deest* IL De paenitentia laici castrati M   13 Apostolus]
deest M   13 anni] annus L annos M   14 insidiator] insidiatur* I insidiatur L   14 extitit]
extetit* I existetit L *deest* M   15 CXLVI] *deest* L CXLVII M   15 De uxore repudiata]
deest IL   16 Apostolus] *deest* M   17 dimissam] demissam L   18 CXLVII] *deest* L
CXLVIII M   18 De ordinatis per ignorantiam] *deest* IL   19 Nicena] Niceni I Synodus
Nicena M   20 contemptu] contentu L   20 disimulatione] desimulationem LM

68   Collectio CCCC capitulorum

enim non praeiudicat regulae ecclesiasticae; cum enim conpertum fuerit deponentur.

CXLVIII   Illis aliqua misericordia
Nicena: <De his qui praeuaricati sunt sine ulla necessitate> placuit sancto
concilio licet indigni sunt misericordiam, tamen aliquid circa eos humanitatis
ostendi.

CXLVIIII   De ordinatis indiscrete
Et iterum: Qui indiscrete ordinati, postmodum uel ipsi uel alii de se aliquod
crimen confessi sunt, degradentur.

CL   Non preferentur diaconi presbiteris
Diaconi presbiteris non preferantur. Neque sedeant in consessu presbiterorum.   *I 164v*

CLI   Sacerdoti secum mulieres non habentes
Nicena: Omnimodis interdicit sancta synodus: neque episcopo, neque presbitero, neque diacono, neque ulli clericorum omnino licere habere permitti
secum mulierem extraneam, nisi forte mater aut soror uel amita uel matertera
sit, in his namque solis personis et horum similibus omnibusque mulieribus
suspitio declinatur. Qui autem preter haec agit, pereclitabitur de clero suo.

4–6 *Nicaea* §11   **8–9** *Nicaea* §11   **11–12** *Nicaea* §20 (Rufin.)   **14–18** *Nicaea* §3

---

1 praeiudicat⌉ predicat IL   **1** ecclesiasticae⌉ ecclesiestica L   **3** CXLVIII⌉ *deest* L CXLVIIII M   **3** Illis aliqua misericordia⌉ *deest* IL   **4** Nicena⌉ Niceni ILM   **5** aliquid circa eos⌉ *deest* L   **7** CXLVIIII⌉ *deest* L CL M   **7** De ordinatis indiscrete⌉ *deest* IL   **8** Et⌉ Niceni et M   **8** aliquod⌉ aliquid L   **9** confessi⌉ professi LM   **10** CL⌉ *deest* L CLI M   **10** Non preferentur diaconi presbiteris⌉ *deest* IL Non preberentur diaconi presbiteris M   **11** Diaconi⌉ Niceni: Diaconi LM   **11** presbiteris⌉ presbiter L   **11** preferantur⌉ preberentur LM   **11** consessu⌉ consesisu* I concessu L consessu M   **13** CLI⌉ *deest* L CLII M   **13** Sacerdoti secum mulieres non habentes⌉ *deest* IL Sacerdotes secum mulieres non habentes M   **14** Nicena⌉ Niceni ILM   **14** Omnimodis⌉ Omnis mundis L   **14** synodus⌉ sinodus L   **15** diacono⌉ diaconi L   **15** ulli⌉ illi L   **16** matertera⌉ materta* I mater L   **17** horum⌉ orum L   **17** omnibusque⌉ omnibus qui L   **17** mulieribus⌉ mulieribus est ILM   **18** suspitio⌉ suspicio LM   **18** haec⌉ *deest* L   **18** pereclitabitur⌉ pclitabitur *corr.* periclitabitur M   **18** suo⌉ *deest* M

Collectio CCCC capitulorum

69

CLII Qui sine electione ordinati abiciantur

M 188r Leonis Papae responsio ad Rusticum episcopum Narbonensis: Nulla ratio sinit
ut inter episcopos habeantur qui nec ab clericis sunt electi, nec a plebibus expe-
titi, nec a prouintialibus episcopis cum metropolitani iuditio consecrati. Unde,
cum sepe quaestio de male accepto honore nascatur, quis ambigat nequaquam 5
I 165r istis esse tribuendum, quae non docetur fuisse conlatum? Si qui autem clerici
ab istis pseudoepiscopis in eis ecclesiis ordinati sunt, quia ad proprios episcopos pertinebant, et ordinatio eorum consensu et iuditio presidentium facta est,
L 103v potest rata haberi, ita ut in ipsis ecclesiis perseuerent. Aliter autem habenda
est una creatio quia nec loco fundata est nec auctore munita. 10

CLIII De monachis qui aut militare coeperint aut uxores acceperint

Propositum monachi proprio arbitrio et uoluntate susceptum deseri non potest absque peccato. Quod enim quis uouit Deo, debet et reddere. Unde qui
derelicta singularitatis professione, ad militiam uel ad nuptias deuolutus est,
paenitentiae publicae satisfactione purgandus est: quia etsi innocens militia et 15
I 165v honestum potest esse coniugium, electionem meliorem deseruisse transgres-
sio est.

2–10 Leo I, *ep. 167, ad Rusticum,* §14   **12–17** Leo I, *ep. 167, ad Rusticum,* §1

---

1 CLII] CLIII M   **1** Qui sine electione ordinati abiciantur] *deest* IL   **2** Leonis Papae
responsio ad Rusticum episcopum Narbonensis] Pape responsio ad Pusticium episcopum Narbonensis Leonis M   **2** responsio] respondet I respondit L   **2** Rusticum] Pusticium I posi-
tium L   **2** episcopum] episcopi L   **2** sinit] sint* I   **3** ut] *superscriptum* M   **3** episcopos]
episcopus L   **3** clericis] cleris M   **3** electi] *deest* L   **4** prouintialibus] prouincialibus LM
4 episcopis] episcopus L   **4** iuditio] iudicio LM   **5** sepe] saepe M   **5** quaestio] questio LM   **6** quae] quod M   **6** docetur] decetur M   **6** qui] quis L   **6** clerici] clericus
L   **7** ecclesiis] clesiis L   **8** ordinatio] ordinati M   **8** iuditio] iuditium L iudicio M
9 potest rata haberi] pro temporata hiberi L poterat habere M   **9** perseuerent] perseue-
rant L   **11** CLIII] CLIIII M   **11** De monachis qui aut militare coeperint aut uxores
acceperint] De proposito monachi proprio M   **11** acceperint] acciperint L   **13** uouit]
nouit L   **13** qui] quid L   **14** militiam] miliciam L   **15** publicae] publice L   **15–16** quia
etsi innocens militia et honestum potest] *deest* L   **16** electionem] dectionem L

70 Collectio CCCC capitulorum

CLIIII De puellis non consecratis si post nupserint

Puelle qui non parentum coactae imperio, sed spontaneo iuditio uirginitatis *M 188v*
propositum atque habitum susceperunt, si postea nuptias elegunt, preuarican-
tur, etiam si consecratio non accessit; cuius itaque non fraudarentur munere,
si in proposito permanerent.

CLV De his qui a parentibus paruuli derelicti sunt, seu ab hostibus capti
et utrum baptizati sint non potest inueniri: an debeant baptizare?

Si nulla extant iuditia inter propinquos aut familiares, nulla inter clericos atque uicinos, a quibus hi de quibus quaeritur baptizati fuisse doceantur, agendum est ut baptizentur: ne manifeste pereant, in quibus quod non ostenditur *I 166r*
gestum, ratio non sinit ut uideatur iteratum.

CLVI Si nesciunt in qua secta sunt baptizati

Non se isti baptizatos nesciunt, sed cuius fidei fuerint qui eos baptizauerunt
se nescire profitentur: unde quoniam quolibet modo formam baptismatis ac- *L 104r*
ceperunt, baptizandi non sunt, sed per manus inpositionem, inuocata uirtute
spiritus sancti, quam ab hereticis accipere non potuerunt, catholicis copulandi
sunt.

2–5 Leo I, *ep. 167, ad Rusticum,* §15 **8–11** Leo I, *ep. 167, ad Rusticum,* §16 **13–17** Leo
I, *ep. 167, ad Rusticum,* §18

---

1 CLIIII] CLV M **1** si post nupserint] *deest* M **1** nupserint] nupserunt L **2** Puelle]
Puellae M **2** coactae] coacte L **2** iuditio] iudicio M **3** habitum] abitum* M
3 susceperunt] susciperunt LM **4** etiam] aetiam L **5** permanerent] permaneant L
6 CLV] *deest* M **6** a] *deest* L **6** paruuli] paruoli L **6** hostibus] ostibus L **7** utrum]
uirum L **7** baptizati] baptiza L **7** sint] sunt LM **7** inueniri] inuenire M **7** an]
ad M **7** baptizare] baptizari L *add.* De discipulo baptismatis M **8** iuditia] iudicia LM
9 hi] hii L **9** quaeritur] queritur L **11** ratio] oratio L **11** uideatur] uideantur L
12 CLVI] CLVII M **12** Si] Qui M **12** sunt baptizati] sunt baptizari L baptizati sunt M **13** Non] Nonne M **14** se nescire] si nescire M **14** quoniam] quem L
14–15 acceperunt] acciperunt LM **15** per] *deest* L **16** ab] *deest* L

Collectio CCCC capitulorum 71

CLVII DE PARUULIS BAPTIZATIS CAPTIUIS A GENTILIBUS CAPTI ET GENTILITER
UIUERUNT

M 189r Si conuiuio solo gentilium et escis immolaticiis usi sunt, possunt ieiuniis et
manus inpositione purgari; ut deinceps idolo ditis abstinentes, sacramentorum
I 166v Christi possint esse participes. Si autem aut idola adorauerunt, aut homicidiis ⁵
uel fornicationibus contaminati sunt, ad communionem eos, nisi per paenitentiam publicam, non oportet admitti. Et ante qui deficientes paenitentiam
accipiunt communionem moriuntur.

CLVIII QUI IN PAENITENTIA MORIUNTUR

Horum causa Dei iuditio reseruanda est, in cuius manu fuit ut talium obitus ₁₀
usque ad communionis remedium differetur. Nos autem quibus uiuentibus
non communicamus, mortuis communicare non possumus.

CLVIIII SI ORDINETUR NON BAPTIZATUS

Sergii Papae: Qui presbiter dicitur si se quidem sciuit non baptizatum et tamquam baptizatus sacerdotii consecrationem accipit, sub longa et districta de- ₁₅
bet paenitentia poni et ecclesiastico baptismo baptizari, nullo modo autem
presbiter estimari ultra, quia obscenis manibus et polluta conscientia misteria
faciebat.

3–8 Leo I, *ep. 167, ad Rusticum,* §19. **10–12** Leo I, *ep. 167, ad Rusticum,* §8

---

1 CLVII⏋ CLVIII M **1** PARUULIS⏋ paruolis L *deest* M **1** BAPTIZATIS⏋ BAPTIZANDIS M
1 A⏋ *deest* L **1** GENTILIBUS⏋ GENTIBUS LM **1–2** CAPTI ET GENTILITER UIUERUNT⏋ *deest*
M **2** UIUERUNT⏋ UIUERE L **3** et escis⏋ et scis *corr.* escis L **3** immolaticiis⏋ immo-
laticis I **4** idolo⏋ idola L **4** ditis⏋ titis M **5** Christi⏋ *deest* M **5** possint⏋ possunt L **5** participes⏋ particeps L **5** aut⏋ aud L **6–7** paenitentiam⏋ penitentiam L
7 paenitentiam⏋ poenitentiam L **9** CLVIII⏋ CLVIIII M **9** QUI IN PAENITENTIA MORIUN-
TUR⏋ *deest* IL **10** iuditio⏋ iudicio M **10** obitus⏋ oblitus I **13** CLVIIII⏋ CLX M **13** SI
ORDINETUR NON BAPTIZATUS⏋ *deest* IL **14** presbiter⏋ plurimi I presbiteri L **14** si se⏋ si
si L **14–15** tamquam⏋ tam quia L **15** sacerdotii⏋ sacerdocii M **15** accipit⏋ accepit
L **16** paenitentia⏋ poenitentia L **16** poni⏋ apponi M **16** ecclesiastico⏋ ecclesiestico L
16 baptismo⏋ baptismatis M **17** estimari⏋ aestimari LM **17** conscientia⏋ constientia
L **17** misteria⏋ mysteria LM

72 Collectio CCCC capitulorum

CLX   Qᴜɪ ᴀᴇsᴛɪᴍᴀᴛɪᴏɴᴇᴍ ʜᴀʙᴇᴛ ǫᴜᴏᴅ ʙᴀᴘᴛɪᴢᴀᴛᴜs ᴇssᴇᴛ   *I 167r*
Si uero aestimationem de se talem habuit quam esset apud ecclesiae paruu-   *M 189v*
lus baptizatus, postea tamen cognouit ac demonstratum est quod non fuerit
baptizatus, indictaque ei temporali penitentia tunc, debet baptizari et nequa-
5 quam ab offitio presbiteri priuandus est sed iterum ordinetur, hi uero qui ab   *L 104v*
eo baptizati sunt sic in ecclesia permanent.

CLXI   Qᴜɪ ᴀᴅᴜʟᴛᴇʀɪᴜᴍ ᴄᴏɴᴍɪsᴇʀɪᴛ
Synodus Anquirinentium: Si quis adulterium commiserit, septem annis penitentiam conpletis perfectione redditur, secundum pristinos gradus.

10 CLXII   Dᴇ ɴᴇᴄᴀɴᴛɪʙᴜs ᴘᴀʀᴛᴜs sᴜᴏs
Mulieres uero quae fornicantur, et partus suos necant, sed et his qui agunt
secum ut utero conceptos excutiant, antiqua quidem definitio usque ad exitum
uitae eos ab ecclesia remouet, humanius autem nunc definimus, ut his x annis
tempus penitentia tribuatur.

15 CLXIII   Qᴜɪ ᴀʙᴏʀᴛɪᴜᴜᴍ ꜰᴀᴄɪᴜɴᴛ
Et in alia: Mulieres quae abortiuum faciunt antequam animam habeant, et   *I 167v*
postea, id est post xʟ dies accepti seminis, ut homicidae peniteant, id est ɪɪɪ

8–9 *Ancyr.* §20   **11–14** *Ancyr.* §21   **16–73.1**   cf. *Iud. Theod.* U I.14.24; *C* 147

---

1 CLX⸋ CLXI M   **1** Qᴜɪ ᴀᴇsᴛɪᴍᴀᴛɪᴏɴᴇᴍ ʜᴀʙᴇᴛ ǫᴜᴏᴅ ʙᴀᴘᴛɪᴢᴀᴛᴜs ᴇssᴇᴛ⸋ *deest* IL   **1** ǫᴜᴏᴅ
ʙᴀᴘᴛɪᴢᴀᴛᴜs ᴇssᴇᴛ⸋ ʙᴀᴘᴛɪsᴍᴀᴍ M   **2** aestimationem⸋ stimationem L   **2** quam⸋ quae L
quod M   **4** ei⸋ ei indicta L   **4** temporali⸋ temporale L   **4** penitentia⸋ paenitentia LM
5 offitio⸋ officio LM   **5** presbiteri⸋ presbiterii M   **5** hi⸋ hii* I hii L   **7** CLXI⸋ CLXII
M   **7** Qᴜɪ ᴀᴅᴜʟᴛᴇʀɪᴜᴍ ᴄᴏɴᴍɪsᴇʀɪᴛ⸋ *deest* IL Qᴜɪ ᴀᴅᴜʟᴛᴇʀɪᴜᴍ ᴄᴏᴍᴍɪsᴇʀɪᴛ M   **8** Synodus
Anquirinentium⸋ Sinodus Quirihensium L   **8** Anquirinentium⸋ Aquiriensium dicit *corr.* Anquirinensium dicit M   **8** commiserit⸋ commisserit L   **8** septem⸋ vɪɪ L   **9** perfectione⸋
perfectionis L   **9** secundum⸋ seci men L   **9** pristinos⸋ praestinus L   **10** CLXII⸋ *se-*
quitur cap. CLXII *post cap.* CLXIII L CLXIII M   **10** Dᴇ ɴᴇᴄᴀɴᴛɪʙᴜs ᴘᴀʀᴛᴜs sᴜᴏs⸋ *deest* IL
Dᴇ ɴᴇᴄᴀɴᴛɪʙᴜs ᴘᴀʀᴛᴏs sᴜᴏs M   **11** Mulieres⸋ Et in alia: Mulieres L   **11** quae⸋ qui IL
11 partus⸋ partos* I partos M   **12** conceptos⸋ conceptus L   **12** excutiant⸋ excuciant
L   **13** remouet⸋ remouit LM   **13** humanius⸋ humanus L   **13** definimus⸋ deuenimus
L   **13** x⸋ decem M   **13** annis⸋ annos M   **14** penitentia⸋ paenitiit L paenitentiae M
15 CLXIII⸋ *praecedit cap.* CLXII *ante cap.* CLXIII L CLXIIII M   **15** Qᴜɪ ᴀʙᴏʀᴛɪᴜᴜᴍ ꜰᴀ-
ᴄɪᴜɴᴛ⸋ *deest* IL Dᴇ ʜɪs ǫᴜɪ ᴀʙᴏʀᴛɪᴜᴜᴍ ꜰᴀᴄɪᴜɴᴛ M   **16** Et in alia⸋ *deest* LM   **16** quae⸋
qui L   **16** abortiuum⸋ adortiuum L   **16** habeant⸋ habeat M   **17** post⸋ *superscriptum*
M   **17** xʟ⸋ quadraginta M   **17** homicidae⸋ homicide LM   **17** peniteant⸋ poenitentiam
L paeniteant M   **17** ɪɪɪ⸋ tres L

Collectio CCCC capitulorum

73

annos, in IIII feria et VI et in tribus XL^{mis}. Si ante XL dies, unum annum peniteat.

CLXIIII QUI HOMICIDIUM FACIUNT
Anquirinensium: Qui uoluntarie homicidium fecerint, ad paenitentiam quidem se iugiter mittant; circa exitum autem uitae communione digni habeantur.

CLXV QUI CASU HOMICIDIUM FACIUNT
Eos uero qui non uoluntate, sed casu homicidium perpetrauerint; haec uero humanior difinitio quincennii tempus tribuit.

CLXVI SI MATER OCCIDAT FILIUM
In alia: Mater si occidat filium suum, si homicidium facit, XV annis et numquam mutat nisi in die Domini peniteat.

CLXVII DE PENITENTIA PAUPERCULAE
Mulier paupercula, si occidat filium suum, VII annis peniteat. In canone dicitur, si homicida sit, X annis peniteat.

CLXVIII QUI NECAT FILIUM SINE BAPTISMO
Qui necat filium suum sine baptismo, in canone: X annis, sed per consilium VII annis peniteat. Si moriatur sine nece hominis et sine baptismo, III annis peniteat.

3–4 *Ancyr.* §22 **6–7** *Ancyr.* §22 **9–10** *Iud. Theod.* U I.14.25; G 102 **12–13** *Iud. Theod.* U I.14.26; G 103 **15–16** *Iud. Theod.* U I.14.30; G 104; C 141 **16–17** *Iud. Theod.* G 106

---

1 annos] annis L   1 IIII] quarta L   1 VI] sexta L   1 XL^{mis}] quadragisimis M   1 Si] *deest* L *superscriptum* M   1 XL] quadraginta M   1 peniteat] poeniteat L paeniteat M   2 CLXIIII] *lacuna* M   2 QUI HOMICIDIUM FACIUNT] *deest* IL *lacuna* M   **3–75.10** Anquirinensium… eique inheserit tamquam] *lacuna* M   3 Anquirinensium] Anquiriensium L   3 uoluntarie] uoluntariae IL   3 paenitentiam] poenitentiam L   4 mittant] mittat L   4 autem] *deest* L   5 QUI CASU HOMICIDIUM FACIUNT] *deest* IL   6 casu] cassu* L   7 humanior difinitio] humani ordinatio L   7 quincennii] quicenni I quinecenni L   8 SI MATER OCCIDAT FILIUM] *deest* IL   9 occidat] occidit L   9 annis] annis paenetiat L   9 numquam] numqua L   10 mutat] motat* I muttat L   10 Domini] dominico L   11 DE PENITENTIA PAUPERCULAE] *deest* IL   12 occidat] occidit L   14 QUI NECAT FILIUM SINE BAPTISMO] *deest* IL   15 necat] negat L   15 baptismo] baptismum I   15 annis] annis paeniteat L   16 annis] *deest* L   16 peniteat] paeniteat L   **16–17** Si moriatur…peniteat] *deest* L

74   Collectio CCCC capitulorum

CLXVIIII Qui auguria et auspitia seruat

Anquirinensium: Qui auguria auspitiaque, siue somnia, uel diuinationes qua-   *L 105r*
slibet secundum mores gentium obseruant, aut in domos suas huiusmodi homines introducunt in exquirendis aliquam artem malefitiorum, aut ut domos
5 suas inlustrent, confessi peniteant, si de clero sunt abiciantur, si uero seculares
v annis agant secundum regulas antiquas constitutas.

In alia: Si mulier in canone v annis et nunc uno anno uel tribus xl^{mis}, uel xl
iuxta qualitatem culpae peniteat.

Mulier si qua ponit filium suum supra tectum uel in fornacem pro sanitate
10 febris, v annis peniteat.

CLXX Qui retro facit cum muliere

Si uir cum muliere sua retro aut in tergo nupserit, penitere debet quasi ille qui   *I 168v*
cum animalibus.

CLXXI Si mulier cum muliere fornicat

15 Si mulier cum muliere, annis iii; id est, si mulier quasi more fornicatoris ad
alteram coniunxerit, iii annis sicut fornicator peniteat.

CLXXII Permiscens semen uiri sui

Sic et illa, quae semen uiri sui in cybo miscens, ut inde plus eius amorem
accipiat, peniteat.

2–6 *Ancyr.* §24; cf. *Iud. Theod. U* I.15.4   **7–8** cf. *Iud. Theod. U* I.15.4; *D* 145   **9–10** cf.
Iud. Theod. U I.15.2; *G* 117; *C* 148   **12–13** cf. *Iud. Theod. U* I.14.21-2; *G* 107   **15** *Iud.
Theod. U* I.2.12; *G* 95   **15–16** *Iud. Theod. U* I.14.15   **18–19** *Iud. Theod. U* I.14.15

---

1 Qui auguria et auspitia seruat⌉ *deest* IL   **2** auspitiaque⌉ auspiciaque L   **3** suas⌉
suos L   **4** aliquam⌉ aliquem L   **4** malefitiorum⌉ maleficiorum L   **4** domos⌉ domus L
5 peniteant⌉ paeniteant L   **5** abiciantur⌉ abiciatur L   **5** si uero⌉ siue L   **6** agant⌉ agat
L   **7** In alia⌉ CLXX In alia L   **7** Si mulier⌉ Similiter L   **7** uel xl⌉ *del.* L   **8** peniteat⌉
paeniteat   **10** peniteat⌉ paeniteat L   **11** CLXX⌉ CLXXI L   **11** Qui retro facit cum
muliere⌉ *deest* L   **14** CLXXI⌉ CLXXII L   **14** Si mulier cum muliere fornicat⌉ *deest*
IL   **15** Si mulier⌉ Similiter L   **15** quasi⌉ quese L   **16** coniunxerit⌉ coniuncxerit L
16 peniteat⌉ paeniteat L   **17** CLXXII⌉ *cap. deest* L   **17** Permiscens semen uiri sui⌉ *deest*
IL   **18–19** Sic et illa...peniteat⌉ *deest* L

Collectio CCCC capitulorum

75

CLXXIII Qui cum uirginem fornicat
Si quis fornicat cum uirgine III annis.

CLXXIIII Si cum maritata fornicat
Si cum maritata, IIII annis: integros II, alios II, in XL^{mis} tribus et tribus diebus
in ebdomata peniteat.

CLXXV Si mulier cum se sola
Mulier sola cum se ipsa coitum habeat, III annis peniteat.

CLXXVI De disponsa sorore
Anquirinensium: Si quis sponsam habens sorori eius forsitan intulerit uiolentiam, eique inheserit tamquam suae: hanc autem deceptam, postea duxerit
uxorem desponsatam, illa uero quae uitium passa est, si forte necem sibi intulerit: omnes hii qui facti huius conscii sunt, x annis in penitentia redigantur
secundum canones constitutos.

CLXXVII Si duobus fratribus nupserit
Canones Cesariensis: Mulier si duobus fratribus nupserit, abici debere usque
ad diem mortis. Sed propter humanitatem in extremis suis sacramentis reconciliari oportet: ita tamen, ut si forte sanitatem recuperit, matrimonio soluto
ad penitentiam admittatur. Quod si defuncta fuerit mulier in huius modi con-
sortio constituta, difficilis erit penitentia remanenti. Qua sententia tam uiros
quam mulieres tenere debebunt.

---

2 cf. *Iud. Theod. U* I.2.1; *D* 82   **4–5** cf. *Iud. Theod. U* I.2.1; *D* 82   **7** cf. *Iud. Theod. U*
I.2.13; *G* 97   **9–13** *Ancyr.* §25.   **15–20** *Neocaes.* §2

---

1 Qui cum uirginem fornicat] *deest* IL   **2** fornicat] fornicator L   **2** annis] paeniteat L
3 Si cum maritata fornicat] *deest* IL   **4** maritata] marita L   **4** IIII] quator L   **4** annis]
annos L   **4** II] v L   **4** in] *deest* L   **4** XL^{mis}] quadragesimus L   **5** ebdomata] ebdomada L   **5** peniteat] paenitiit L   **6** Si mulier cum se sola] *deest* IL   **7** peniteat] paeniteat
L   **8** De disponsa sorore] *deest* IL   **9** Anquirinensium] Anquiriensium L   **9** eius] cuius
corr. uius L   **9** intulerit] intullerit L   **9–10** uiolentiam] uiolentia L   **11** desponsatam]
disponsatam LM   **11** quae uitium] quicumque L   **11** quae] qui M   **11** necem] decem
L   **12** penitentia] paenitentia LM   **12** redigantur] redigentur L   **13** secundum] sicut L
13 canones] cannones L   **14** CLXXVII] CLXXVI L   **14** Si duobus fratribus nupserit]
deest IL   **17** recuperit] recuperauerit M   **17** soluto] solito L   **18** penitentiam] poenitentiam L paenitentiam M   **18** admittatur] mittatur M   **18** Quod] Que L   **19** penitentia]
paenitentia LM   **19** Qua sententia] Que sentia L   **20** quam] quem L   **20** tenere] teneri
L   **20** debebunt] debent M

76   Collectio CCCC capitulorum

CLXXVIII   Presbiter secundis nuptiis non debet inesse
Presbiterum conuiuio secundarum nuptiarum interesse non debere, maxime
cum petatur secundis nuptiis penitentiam tribuere. Quis ergo est presbiter qui
propter conuiuium illis consentiat nuptiis

5 CLXXVIIII   Presbiter qui admiserit corporale peccatum
Qui admiserit corporale peccatum, et hic postea presbiter ordinatus est, si con-   *I 169v*
fessus fuerit quod ante ordinationem suam peccauerit, non quidem offerat; maneat autem in aliis offitiis propter eius studii utilitatem. Nam cetera peccata
censuerunt plurimi etiam ordinationem priuari. Quod si de his non fuerit con-   *M 190v*
10 fessus, nec ab aliquo poterit manifeste conuinci, huic ipsi de se potestas est
permittenda.

CLXXX   Qui commonia ieiunia contemnit
Gangrensium canonum: Si quis iudicans, die dominica ieiunauerit, eius die
contemptu; anathema sit.

15 [CLXXXI]
Si quis eorum, qui in proposito sunt continentiae, preter necessitatem corpo-
ralem superbia, ieiunia communia totius ecclesiae putauerit contempnenda, et
suo sensu dicat non esse perfecta; anathema sit.

CLXXXI   De tribus gradibus continentium
20 Statuta Cartaginensis: Cum preterito concilio de continentiae et castitatis
moderamine tractaretur, gradus isti tres qui constrictione quaedam castitatis   *I 170r*

2–4 *Neocaes.* §7   **6–11** *Neocaes.* §9   **13–14** *Gangrens.* §18   **16–18** *Gangrens.* §19
20–77.4 *Carthag.* (390) §2

---

1 CLXXVIII] *cap. deest* L   1 Presbiter secundis nuptiis non debet inesse] *deest* IL
2–4 Presbiterum…nuptiis] *deest* L   **2** maxime] maximae M   **3** penitentiam] paenitentiam M   **5** CLXXVIIII] CLXXVII L   **5** Presbiter qui admiserit corporale pec-
catum] *deest* IL Presbiter qui commiserit corpore peccatum M   **6** corporale] corpore
L   **6–7** confessus] confesus L   **7** quod] qui L   **8** offitiis] officiis LM   **8** studii]
studiis M   **9** censuerunt] consuerunt M   **9** plurimi] pluri M   **10** aliquo] alico L
10 ipsi] ipse LM   **10** se] *deest* L   **11** permittenda] permittendam L   **12** CLXXX]
deest L   **12** Qui commonia ieiunia contemnit] *deest* IL Quicqua communia ieiunia contemna
M   **13–14** Si quis…sit] *deest* L   **15** [CLXXXI]] *deest* M   **16** proposito] propositu I
16–17 corporalem] corporali I   **17** communia] commonia L   **17** contempnenda] con-
temnenda M   **19** CLXXXI] CLXXXII IL   **19** De tribus gradibus continentium] *deest*
IL   **21** moderamine] modoramine L   **21** isti] iste L   **21** quaedam] quedam L

Collectio CCCC capitulorum

77

per consecrationis adnixi sunt, episcopus inquam, presbiter et diaconus. Ita placuit, ut condecet sacros antestites ac Dei sacerdotes necnon et leuitas uel qui sacramentis diuinis inseruiunt, continentes esse in omnibus, quo possint simpliciter quod a Domino postulant impetrare.

CLXXXII   Si clericus commodauerit

Et ut clericus si commodauerit pecuniam, pecuniam recipiat; si speciem, ean-
M 191r   dem speciem, quantum ei debetur, accipiat.

CLXXXIII   Ut non sint sacerdotes procuratores

L 106r   Et ut episcopi, presbiteri, diaconi non sint ductores aut procuratores neque ul-
lo turpi negotio et inhonesto uictum quaerant, prospicere enim debent scriptum esse: nullus militans Deo inplicat se negotiis secularibus.

CLXXXIIII   Ut episcopi trans mare non proficiscantur

Ut episcopi trans mare non proficiscantur, nisi consulto primae sedis episco-
I 170v   pum suae cuiusque prouintiae, ut ab eo precipue possint sumere formatas uel
conmendaticias epistolas.

6–7   *Can. in causa Apiarii A* §16   **9–11**   *Can. in causa Apiarii A* §16   **13–15**   *Can. in causa Apiarii A* §23

1 consecrationis⁊ consegrationis* L   1 adnixi⁊ adnexi L   2 condecet⁊ cumdecet L
2 sacros⁊ seros M   2 antestites⁊ intestites L   3 possint⁊ possunt L   4 Domino⁊ Deo
M   4 postulant⁊ postolant L   4 impetrare⁊ inpetrare M   5 CLXXXII⁊ CLXXXIII IL
5 Si clericus commodauerit⁊ *deest* IL Si clericus commendauerit M   6 clericus⁊ clerico L
6 pecuniam⁊ paecuniam M   6 pecuniam⁊ *superscriptum* I paecunia M   6 recipiat⁊ recepit
L   6 si speciem⁊ suscipem L   8 CLXXXIII⁊ *deest* L CLXXXIIII I   8 Ut non sint sacerdotes procuratores⁊ *deest* IL   9 episcopi⁊ episcopus L   9 sint⁊ sunt L   9 aut procura-
tores⁊ *deest* L   9–10 ullo⁊ illo L   10 inhonesto⁊ inhonestum M   10 quaerant⁊ querant
L   10 prospicere⁊ reprospicere L respicere M   11 inplicat⁊ implicat L   11 secularibus⁊
saecularibus M   12 CLXXXIIII⁊ CLXXXV IL   12 Ut episcopi trans mare non pro-
ficiscantur⁊ *deest* IL Episcopi trans mare non proficiscantur M   13 primae⁊ prime L
13–14 episcopum⁊ episcopi L   14 prouintiae⁊ prouinciae LM   14 precipue⁊ precipuae
L   14 formatas⁊ formatos* I   15 conmendaticias⁊ commendaticas L   15 epistolas⁊
epistulas M

78   Collectio CCCC capitulorum

CLXXXV Non licet episcopo uendere pretia ecclesiae
Ita etiam placuit ut presbiteri non uendant rem ecclesiae ubi sunt constituti,
nescientibus episcopis suis, quomodo nec episcopo licet uendere pretia ecclesiae, inconsulto consilio uel cuncto presbiterio sine necessitate ulla.

CLXXXVI De benedictione sponsi et sponsae
Sponsus et sponsa cum benedicti fuerint, pro reuerentia benedictionis episcopi
eadem nocte in uirginitate permaneant.

CLXXXVII De ueste sanctaemonialis feminae
Sanctimonialis uirgo, cum ad consecrationem suo episcopo offertur, in talibus uestibus adplicetur, qualibus sempter usura est, professioni et sanctimonia
aptis.

CLXXXVIII De subdiacono
Subdiaconus cum ordinatur, accepit patenam de manu episcopi uacuam et calicem uacuum, de manu uero archidiaconi accipiat urciolum cum aqua et aquaemanilem ac manutergium.

M 191v

I 171r

CLXXXVIII Quid sit acholitus
Acholitus cum ordinatur, ab episcopis quidem doceatur qualiter se in offitio
suo agere debeat, sed ab archidiacono accipiat ceroferariam cum cereo, ut sciat

---

2–4 *Can. in causa Apiarii A* §33   **6–7** cf. *Stat. eccl. ant.* §101   **9–11** *Stat. eccl. ant.* §99
13–15 *Stat. eccl. ant.* §93   **17–79.2** *Stat. eccl. ant.* §94

---

1 CLXXXV⟧ CLXXXVI IL   **1** Non licet episcopo uendere pretia ecclesiae⟧ *deest* IL
Ne licet episcopis uendere pretia ecclesiae M   **2** uendant⟧ uindent L   **2** sunt⟧ sum
L **3** episcopo⟧ episcopis L **3** uendere⟧ uindere L **3** pretia⟧ precia L **4** presbiterio⟧
presbitero L **4** sine necessitate⟧ si necessitate L **4** ulla⟧ illa L **5** CLXXXVI⟧ *deest*
I CLXXXVII L **5** De benedictione sponsi et sponsae⟧ *deest* IL **7** eadem⟧ eandem L
7 nocte⟧ docte *corr.* octe L **8** CLXXXVII⟧ CLXXXVIII L **8** De ueste sanctaemonialis
feminae⟧ *deest* IL **9** Sanctimonialis⟧ Sanctaemonialis M **9** consecrationem⟧ secrationem I **9** suo⟧ fui I sui L **10** sempter⟧ semper LM **10** usura⟧ ᶦt M **10** professioni⟧
professione L **10** sanctimonia⟧ sanctimoniae L **12** CLXXXVIII⟧ CLXXXVIIII L
12 De subdiacono⟧ *deest* IL **13** Subdiaconus⟧ Subdiaconos* M **13** ordinatur⟧ ordinator L **13** accepit⟧ accipiet M **13** patenam⟧ patnam* M **14** archidiaconi⟧ arcidiacono L **14** urciolum⟧ ortiolum L orciolum M **14–15** aquaemanilem⟧ aeaquemanilem L **16** CLXXXVIII⟧ CXC L **16** Quid sit acholitus⟧ *deest* IL Quid sit acolitus
M **17** Acholitus⟧ Acolitus M **17** ab⟧ ad L **17** episcopis⟧ episcopo L episcopi M
17 offitio⟧ officio LM **18** ab⟧ *deest* L **18** ceroferariam⟧ teroferariam I cerofrariam L
cerofacriam M

Collectio CCCC capitulorum 79

se ad accendenda ecclesiae luminaria mancipari; accipiat et urciolum uacuum ad suggerendum uinum in eucharistiam corporis Christi.

CXC DE EXORCISTA

L 106v Exorcista cum ordinatur, accipiat de manu episcopi libellum in quo scripti sunt exorcismi, dicente sibi episcopo: Accipe et conmenda, et habeto potestatem 5 inponendi manus super inerguminum siue baptizandum siue caticuminum.

CXCI DE LECTORE

Lector cum ordinatur, faciat uerbum episcopus de eo ad plebem, indicans eius *I 171v* fidem ac uitam et ingenium; post haec, expectante plebe, tradat ei codicem de quo lecturus est, dicens ad eum: Accipe, et esto uerbi Dei lector, habitu- 10 rus, si fideliter et utiliter impleueris offitium, partem cum his qui uerbum Dei ministrauerint.

CXCII DE OSTIARIO

Ostiarius cum ordinatur, postquam ab archidiacono instructus fuerit qualiter *M 192r* in domo Dei conuersare debeat, ad suggestionem archidiaconi tradet ei episco- 15 pus claues ecclesiae de altari, dicens: Sic age, quasi redditurus Deo rationem pro his rebus quae istis clauibus recluduntur.

4–6 *Stat. eccl. ant.* §95   **8–12** *Stat. eccl. ant.* §96   **14–17** *Stat. eccl. ant.* §97

---

1 accendenda�️] accenda L accenda* M   **1** ecclesiae] ecclesia L   **1** urciolum] orciolum LM   **2** suggerendum] segregendum L   **3** CXC] *deest* L   **3** DE EXORCISTA] *deest* IL   **4** ordinatur] ordinator L   **5** exorcismi] exorcissimi L   **5** dicente] dicentes L **5** episcopo] Christo L   **5** conmenda] commendo L commenda M   **6** inerguminum] energumenum M   **6** baptizandum] baptizatum L   **7** CXCI] CXCII L   **7** DE LECTORE] *deest* IL **8** de eo] deco L   **8–9** eius fidem] eiusdem* M   **9** ac uitam] ac ciuitatem L   **9** et] ex L   **10** esto] ista L   **10** uerbi] uerba L uerbo M   **11** utiliter] uliter* M   **11** impleueris] impleberis M   **11** offitium] officium LM   **13** CXCII] CXCIII L   **13** DE OSTIARIO] *deest* IL DE HOSTARIO M   **15** conuersare] conuersari L   **15** suggestionem] suggessionem L   **15** tradet] tradat LM   **16** altari] altare L   **17** quae] que L   **17** recluduntur] recludentur L

80 Collectio CCCC capitulorum

CXCIII De cantatore

Psalmista, id est cantator, potest absque scientia episcopi, sola iussione presbiteri, offitium suscipere cantandi, dicente sibi presbitero: Uide ut quod ore
cantas, corde credas et quod corde credis operibus probes.

CXCIIII De dispendio uiduae

Uiduae quae ecclesiae stipendio sustentantur, tam adsiduae in Dei opere esse   *I 172r*
debent, quia et meritis et orationibus suis ecclesiam iuuent.

CXCV Ne quis clericus ad iudicia saecularia eat

Synodus Calcidonensis: Si quis clericus cum clerico causam habeat, placuit ut
episcopum suum non deserant, et ad iuditia secularia currant, sed prius, ut
dictum est, apud episcopum suum examinent causam, aut certe cum uolun-   *L 107r*
tate ipsius episcopi causa uentiletur aut quos partes utrasque uoluerint. Si
quis autem contra haec uenire temptauerit, canonicis interdictis subiacebit. Si
uero clericus quis habeat causam cum extraneo episcopo, uel cum suo, apud
synodum prouintiae iudicetur.

CXCVI Qui contra metropolitanum causam habet

Si autem episcopus aut clericus disceptationem habeat cum metropolitano epi-   *M 192v*
scopo ad primam sedem recurrant, aut ad sedem <Constantinopolitanam> et
ibi causam definiant.

2–4   *Stat. eccl. ant.* §98   6–7   *Stat. eccl. ant.* §102   9–15   *Chalced.* §9   17–19   *Chalced.*
§9

---

1 CXCIII] CXCIIII L   1 De cantatore] *deest* IL   2 scientia] sententiam L
2–3 presbiteri] presbiter L   3 offitium] officium LM   4 credis] credes L   5 CXCIIII]
CXCV L   5 De dispendio uiduae] *deest* IL De dispendo* uiduae M   6 Uiduae] Uide L
6 quae] que L   6 sustentantur] sustentur* I   7 quia] quam M   8 CXCV] CXCVI
L   8 Ne quis clericus ad iudicia saecularia eat] *deest* IL   9 Synodus Calcidonensis]
Sinodus Calcidonensium L   9 Calcidonensis] Calcidonensis ait M   9 habeat] habeant
L   10 iuditia] iudicia LM   10 secularia] saecularia LM   11 aut] ut L   12 utrasque]
utrosque L   13 haec] hec L   15 synodum] sinodum L   15 prouintiae] prouincie
M   16 CXCVI] CXCVII L   16 Qui contra metropolitanum causam habet] *deest* IL
17–18 episcopo] uel conspirationis crimen apud episcopo L   18 primam] propriam L
18 Constantinopolitanam] *deest* ILM   19 definiant] difiniant L

Collectio CCCC capitulorum 81

CXCVII Peregrinos non ministrare

I 172v Peregrinos clericos et lectores in aliena ciuitate sine synodicis litteris episcopi sui penitus nusquam ministrare debere.

CXCVIII Ad abicienda crimina conspirationis

Coniurationis uel conspirationis crimen apud extrinsecas leges penitus amputari solere; multo magis in ecclesia Dei hoc ne fiat prohiberi oportet. Igitur clerici aut monachi fuerint inuenti coniurati et per coniurationem calumniam facientes episcopo uel quibuslibet clericis, proprium amittunt gradum.

CXCVIIII Post mortem episcopi non licet predare

Clericis non licere post mortem episcopi sui diripere ea que illi competere non possunt, sicut et anterioribus canonibus cautum est; alioquin eos de gradibus suis posse pereclitari.

CC De monasteriis consecratis

Quae semel Deo sacrata sunt monasteria post episcoporum consensum, oportet in perpetuum monasteria nuncupari, et eorum res monasteriis reseruari et

I 173r;
M 193r non debere ulterius caenacula secularia fieri. Si quis uero hoc fieri permiserit, canonicis interdictis subiaceat.

2–3 *Chalced.* §13   **5–8** *Chalced.* §18   **10–12** *Chalced.* §22   **14–17** *Chalced.* §24

1 CXCVII] *cap. deest* L   1 Peregrinos non ministrare] *deest* IL   **2–3** Peregrinos clericos...debere] *deest* L   3 nusquam] numquam M   4 Ad abicienda crimina conspirationis] *deest* IL Ad adicienda crimina conspirationis M   5 extrinsecas] extrinsecus L   5 penitus] poenitus L   **5–6** amputari] amputare M   6 hoc ne fiat] honefiat L   7 monachi] clerici monachi L   7 coniurationem] coniuratione M   8 episcopo] episcopis L   8 amittunt] ammittunt* L   9 Post mortem episcopi non licet predare] *deest* IL Post mortem episcopi non licet praedicare M   10 Clericis] Clericus L   10 non licere] *deest* L   10 post] propter IL   10 que] quae M   10 competere] conpetere LM   12 pereclitari] pereclitare L periclitari M   13 CC] *deest* L   13 De monasteriis consecratis] *deest* IL De monasteriis secratis M   14 Quae] Que L   14 post] *deest* L per M   15 perpetuum] perpetuam L   15 monasteria] *deest* L   15 nuncupari] noncupari L   16 caenacula] cenacula M   16 secularia] saecularia M

82 Collectio CCCC capitulorum

CCI Non transgredi fidem sanctorum
Canones Constantinopoli: Non transgredi fidem sanctorum patrum ccc xviiii,
qui in Nicea Bythiniae conuenerunt: sed permanere eam firmam, et dominam
censemus.

CCII De principatu Constantinopolitani episcopi
Constantinopolitanum episcopum habere primatum honoris post Romanorum   *L 107v*
episcopum, propterea quod urbs ipsa sit iunior Roma.

CCIII De primatu Alexandrini episcopi
Alexandrinum quidem episcopum, qui in Aegypto gubernare, et orientales
episcopos orientem solum gubernare, seruatis quae in Nicenis canonibus.

CCIIII De primatu Antiochenae <episcopi>
Primatus Antiochenae ecclesiae et Asiae gubernationis episcopi, quia per Asiam
sunt, parochias solum gubernare.

CCV De Ponto <et> Ponticae
Qui uero sunt Ponto, Ponticae tantum; qui sunt Traciae, Traciarum solum.   *I 173v*

CCVI De principe barbaricis
Quae autem in barbaricis gentibus sunt ecclesiae Dei, ita gubernari oportet,
secundum quod obtinuit a patribus consuetudo.

2–4 Conc. Constant. (381), §1   **6–7** *Constantin. (381)* §3   **9–10** *Constantin. (381)* §3
12–13 *Constantin. (381)* §3   **15** *Constantin. (381)* §3   **17–18** *Constantin. (381)* §3

---

1 CCI] *deest* L   1 Non transgredi fidem sanctorum] *deest* IL   2 Constantinopoli] Constantini episcoporum L Constantinopolitani M   **2** ccc xviiii] ccc xviii L actos x et octo M   **3** Nicea] Nice* I Nicena M   **3** Bythiniae] Bithiniae L Bithyniae M   **5** CCII] CCI L   **5** De principatu Constantinopolitani episcopi] *deest* IL   **6** episcopum] episcopis L   7 episcopum] episcopis L episcoporum M   **7** urbs] ubrs L   **8** De primatu Alexandrini episcopi] *deest* IL De Alexandrini episcopo *corr.* De Alexandrino episcopo M   **9** Aegypto] Egypto L   **10** episcopos] episcopus L   **10** gubernare] gubernari L   **10** seruatis quae] seruatisque M   **10** quae] que L   **11** CCIIII] CCIII L   **11** De primatu Antiochenae <episcopi>] *deest* IL   **12** Antiochenae] Nicene L   **12** Asiae] Asie L   **13** parochias] parrochias M   **14** De Ponto <et> Ponticae] *deest* IL De Ponto Pontiae* M   **15** Ponticae] Pontifice L Pontice M   **15** qui] que L   **15** Traciae] Tracie L Trachiae M   **15** Traciarum] Trachiarum M   **16** De principe barbaricis] *deest* IL   **17** Quae] Que L   **17** ecclesiae] ecclesias I ecclesiis L   **17** gubernari] gubernario L   **17** oportet] optet L   **18** secundum] secondum* L

Collectio CCCC capitulorum 83

CCVII Sɪ ᴅᴇᴘᴏsɪᴛᴜs ꜰᴜᴇʀɪᴛ ᴇᴘɪsᴄᴏᴘᴜs
Canones Sardicensis: Ut cum aliquis episcopus depositus fuerit eorum episcoporum iuditio, qui in uicinis locis commorentur, et proclamauerit agendum
sibi negotium in urbe Roma, alter episcopum in eius cathedram, post apella-
tionem eius qui uidetur esse depositus, omnino non ordinetur in loco ipsius,   5
nisi causa fuerit in iuditio Romani episcopi terminata, et si remittendus sit cum
commendaticiis epistolis aut a latere suo presbiterum mittat, quia omnia erit
in arbitrio suo.

CCVIII Nᴜʟʟᴜs sᴏʟʟɪᴄɪᴛᴀᴛ ᴀʟᴛᴇʀɪᴜs ᴄʟᴇʀɪᴄᴜᴍ
Nulli episcopo liceat alterius ciuitatis clericum sollicitare et in suis parrochiis   10
ordinare. Uniuersi dixerunt: quia ex his contentionibus solet discordia nasci
prohibet omnium sententia ut ne quis hoc facere audeat.

CCVIIII Dᴇ ᴀᴄᴄᴜsᴀᴛᴏ ᴇᴘɪsᴄᴏᴘᴏ
Statuta Antiocensium: Si quis episcopus in aliquibus criminibus accusatus et
iudicatus, postmodum eueniat ut pro eo dissonare qui sunt in prouintia epi-   15
scopi, alii eorum innocentem qui iudicantur adserentes, alii eorum reum; pro
elimatione discussionis totius causae, placuit sanctae synodo ut metropolitanum episcopum, et qui ex uicina prouintia conuocantur, et collegas aliquos, qui
iudicent, et dubietatem dissoluant, et per hoc firmari cum comprouintialibus,
quae eis recte uidentur.   20

2–8 *Sardica* §4   **10–12** *Sardica* §18   **14–20** *Antioch* §14

---

1 Sɪ ᴅᴇᴘᴏsɪᴛᴜs ꜰᴜᴇʀɪᴛ ᴇᴘɪsᴄᴏᴘᴜs] *deest* IL   **2** episcopus] episcopis L   **3** iuditio] iudicio M   **3** commorentur] commorantur M   **4** negotium] negotio L   **4** Roma] romana
M   **4** episcopum] episcopis *corr.* episcopus L episcopus M   **4** cathedram] catheram* I
4–5 apellationem] apellatione L   **5** ipsius] ipsios L   **6** causa] *deest* L   **6** fuerit] fuerint
M   **6** iuditio] iudicio M   **7** commendaticiis] commendaticis L   **7** presbiterum] presbiterorum LM   **9** Nᴜʟʟᴜs sᴏʟʟɪᴄɪᴛᴀᴛ ᴀʟᴛᴇʀɪᴜs ᴄʟᴇʀɪᴄᴜᴍ] *deest* IL Nᴜʟʟᴜs sᴏʟʟɪᴄɪᴛᴇᴛ ᴀʟᴛᴇʀɪᴜs
ᴄʟᴇʀɪᴄᴜᴍ M   **10** episcopo] episcopi M   **10** sollicitare] sollicitari L   **10** parrochiis]
parochiis L   **11** ordinare] ordinari L   **12** audeat] autdeat L   **13** CCVIIII] *deest*
L   **13** Dᴇ ᴀᴄᴄᴜsᴀᴛᴏ ᴇᴘɪsᴄᴏᴘᴏ] *deest* IL   **14** Antiocensium] Antionens L Anthiocensium M   **15** eueniat] ueniat L   **15** prouintia] prouincia M   **16** iudicantur] iudicatur
L   **16** adserentes] deserentes M   **16** reum] rerum L   **17** elimatione] elymatione M
17 sanctae] sancto LM   **17** synodo] sinodo L   **17–18** metropolitanum] metropolitano*
I   **18** prouintia] provincia M   **18** collegas] colligas LM   **18** aliquos] alios L   **18** qui]
quis L   **19** comprouintialibus] conprouincialibus LM   **20** quae] que L   **20** recte] recta
M

84 Collectio CCCC capitulorum

CCX Si quis in aliquibus episcopus accusatus
Si quis episcopus in aliquibus criminibus accusatus ab omnibus iudicetur, qui
sunt in prouintia episcopis, si omnes ex uno consensu unam contra eum proferant sententiam; hunc nullomodo ab alio se iudicari, sed permanere firmam
5 et consonantem, quae a prouintialibus episcopis data sententia.

M 194r

I 174v

CCXI Ut nullus episcopus eligat successorem in exitum uitae
Nulli episcoporum licere sibi constituere successorem in exitu uitae suae. Et
si aliquid tale factum fuerit, infirma esse debet electio uel ordinatio eius. Illud autem obseruare depositione ecclesiastica instituente non aliter fieri, nisi
10 aut cum synodo et iuditio episcoporum et maxime electio clericorum, ut post
transitum quiescentis potestatem habeant elegere et ordinare eum qui dignus
est.

CCXII Ut nullus gradus aduersus alium
Synodus Siluestri in Roma cum cclxxxiiii episcopi et Constantino et Helena:
15 Presbiter non aduersus episcopum, non diaconus aduersus presbiterum, non
acolitus aduersus subdiaconum, non exorcista aduersus acolitum, non lector
aduersus exorcistam, non ostiarius aduersus lectorem det accusationem aliquam. Et non damnabitur presul, nisi in lxxii testibus. Neque presul sum-

I 175r; 108v

2–5 *Antioch* §15   **7–12** *Antioch* §23   **15–85.2** *Const. Sylv.* ll. 105-11

---

1 Si quis in aliquibus episcopus accusatus⌉ *deest* IL Si quis in aliquibus episcopus accusatus est M   **2** accusatus ab omnibus⌉ *deest* L   **3** prouintia⌉ prouincia LM   **3** episcopis⌉
episcopus L   **3** unam⌉ una L *superscriptum* M   **3–4** proferant⌉ proferat* M   **5** quae⌉
que L   **5** a prouintialibus⌉ ea prouincialibus L prouincialibus M   **5** episcopis⌉ *deest* L
5 data⌉ datam M   **6** Ut nullus episcopus eligat successorem in exitum uitae⌉ *deest* IL
Ut nullus episcopus elegat successorem sibi in exitu uitae M   **7** constituere⌉ construere L
7 exitu⌉ exitum LM   **9** ecclesiastica⌉ ecclesiestica L   **10** synodo⌉ sinodo L   **10** iuditio⌉
iudicio M   **10** maxime⌉ maximae M   **10** electio⌉ electior L   **11** quiescentis⌉ quiescen-
tes L   **11** et⌉ ad L   **13** Ut nullus gradus aduersus alium⌉ *deest* IL Ut nullus gradus
intret in curia M   **14** Synodus…Helena⌉ *praecedit rubricum* M   **14** Synodus⌉ Sinodus
L   **14** Roma⌉ Romana M   **14** episcopi⌉ episcopis LM   **14** Constantino⌉ contantino*
L   **14** Helena⌉ Eliana M   **15** Presbiter non⌉ Non presbiter M   **16** acolitus⌉ acholitus
L   **16** subdiaconum⌉ diaconum L   **16** acolitum⌉ acholitum L   **17** accusationem⌉ acu-
sationem L   **17–18** aliquam⌉ aliquem L   **18** lxxii⌉ septuaginta duobus M   **18** testibus⌉
deest IL   **18** presul⌉ praesul M

Collectio CCCC capitulorum

85

M 194v mus a quemquam iudicabitur, quoniam scriptum est: Non est discipulus super magistrum.

CCXIII Presbiter cum xliiii testimoniis damnabitur

Presbiter autem nisi in xliiii testimonia non damnabitur. Diaconus cardina-
rius constructus urbis Romae, nisi in xxxvi, non condemnabitur. Subdiaconus, $\quad$ 5
acolitus, exorcista, lector, nisi, sicut scriptum est, ii uel tria. Sic datur mistica
ueritas in testimonia.

I 175v Testimonium clerici aduersus laicum nemo recipiat. Nemo enim clericum quemlibet in publico et examinet, nisi in ecclesia.

CCXIIII Ut nullus gradus intrat in curia $\quad$ 10

Nemo enim clericus uel diaconus aut presbiter propter quamlibet intrat in cu-
ria, quoniam omnis curia a cruere dicitur, et immolatione simulacrorum. Quia
si quis clericus, accusans clericum, in curia introierit anathemate suscipiat,
numquam matrem redigens ecclesiam. A communione non priuetur.

CCXV Nemo clericum caedat $\quad$ 15

Nemo enim quisquam peccantem clericum caede adtingat; non presbiterum,
non diaconum, non episcopum supra clericum uel seruitorem ecclesiae ad ce-
dem perducat. Sed si ita causa exigit clerici, triduo priuentur honore, ut pae-
nitens redeat ad matrem ecclesiam.

4–7 *Const. Sylv.* ll. 111-16 $\quad$ **8–9** *Const. Sylv.* ll. 187-9 $\quad$ **11–14** *Const. Sylv.* ll. 190-4
16–19 *Const. Sylv.* ll. 195-8

---

1 iudicabitur, quoniam scriptum est: Non est discipulus⌉ *deest* L $\quad$ **3** CCXIII⌉ CCXII I
3 Presbiter cum xliiii testimoniis damnabitur⌉ *deest* IL Presbiterum cum xiiii testimoniis
M $\quad$ **4** xliiii⌉ quadraginta iiii M $\quad$ **5** xxxvi⌉ xxxv L uiginti et sex M $\quad$ **6** acolitus⌉ acho-
litus L $\quad$ **6** sicut⌉ si aut M $\quad$ **6** ii⌉ duo LM $\quad$ **6** tria⌉ tres M $\quad$ **6** mistica⌉ mystica L
9 et⌉ *deest* L $\quad$ **9** examinet⌉ examinent M $\quad$ **10** Ut nullus gradus intrat in curia⌉ *deest*
IL Ut nullus gradus introt* in curia M $\quad$ **12** cruere⌉ cruore LM $\quad$ **12** dicitur⌉ dixe-
runt L $\quad$ **12** simulacrorum⌉ sumulacrorum* L $\quad$ **13** si quis⌉ sicut M $\quad$ **13** curia⌉ curiam
M $\quad$ **13** anathemate⌉ anathematae L anathema M $\quad$ **14** redigens⌉ rediens L $\quad$ **15** Nemo
clericum caedat⌉ *deest* IL Nemo clericum cedat M $\quad$ **16** quisquam⌉ clericus quisquam*
L $\quad$ **16** peccantem⌉ peccatum M $\quad$ **16** caede⌉ cede LM $\quad$ **16** adtingat⌉ adtinguat L at-
tingat M $\quad$ **17** uel⌉ ad L $\quad$ **17** seruitorem⌉ seruitiorem M $\quad$ **18** priuentur⌉ priuenter I
18–19 paenitens⌉ poenitens LM

86   Collectio CCCC capitulorum

CCXVI   Sɪ ᴘʀᴇsʙɪᴛᴇʀ sᴜᴍᴀᴛ ᴄᴏɴɪᴜɢɪᴜᴍ ᴘᴏsᴛ xɪɪ ᴀɴɴᴜᴍ sᴀᴄʀɪꜰɪᴄᴀᴛ
Nemo enim presbiter a die honoris presbiterii sumat coniugium, quod si quis
neglecto egerit, xɪɪ anni eum dicimus priuari honore. Quod si quis hoc publice   *M 195r*
egerit dictum contempnetur in perpetuum.   *L 109r*

5   CCXVII   Nᴇᴍᴏ ɪᴜᴅɪᴄᴀʙɪᴛ ᴘʀɪᴍᴀᴍ sᴇᴅᴇᴍ
Nemo enim iudicabit primam sedem quoniam omnes sedes a prima sede iusti-   *I 176r*
tiam desiderant temperari, neque ab Augusto, neque ab omni clero, neque a
regibus, neque a populo iudex iudicabitur.

CCXVIII   Nᴜʟʟᴜs ᴇʟɪɢᴀᴛᴜʀ ᴅᴇ ᴀʟᴛᴇʀᴀ ᴇᴄᴄʟᴇsɪᴀ
10   Caelestinus Papa: Tunc alter de altera elegatur ecclesia, si de ciuitatis ipsius
clericis cui est episcopus ordinandus, nullus dignus, quod euenire non credimus, poterit repperiri. Primum enim illi reprobandi sunt, ut aliqui de alienis
ecclesiis merito proferantur.

CCXVIIII   Fᴀᴄᴜʟᴛᴀs ʀᴇsɪsᴛᴇɴᴅɪ
15   Sit facultas clericis resistendi, si se uiderint praegrauari; et quos sibi ingeri
extraneorum agnouerint, non timeant refutare. Qui si non debitum premium,
uel liberum de eis qui eos recturi sunt, debent habere iuditium.

2–4   *Const. Sylv.* ll. 201-4   **6–8**   *Const. Sylv.* ll. 205-7   **10–13**   Cael., *ep.* 4, §5   **15–17**
Cael., *ep.* 4, §5

---

1 CCXVI] CCXV L   **1** Sɪ ᴘʀᴇsʙɪᴛᴇʀ sᴜᴍᴀᴛ ᴄᴏɴɪᴜɢɪᴜᴍ ᴘᴏsᴛ xɪɪ ᴀɴɴᴜᴍ sᴀᴄʀɪꜰɪᴄᴀᴛ] *deest*
IL Dᴇ ᴘᴀᴇɴɪᴛᴇɴᴛɪᴀ ᴘʀᴇsʙɪᴛᴇʀɪ M   **2** presbiterii] presbiterirs L   **3** neglecto] neclecto L
3 xɪɪ] duodecim M   **3** anni] annos M   **3** dicimus] decimus L   **4** contempnetur] con-
demnetur L contempnet M   **5** CCXVII] *deest* M   **5** Nᴇᴍᴏ ɪᴜᴅɪᴄᴀʙɪᴛ ᴘʀɪᴍᴀᴍ sᴇᴅᴇᴍ] *deest*
IL   **7** temperari] tempora L   **9** CCXVIII] CCXIII I   **9** Nᴜʟʟᴜs ᴇʟɪɢᴀᴛᴜʀ ᴅᴇ ᴀʟᴛᴇʀᴀ
ᴇᴄᴄʟᴇsɪᴀ] *deest* IL   **9** ᴇᴄᴄʟᴇsɪᴀ] *deest* M   **10** Caelestinus] Celestinus LM   **10** Papa]
Papa ait M   **10** ecclesia] ecclesiam L   **11** clericis] clericus L   **11** quod euenire] que-
uenire L   **12** repperiri] reperiri L   **12** Primum] Primam L   **13** merito] merite L
13 proferantur] praeferantur M   **14** Fᴀᴄᴜʟᴛᴀs ʀᴇsɪsᴛᴇɴᴅɪ] *deest* IL   **15** et quos sibi inge-
ri] *deest* L   **16** premium] praemium M   **17** debent] debeant L   **17** iuditium] iudicium
L *deest* M

Collectio CCCC capitulorum

87

CCXX Episcopus ab omni labe securus

Episcopus ab omni labe saeculi istius inmunis, ante Dei conspectum et securus, ut populum doceat, inueniaris. Cui enim multum creditur, plus ab eo exigitur in usura poenarum.

CCXXI Caelestinus papa de ultima penitentia

Perdidisset latro premium in cruce ad Christi dexteram pendens, si illum unius horae poenitentiae non iuuasset. Et cum esset in poena, penituit, et per unius sermonis professionem habitaculum paradisi Deo promittente promeruit. Uera ergo ad Deum conuersio in ultimis positorum, mente potius est aestimanda, non tempore, propheta hoc taliter adserente: In quacumque die conuersus fuerit peccator, uita uiuet et reliqua. Et iterum: cum eum conuersus ingemueris, tunc saluus eris. Cum ergo sit Dominus cordis inspector, quouis tempore non est deneganda paenitentia postulanti, cum illi se obliget iudici cui occulta omnia nouerit reuelari.

CCXXII Nemo gradatis manus inponent

<Sententia> Leonis non inponendis manibus penitenti diaconis uel presbiteris: Alienum est a consuetudine ecclesiastica, ut qui presbiterali honore ac diaconi gradu fuerint consecrati, hi pro crimine aliquo suo per manus impositionem remedium accipiant penitendi, quod sine dubio ex apostolica traditione descendit. Secundum quod scriptum est: Sacerdos si peccauit, quis orauit pro

---

3–4 Innocentius I, *ep. 2, ad Victricium*, §2   6–14 Cael., *ep.* 4, §2   17–88.2 Leo I, *ep. 167, ad Rusticum*, §2

---

1 Episcopus ab omni labe securus] *deest* IL   2 ab omni labe] abominabile L   2 istius] huius M   2 inmunis] inmunus L   3 ut] uti L   3 populum] episcopum populum L episcopus populum M   4 poenarum] paenatur L   5 Caelestinus papa de ultima penitentia] *deest* L   5 Caelestinus] Celestinus M   5 penitentia] paenitentia M 6 Perdidisset] Perdedisset L   7 horae] hore L   7 poenitentiae] penitentie* L paenitentiae M   7 iuuasset] inuasset L   7 poena] paena L   7 penituit] paenetuit L   8 paradisi] paradyso L paradysi M   8 Deo] Dei L   8 promeruit] meruit M   9 ergo] enim M   9 aestimanda] aestimenda L   11 uiuet] uiuit LM   11 cum eum] *superscriptum* I 11 eum] *deest* M   13 paenitentia] paenitens L   13 obliget] obligat M   13 iudici] iudicii LM   15 Nemo gradatis manus inponent] *deest* IL   16 Sententia] *deest* ILM 16 penitenti] paenitenti M   16 diaconis] diaconus L   16–17 presbiteris] presbiter L 17 a] *deest* L   17 presbiterali] prespiritali I presbiter tali L   18 hi] hii L   18 aliquo] alico L   19 accipiant] accipiunt L   19 penitendi] paenitendi LM   19 quod] qui L 20 descendit] discendit L   20 Sacerdos] Sacerdus M

88   Collectio CCCC capitulorum

illo? Unde huiusmodi lapsis ad promerendam misericordiam Dei priuata est
expetenda secessio, ubi illis satisfactio si fuerit digna sit etiam fructuosa.

CCXXIII   Statuta ecclesia unica incipiunt
Episcopus in ecclesia in consessu presbiterorum sublimior sedeat, intra domum uero collegam se presbiterorum esse agnoscat.

CCXXIIII   Episcopus non longe ab aecclesia hospitiolum habeat
Ut episcopus non longe ab ecclesia hospitiolum habeat.

CCXXV   Episcopus hereticorum libros non legat
Episcopus gentilium libros non legat hereticorum autem pro necessitate et
tempore perlegat.

CCXXVI   Episcopus in synodo non litiget
Episcopus nec prouocatus pro rebus transitoriis litiget.

CCXXVII   Episcopus legatum mittat pro se ad synodum
Episcopus ad synodum ire satis graui necessitate inhibeatur, sic tamen et in
persona sua legatum mittat suscepturus salua fidei ueritate quicquid synodus   *I 177v*
statuerit.

CCXXVIII   De penitentia
Is qui penitentiam in infirmitate petit, si casu dum ad eum sacerdos inuitatus uenit, oppressus infirmitate obmotuerit uel in frenisin uersus fuerit, dent   *L 110r*
testimonium hi qui eum audierunt et penitentiam accipiant eius. Si continuo

---

4–5   *Stat. eccl. ant.* §2   7   *Stat. eccl. ant.* §1   9–10   *Stat. eccl. ant.* §5   12   *Stat. eccl. ant.*
§8   14–16   *Stat. eccl. ant.* §9   18–89.4   *Stat. eccl. ant.* §20

---

1 lapsis⌉ lapsus M   1 priuata⌉ priuatas* L   2 secessio⌉ successio L   3 Statuta ecclesia unica incipiunt⌉ Incipit statuta ecclesiastica M   4 consessu⌉ confessu* I concessu L
4 presbiterorum⌉ presbiterum L presbiterium M   5 collegam⌉ colligam LM   6 Episcopus
non longe ab aecclesia hospitiolum habeat⌉ *deest* IL Episcopus non longe ab ecclesia M
7 ab⌉ *deest* L   7 ecclesia⌉ ecclesiae L   7 hospitiolum⌉ hospiciolum L   8 Episcopus hereticorum libros non legat⌉ *deest* IL   9 autem⌉ *deest* M   11 Episcopus in synodo non
litiget⌉ *deest* IL   12 transitoriis⌉ transiturus L   13 Episcopus legatum mittat pro se
ad synodum⌉ *deest* IL   14 synodum⌉ sinodum L   14 et⌉ ut L   15 synodus⌉ sinodus L   17 penitentia⌉ paenitentia in infirmitate M   18 Is⌉ His L   18 penitentiam⌉
paenitentiam M   18 casu⌉ cassu L   18 sacerdos⌉ sacerdus M   19 oppressus⌉ ob-
pressus L   19 obmotuerit⌉ obmutuerit LM   20 hi⌉ hii L   20 audierunt⌉ adierunt L
20 penitentiam⌉ paenitentiam LM

Collectio CCCC capitulorum

89

M 196v creditur moriturus, reconcilietur per manus inpositionem et infundatur ori eius eucharistia. Si superuixerit, admoneatur a supradictis testibus petitionis suae satisfactum et subdatur statutis paenitentiae, quamdiu sacerdos qui eucharistiam dedit ei statuerit.

CCXXVIIII   In fine uitae commonio ne denegetur

Innocenti Papae: Paenitentibus etiam in extremo fine uitae communio non denegatur.

CCXXX   De auditorio nullus egrediatur

Unica: Sacerdote faciente uerbum in ecclesia, qui egressus de auditorio fierit, excommunicetur.

CCXXXI   Clericus se ipsum ubique ostendat

I 178r Clericus professionem suam habitu et incessu probet et ideo nec uestibus nec calciamentis decorem quaerat.

CCXXXII   De artifitio debet uestire

Clericus uictum et uestimentum sibi artifitio uel agricultura absque offitii sui dumtaxat detrimento preparat.

CCXXXIII   De artifitio uictum quaerat

Clericus quamuis uerbi Dei eruditus, artifitio tamen uictum quaerat.

6–7 cf. Innocentius I, *ep. 6, ad Exsuperium*, §2   **9–10** *Stat. eccl. ant.* §31   **12–13** *Stat. eccl. ant.* §26   **15–16** *Stat. eccl. ant.* §29   **18** *Stat. eccl. ant.* §79

---

1 inpositionem⌉ inpositione M   **2** admoneatur⌉ amoneatur L   **3** statutis⌉ statutas L **3** paenitentiae⌉ penitentiae L   **3** sacerdos⌉ sacerdus M   **4** eucharistiam⌉ enuchar L **4** ei⌉ *deest* L   **5** In fine uitae commonio ne denegetur⌉ *deest* IL In fine uitae communio non denegetur M   **6** Innocenti Papae⌉ Innocentio Pape L *deest* M   **6** Paenitentibus⌉ Poenitentibus L   **6** extremo⌉ extremis M   **6** fine⌉ finem L   **6** communio⌉ commoneo L communionem M   **8** De auditorio nullus egrediatur⌉ *deest* IL   **9** Unica⌉ *deest* M **9** auditorio⌉ adiutorio L   **9** fierit⌉ fuerit LM   **11** Clericus se ipsum ubique ostendat⌉ *deest* IL   **13** quaerat⌉ querat L   **14** De artifitio debet uestire⌉ *deest* IL De artificio debet uestire M   **15** uestimentum⌉ uestitum L   **15** artifitio⌉ artificio M   **15** offitii⌉ officii LM   **16** preparat⌉ praeparet M   **17** De artifitio uictum quaerat⌉ *deest* IL De artifitio uictum querat M   **18** Dei⌉ sit M   **18** artifitio⌉ artificio M   **18** quaerat⌉ querat LM

90 Collectio CCCC capitulorum

CCXXXIIII Qui episcopum contemnet recurrat ad synodum
Clericus qui episcopi erga districtionem iniustam putat, recurrat ad synodum.

CCXXXV Qui cantat in epulis clericus excommunicatur
Clericus inter epulas cantans, fidem utique non edificans, sed auribus tantum
pruriens, excommunicetur.   *M 197r*

CCXXXVI Paenitentes sepeliantur aecclesia
Mortuos ecclesiae paenitentes et efferant et sepeliant.

CCXXXVII De honore confessoris
Christianus, qui pro catholica fide tribulationes patitur, omni honore a sacerdotibus honorandus.

CCXXXVIII De uidua adulescentula
Uiduae adulescentes, quae corpore debiles sunt; sumptu ecclesiae, cuius uiduae   *L 110v*
sunt, sustentent.

CCXXXVIIII De clerico adulatore
Clericus qui adulationibus uacare deprehenditur, ab offitio suo degradetur.   *I 178v*

CCXL Maledicus degradetur
Clericus maledicus si non sinat, degradetur.

---

2 *Stat. eccl. ant.* §88   4–5 cf. *Stat. eccl. ant.* §75   7 *Stat. eccl. ant.* §66   9–10 cf. *Stat. eccl. ant.* §70   12–13 *Stat. eccl. ant.* §36   15 *Stat. eccl. ant.* §43   17 cf. *Stat. eccl. ant.* §44

---

1 Qui episcopum contemnet recurrat ad synodum] *deest* IL   2 iniustam] iniustitiam
corr. iniustiiam L   2 synodum] sinodum L   3 Qui cantat in epulis clericus excom-
municatur] *deest* IL Qui cantat in aepulis clericus excommunicatur M   4 epulas] ae-
pulans L aepulas M   4 cantans] cantas* M   4 utique] itaque L   4 edificans] ae-
dificans M   5 excommunicetur] excommunitur I   6 Paenitentes sepeliantur aec-
clesia] *deest* IL   7 paenitentes] penitentes L   8 De honore confessoris] *deest* IL
9 tribulationes] tribulationes *corr.* tribulationis L   10 honorandus] honorandis L honorandus est M   11 De uidua adulescentula] *deest* IL   11 adulescentula] aduliscentula M
12 adulescentes] aduliscentes LM   12 quae] qui L   12 ecclesiae] ecclesies I   13 sunt]
deest L   13 sustentent] sustentur L   14 De clerico adulatore] *deest* IL   15 offitio]
officio LM   16 Maledicus degradetur] *deest* IL   17 maledicus] maledictus I

Collectio CCCC capitulorum 91

CCXLI Populus docendus est

Docendus populus, non sequendus est. Nos quoque, sciant quid liceat quidue non liceat, commonere, non his consensum prebere debemus.

CCXLII Si monachi procreantes filios

Monachi procreantes filios in carcere recludantur, tantum facinus continua lamentatione deflentes, ut uel eis ad mortem solius misericordiae intuitu communionis gratia possit indulgeri.

CCXLIII De uirginibus habitantibus in monasterio

Similiter uirgines nubere prohibe, plurimis in monasteriis aetatem peregisse contigeret.

CCXLIIII De uiduis diu permansuris

M 197v Nec uiduas ad nuptias transire patimur, quae in religioso preposito diu permanserint.

CCXLV Qui ab hereticis baptizati

Qui ab hereticis in nomine sanctae trinitatis baptizati sunt, non rebaptizentur
I 179r a nobis, sed manus inpositione confirmentur.

2–3 Cael., *ep. 5*, §3   **5–7** *Hibernensis* 38.14 (p. 297, ln. 9-11)   **9–10** Symmachus, *ep. 15, ad Caesarium Arelatensem*, §5   **12–13** Symmachus, *ep. 15, ad Caesarium Arelatensem*, §5   **15–16** cf. Leo I, *ep. 159, ad Nicetam*, §7; cf. Bonifatius, *ep. 68*

---

1 Populus docendus est] *deest* IL   **2** sequendus] sequendum L   **2** liceat] liceant L **2** quidue] quid duae L   **3** liceat] liceant L   **4** Si monachi procreantes filios] *deest* IL Si monachi procreandis filios M   **5** procreantes] proscreantes L   **5** carcere] cercere L   **6** lamentatione] lamentatio M   **6** eis] *superscriptum* M   **6** solius] *deest* L **6–7** communionis] commonionis* I   **7** indulgeri] indulgere L   **8** De uirginibus habitantibus in monasterio] *deest* IL   **9** uirgines] uirginis L   **10** contigeret] contingerit L **11** De uiduis diu permansuris] *deest* IL   **12** quae] que L qui M   **12** religioso] relegioso LM   **12** preposito] proposito LM   **14** Qui ab hereticis baptizati] *deest* IL Qui ab hereticis scis baptizati sunt M   **15** hereticis] heretis* I   **15–16** in nomine…confirmentur] ut supra r[esponsum] retro L   **15** nomine] nominae* I   **15** rebaptizentur] rebaptizaentur* M   **16** confirmentur] firmentur M

92 Collectio CCCC capitulorum

CCXLVI Qui pascha uno die caelebratur
Arelatenses dc episcoporum Pascha uno die et uno tempore per totum orbem
deberet celebrari statuit: Primo in loco de obseruatione paschae dominicae,
ut uno die et uno tempore per omnem orbem a nobis obseruaretur, ut iuxta
5 consuetudinem litteras ad omnes tu dirigas.

CCXLVII Duo episcopi non sint in una ciuitate
De Nicena: Ne in una ciuitate duo sint episcopi.

CCXLVIII De amentibus
Synodus Arausicanum: Amentibus quaecumque pietatis sunt conferenda.

10 CCXLVIIII De inerguminis
Inergumini baptizati religiosique communicent, clerici inergumini degradentur.

CCL De publicis odiis exarsis
Synodus Aralatensis: Hi qui publicis inter se odiis exardescant, ab ecclesie
15 conuentu remouendi sunt, donec ad pacem recurrant.

CCLI De laicis tribus temporibus non communicant
Synodus Agatensis: Saeculares uero qui in Natale Domini et Pascha et Pentecosten non communicauerint, catholici esse non credantur.

2–5 *Arelat.* §1   7 *Nicaea* §8   9 *Araus.* §12 (13); *Arelat. II* §38 (37)   11–12 cf. *Araus.*
§§13, 15 (14, 16); *Arelat. II* §§39-40 (38-9)   14–15 *Arelat. II* §50   17–18 *Agath.* §18

---

1 Qui pascha uno die caelebratur] *deest* IL   2 Arelatenses dc episcoporum] *deest* M
2 Arelatenses] Aratentes I Artensis L   3 deberet] debere LM   3 celebrari] celebrare LM   3 statuit] statuitur L   3–5 Primo in loco…dirigas] *deest* LM   6 CCXLVII]
cap. deest L   6 Duo episcopi non sint in una ciuitate] *deest* IL   7 De Nicena: Ne in una
ciuitate duo sint episcopi] *deest* L   7 De Nicena] *deest* M   8 De amentibus] *deest* IL De
amantibus M   9 Synodus Arausicanum] *deest* LM   9 quaecumque] quicumque L   10 De
inerguminis] *deest* IL De energuminis M   11 Inergumini] Inergulmini L Energumini M
11 baptizati] baptizare L   11 religiosique] relegiosique L   11 inergumini] energumini
M   13 CCL] *deest* L   13 De publicis odiis exarsis] *deest* IL   13 exarsis] exardescant
M   14 Synodus] Sinodus L *deest* M   14 Aralatensis] Araladensis I *deest* M   14 Hi]
Hii L   14 ecclesie] ecclesiis L ecclesiae M   15 remouendi] remonendi L   15 recurrant]
recurrint L   16 De laicis tribus temporibus non communicant] *deest* IL   17 Synodus Aga-
tensis] *deest* M   17 Synodus] Sinodus L   17 Saeculares] Seculares L   17 in] inter L
18 catholici] catholicam L   18 credantur] degradentur L

Collectio CCCC capitulorum 93

CCLII MONASTERIUM EPISCOPUM TESTE FUNDANDUM EST

L 111r Monasterium nouum nisi episcopo permittente aut probante nullus fundare presumat.

CCLIII DE MONACHO UAGO

I 179v Monachus uagans sine abbatis sui testimonio clericus non ordinetur. 5

CCLIIII NULLUS ALTERIUS MONACHUM ACCIPIAT

Monachum sine permissu abbatis sui nullus accipiat.

CCLV NULLUS EPISCOPUM PRETER IN UILLA III TEMPORIBUS CELEBRAT

Synodus Aurialianensis: Nulli liceat Paschae, Natale Domini, Pentecosten solemnitate in uilla celebrare nisi quem infirmitas inpediat. 10

CCLVI EPISCOPUS CORRIGAT ABBATES

Abbates per humilitatem religionis in episcoporum potestate consistant et, si quid extra regulam fecerint, ab episcopo corrigantur.

CCLVII DE DONO DATO PRO ANIMABUS

Hieronimus in capitulis canonis: Donum quod pro animabus datur sacerdo- 15 ti non licet propriis usibus, sed ecclesie erogare. Casellas ecclesiae uel uasa unde pauperes uiuant uendere uel donare pastoris potestati non subiaceat, cui dictum est: Pasce oues meas meosque agnos.

2–3 *Agath.* §27   **5**   cf. *Agath.* §27   **7**   cf. *Agath.* §27   **9–10**   *Aurel.* §25   **12–13**   *Aurel.* §19   **15–18**   cf. *Agath.* §7

---

1 MONASTERIUM EPISCOPUM TESTE FUNDANDUM EST⌉ *deest* IL   **2** probante⌉ probate L proban- tem M   **4** DE MONACHO UAGO⌉ *deest* IL   **5** sui⌉ suis* M   **5** testimonio⌉ testimonium L **5–95.6** clericus non ordinetur...qui perfecte⌉ *lacuna* M   **5** clericus⌉ clerici L   **6** NULLUS ALTERIUS MONACHUM ACCIPIAT⌉ *deest* IL   **7** Monachum⌉ Monachus L   **7** permissu⌉ permi- sio L   **8** NULLUS EPISCOPUM PRETER IN UILLA III TEMPORIBUS CELEBRAT⌉ *deest* IL   **9** Synodus⌉ Sinodus L   **9** Paschae⌉ Pascha L   **10** solemnitate⌉ sollemnitate L   **11** EPISCOPUS CORRI- GAT ABBATES⌉ *deest* IL   **12** humilitatem⌉ humilite L   **12** religionis⌉ relegionis L   **14** DE DONO DATO PRO ANIMABUS⌉ *deest* IL   **15** capitulis⌉ capitulum L   **15** canonis⌉ canones L   **15** Donum quod⌉ donumque L   **16** ecclesie⌉ ecclesiae L   **16** Casellas⌉ cassellas I   **16** ecclesiae⌉ ecclesia I   **17** unde pauperes uiuant⌉ *deest* L   **17** uendere⌉ uindere L **17–18** cui dictum⌉ uindictum L   **18** Pasce⌉ paschae L   **18** agnos⌉ agnus L

94 Collectio CCCC capitulorum

CCLVIII Qui morte dignus subiciendus seruituti
Qui dignus est morte seruituti alterius subiciendus est.

CCLVIIII De inhabitante sine uoto
Qui fuerit inter fratres sine uoto monachi, utatur incommunita fratrum, nisi
5 dederit confessionem abbati.

CCLX Interrogandae Romanis
De cohabitationem cum peccatoribus audite apostolum dicentem: Cum huiu- *I 180r*
smodi nec cibum sumere. Nec eius escam prohibet, sed cum eo simul accedere
ad mensam.

10 De excommunicationem audi Dominem dicentem: Si te non audierit, sit tibi sicut ethnicus et publicanus. Non maledices; sed repelles excommunica-
tum a communione et mensa et missa et pace, et si hereticus est post unam
correptionem deuita.

CCLXI De penitentibus post ruinas
15 Statuitur ut abbas uideat, cui a Deo tribuitur potestas alligandi et soluendi.
Sed aptior est ad ueniam, iuxta scripturae exempla, si cum lacrimis et lamentatione et lugubri ueste sub custodia melior est penitentia breuis quam longa *L 111v*
et remissa cum tempore mentis.

CCLXII De suspectis causis
20 Audi Dominum dicentem: Sinite utraque crescere usque ad messem, hoc est,
donec ueniat qui manifestabit consilia cordium, ne iuditium ante diem iuditii *I 180v*
facias. Uide Iudam ad mensam Ihesum et latronem in paradiso.

7–9 *Syn. II Patr.*§1   10–13 *Syn. II Patr.*§4   15–18 *Syn. II Patr.*§3   20–22 *Syn. II Patr.*§5

---

1 Qui morte dignus subiciendus seruituti] *deest* IL   2 subiciendus] subciendus L   3 De
inhabitante sine uoto] *deest* IL   4 incommunita] incommonita I   4 nisi] sine L
5 abbati] abbatis sui L   6 Interrogandae] Interrogande L   7 cohabitationem] coabi-
tione L   8 Nec] Non L   10 excommunicationem] excommunicatione L   11 ethnicus] et
inimicus L   11 et] uel L   12 post unam] postuam L   13 deuita] diuitam L   14 post]
propter L   14 ruinas] uinus L   15 soluendi] dissoluendi L   16 si cum] sicut L
17 lugubri] lucubri L   17 penitentia] paenitentia L   18 mentis] mentes L   20 crescere
usque] usque L   21 manifestabit] manifestauit IL   21 ne] nec L   21 iuditium]
iudicium L   21 iuditii] iudicii L   22 Iudam] uiduam L   22 paradiso] paradyso L

Collectio CCCC capitulorum

95

CCLXIII DE LAPSIS POST GRADUM
Qui cum gradum cecidit, sine gradu consurgat. Contentus nomine tantum amittat ministerium, nisi qui tantum a conspectu Dei peccans non recessit.

CCLXIIII DE TRIBUS SEMINIBUS EUANGELIORUM
Centesimi sunt episcopi et doctores, quia omnibus omnia sunt; LX clerici et 5
M 198r uiduae continentes sunt; XXX laici fideles qui perfecte Trinitati credunt. His amplius non est in messe Dei. Monachos uero et uirgines cum centesimis iungamus.

CCLXV DE CONFITENTIBUS
Si quis uult confiteri peccata sua episcopo aut presbitero, si furtum faciebat, 10
debet restituere et reconciliare cum illo quem offendebat et multum breuiabat
I 181r penitentiam eius; si noluerit aut non potest, constitutum tempus peniteat per omnia.

CCLXVI QUI POST RENUNTIATIONEM REUERSURUS
Si quis renuntiauerit saeculo, postea reuersus in saecularem habitum, si mona- 15
chus esset et postea penitentiam egerit, X annis peniteat; post primum trien-
nium, si probatus fuerit in omni penitentia, in lacrimis et in orationibus, humanius circa eum episcopus potest facere.

CCLXVII DE ADULTERA
Uir qui uxorem suam inuenit adulteram et non uult dimittere eam, sed in ma- 20
trimonio suo adhuc habere, annos duos peniteat, et ieiunia relegiosa exerceat

---

2–3 *Syn. II Patr.*§10 **5–8** *Syn. II Patr.*§18 **10–13** *Iud. Theod. G* 38b-39 **15–18** *Iud. Theod. U* I.8.12 **20–96.2** *Iud. Theod. U* I.14.4

---

2 gradum] gradu L **5** Centesimi] centissime L **6** Trinitati] Trinitate LM **7** Dei] Domini M **7** Monachos] Monachus L **7** uirgines] uirginis L **7** centesimis] centissimis L **9** CCLXV] CCLXIIII M **9** DE CONFITENTIBUS] DE FURTIS RESTITUENDIS M **10** aut] uel L **11** breuiabat] breuiabit M **12** penitentiam] paenitentiam M **12** peniteat] paeniteat LM **14** CCLXVI] CCLXV M **14** QUI POST RENUNTIATIONEM REUERSURUS] *deest* IL **15–16** si monachus] simachus L **16** penitentiam] paenitentiam LM **16** egerit] aegerit L **16** annis] annos M **16** peniteat] paeniteat LM **16** post] postea L **17** penitentia] paenitentia M **17** lacrimis] lacromis* L **17** orationibus] horationibus L **19** CCLXVII] CCLXVI M **20** inuenit] inuenerit L **21** peniteat] paeniteat LM **21** relegiosa] relegiosaque I

96 — Collectio CCCC capitulorum

aut quamdiu ipsa peniteat, se abstineat a matrimonio eius, quia adulterium illa perpetrauerit.

L 112r

CCLXVIII De lauatione matrimonii
Maritus qui cum uxore sua dormierit, lauet se antequam intret ecclesiam.

5 **CCLXVIIII** De muliere adultera
Mulier adultera si est et uir eius non uult habitare cum ea, si uult illa monasterium intrare, quartam partem suae hereditatis obtineat, si non uult, nihil habeat.

I 181v;
M 198v

CCLXX De uiro non posse nubere
10 Uir et mulier coniunxerint se in matrimonio, et postea dixerit mulier de uiro, non posse nubere cum ea, si quis potest probare quod uerum est, accipiat alium.

CCLXXI Ab hostibus capta
Cuius uxorem hostis abstulerit et non potest repetere eam, licet ei aliam accipere. Melius est, quam fornicare. Si postea reditur uxor, non debet recipere
15 eam, si aliam habet, sed ipsa accipiat alterum, si unum ante habuerit. Eadem sententia stat de seruis transmarinis.

CCLXXII Si in captiuitatem perducta
Si in captiuitatem per uim ducta aut ductus, redemi non potest, post annum potest accipere alteram mulierem aut alterum uirum.

---

4 *Iud. Theod. U* II.12.30   **6–8** *Iud. Theod. U* II.12.11   **10–11** *Iud. Theod. U* II.12.33
13–16 cf. *Iud. Theod. U* II.12.24–5   **18–19** cf. *Iud. Theod. U* II.12.21

1–2 aut...perpetrauerit] *deest* M   **1** aut] uel L   **1** peniteat] paeniteat L   **1** se abstineat] abstineat se L   **1** abstineat] abisti I   **1** quia] qui L   **3** CCLXVIII] CCLXVII M   **3** De lauatione matrimonii] *deest* IL   **4** sua] *deest* M   **4** ecclesiam] in ecclesiam L in ecclesia M   **5** CCLXVIIII] CCLXVIII M   **5** De muliere adultera] *deest* IL   **6** ea] illa L **6–7** monasterium] in monesterio L   **9** CCLXX] CCLXVIIII M   **9** De uiro non posse nubere] *deest* IL   **10** coniunxerint] coniuncxerunt L qui coniunxerint M   **10** uiro] uiri L **11** potest] post L   **12** CCLXXI] *deest* M   **12** Ab hostibus capta] De uxore capta ab hostibus M   **13** repetere] repetire L   **13** aliam] alia L   **13–14** accipere...postea] *deest* L   **14** reditur] redditur L   **15** habet] babet L   **16** seruis] feruis M   **17** CCLXXII] CCLXX M   **17** Si in captiuitatem perducta] *deest* IL Si in captiuitate perducta M   **18** Si] In alio loco: Si L Si mulier M   **18** uim ducta] uindictam L   **18** aut ductus] aut uir ductus fuerit M   **18** redemi] remedi L   **19** alteram mulierem aut] *deest* L

Collectio CCCC capitulorum

97

CCLXXIII   Qui uouit post mortem uiri

Mulier nupta uni uiro, quae uouet Deo, ut post mortem uiri eius non accipiat alium et mortuo preuaricatrix uoti acceperit alterum, iterumque nupta cum eo, paenitentia mota, implere uota sua uult, in potestate uiri eius est, utrum impleat, an non. Ergo unam licentiam dedit nubere cum illo uiro, quae confessa est uota, post xi annos.

CCLXXIIII   De muliere mortua

Muliere mortua licet uiro post mensem alteram accipere.

CCLXXV   De uiro mortuo

Post annum licet mulieri tollere uirum.

CCLXXVI   De uoto mulieris

Si quis maritus uel si qua mulier uotum habens uirginitatis adiungitur matrimonio non dimittat illud sed peniteat tribus annis.

Mulieri non licet uotum uouere sine consensu uiri sui, sed etsi uouerit, dimitti potest.

Maritus non debet uxorem suam nudatam uidere.

CCLXXVII   De reconciliatione mulieris

Quaecumque mulier adulterium perpetrauerit, in potestate uiri est, si uellit reconciliari mulieri adulteratae. Si reconciliauerit, in clero non proficit uindicta illius, ad primum uirum pertinet non ad regem.

2–6 cf. *Iud. Theod. U* II.12.14-5   **8**   cf. *Iud. Theod. U* II.12.10   **10**   cf. *Iud. Theod. U* II.12.10   **12–13**   *Iud. Theod. U* I.14.5   **14–15**   *Iud. Theod. U* I.14.7   **16**   *Iud. Theod. U* II.12.31   **18–20**   *Iud. Theod. U* II.12.12

---

1 CCLXXIII] CCLXXI M   **1** Qui uouit post mortem uiri] *deest* IL   **2** quae] qui L   **2** uouet] uocet L   **3** acceperit] acciperit LM   **3** iterumque] iterum quem L   **4** paenitentia] penitentia L   **4** mota] motus L   **5** unam] una L   **5** quae] qui L   **6** xi] x L   **7** CCLXXIIII] CCLXXII M   **7** De muliere mortua] *deest* IL   **8** Muliere] Mulier M   **8** alteram] altera L   **9** CCLXXV] CCLXXIII M   **9** De uiro mortuo] *deest* IL   **10** mulieri] muliere L   **10** uirum] uirum alium M   **11** CCLXXVI] CCLXXIIII M   **11** De uoto mulieris] De uoto uirginitatem M   **13** dimittat] demittat L   **13** peniteat] paeniteat LM   **13** tribus] iii L   **14** Mulieri] Mulier L   **17** CCLXXVII] CCLXXV M   **17** De reconciliatione mulieris] *deest* IL   **18** Quaecumque] Quicumque L   **18–19** reconciliari] reconciliare LM   **19** adulteratae] adulterate L

98 Collectio CCCC capitulorum

CCLXXVIII De penitentia intima
Paenitentes secundum canones non debent communicare ante consummatio- *I 182v*
nem paenitentiae; nos autem pro misericordia miserantis Dei post annum uel
vi menses licentiam damus.

5 CCLXXVIIII Una penitentia puellae et uiduae
Una paenitentia est puellae et uiduae; vii annos. Maiorem meruit, quae uirum
habet, si fornicationis crimen admiserit.

CCLXXX Si occidat filium
Mulier si occidat filium suum et homicidium facit, xv annos peniteat, et num- *L 113r*
10 quam mutat nisi diebus dominicis.

CCLXXXI Si paupercula occidat
Mulier paupercula si occidat filium suum, vii annos peniteat.
In canonibus dicitur, si homicida sit, x annos.

CCLXXXII Ante baptismum
15 Si moritur infans sine baptismo tres annos habens, pater et mater, iii annos
paeniteant.

CCLXXXIII Qui necat sine baptismo
Qui necat filium suum sine baptismo, in canone x annos, sed per consilium vii *M 199v*
annos peniteat.

2–4 *Iud. Theod. U* I.12.4 6–7 *Iud. Theod. U* I.2.14 9–10 *Iud. Theod. U* I.14.25 12–13 *Iud. Theod. U* I.14.26 15–16 cf. *Iud. Theod. U* I.14.29 18–19 *Iud. Theod. U* I.14.30

---

1 CCLXXVIII⌉ *cap. deest* M 1 penitentia⌉ paenitentia L 2–4 Paenitentes…damus⌉ *deest* M 2 secundum⌉ secontra L 2 communicare⌉ commonicare* I 3 paenitentiae⌉ penitentiae L 3 Dei⌉ *deest* L 5 CCLXXVIIII⌉ CCLXXVI M 5 Una penitentia puellae et uiduae⌉ *deest* L De paenitentia intima M 6 puellae⌉ puelle L 6 uiduae⌉ uidue L 6 vii⌉ vi L 6 annos⌉ annis L 6 quae⌉ qui LM 7 si⌉ et si L 8 CCLXXX⌉ CCLXXVII M 8 Si occidat filium⌉ *deest* IL 9 occidat⌉ occidit L 9 peniteat⌉ paeniteat M 10 mutat⌉ motat* I muttat L mutet M 10 diebus⌉ in diebus M 11 CCLXXXI⌉ CCLXXVIII M 11 Si paupercula occidat⌉ *deest* IL 12 occidat⌉ occidit LM 12 peniteat⌉ paeniteat M 13 dicitur⌉ dixerunt L 14 CCLXXXII⌉ CCLXXVIIII M 14 Ante baptismum⌉ *deest* L Si moritur sine baptismo M 15 moritur⌉ moriatur L 15 tres annos habens, pater et mater⌉ *deest* L 15 iii⌉ tres M 17 CCLXXXIII⌉ CCLXXX M 17 Qui necat sine baptismo⌉ *deest* IL 18 necat⌉ negat L necant M 19 peniteat⌉ *deest* L

Collectio CCCC capitulorum

CCLXXXIIII Si aliter moritur sine baptismo
Si moriatur sine nece hominis et sine baptismo, iii annos peniteat.

CCLXXXV De penitentia si alteram duxerit

I 183r Qui dimiserit uxorem suam alteri coniungens se, vii annis cum tribulatione
peniteat uel quindecim leuius.

CCLXXXVI Si menstruo coierit
Si menstruo tempore coierit cum ea, xl diebus ieiunet.

CCLXXXVII
Si uir cum muliere sua retro aut in tergo nupserit, penitere debet quasi ille qui
cum animalibus.

CCLXXXVIII Si cum sorore
Qui cum sorore sua fornicatur, xii, alii xv annos peniteat.

Si cum matre
Si cum matre fornicat, xv annos et numquam mutat nisi diebus dominicis.

CCLXXXVIIII Si saepe faciens fornicationem
Fornicationem saepe faciens, vii annos peniteat; alii iudicant per consilium iii
annos.

---

2 *Iud. Theod. U* I.14.27; *G* 106   **4–5** *Iud. Theod. U* I.14.8   **7** *Iud. Theod. U* I.14.23
9–10 cf. *Iud. Theod. U* I.14.21-2   **12** cf. *Iud. Theod. U* I.2.17   **14** cf. *Iud. Theod. U* I.2.16
16–17 cf. *Iud. Theod. G* 96

---

1 CCLXXXIIII] CCLXXXI M   **1** Si aliter moritur sine baptismo] *deest* IL   **2** Si moriatur sine nece hominis et sine baptismo, iii annos peniteat] *in margine* I   **2** iii] tres M
2 peniteat] paeniteat M   **3** CCLXXXV] CCLXXXII M   **3** De penitentia si alteram
duxerit] *deest* IL   **3** penitentia] paenitentia M   **4** annis] annos M   **5** peniteat] paeniteat LM   **5** quindecim] xv LM   **6** CCLXXXVI] CCLXXXIII M   **6** Si menstruo
coierit] *deest* IL   **7** coierit] coierit uir M   **7** ea] muliere M   **7** ieiunet] ieiunium L
8 CCLXXXVII] *cap. deest* M   **9–10** Si uir...animalibus] *deest* M   **11** CCLXXXVIII]
CCLXXXIIII M   **11** Si cum sorore] *deest* IL   **12** Qui] Qui fornicatur L   **12** sorore]
uxore I   **12** fornicatur] fornicator* I *deest* L   **12** peniteat] paeniteat M   **13** Si cum ma-
tre] *deest* IL *praecedit* CCLXXXV M   **14** matre] matrem L   **14** annos] annos peniteat
L   **14** mutat] motat* I   **14** diebus] in diebus LM   **15** CCLXXXVIIII] CCLXXXVI M
15 Si saepe faciens fornicationem] *deest* IL   **16** saepe] sepe L   **16** faciens] faciaens L
16 peniteat] paeniteat M   **16–17** alii iudicant per consilium iii annos] *deest* L   **16–17** iii
annos] annos tres M

100   Collectio CCCC capitulorum

CCXC   Sɪ sᴇᴍᴇɴ ɪɴ ᴏs ᴍɪsᴇʀɪᴛ

Si semen in os miserit, vɪɪ annos, alii ɪɪɪɪ peniteat.

CCXCI   Dᴇ ɢᴜsᴛᴀɴᴅᴏ sᴀɴɢᴜɪɴɪs

Mulier, quae sanguinem uiri sui gustauerit pro remedio, xʟ plus minus ue ieiunet dies.

CCXCII   Dᴇ ᴀʙsᴛɪɴᴇɴᴛɪᴀ ᴀɴᴛᴇ ᴘᴀsᴄʜᴀ

Uir abstineat se ab uxore sua xʟ dies ante pascha, ut in apostolo: Ut uacetis
orationi.

CCXCIII   Dᴇsᴘᴏɴsᴀᴛᴀ ᴘᴜᴇʟʟᴀ

Disponsatam puellam non licet parentibus dare altero uiro, nisi illa omnino   *M 200r*
resistat, tamen ad monasterium licet ire, si uoluerit.   *I 183v*

CCXCIIII   Dᴇ sᴀɴᴄᴛᴀᴍᴏɴɪᴀʟᴇ

Sanctaemoniales autem et basilicae cum missa debent semper consecrari.

CCXCV   Dᴇ ꜰᴏʀɴɪᴄᴀʀɪᴀ ᴄᴜᴍ ɪʟʟᴀ

Si quis fornicauerit cum sanctamoniale uel Deo consecrata, sicut in superiore
sententia unusquisque iuxta ordinem suum peniteat, diaconus et presbiter et
episcopus.

---

2   cf. *Iud. Theod. U* I.2.15; *G* 100   **4–5**   *Iud. Theod. U* I.14.16   **7–8**   cf. *Iud. Theod. U*
II.12.2   **7–8**   1 Cor 7:5   **10–11**   *Iud. Theod. U* II.12.34   **13**   *Iud. Theod. U* II.3.6   **15–17**
cf. *P. Bobb.* §12; *P. Merseb. a* §13

---

1 CCXC] CCLXXX I CCLXXXVII M   **1** Sɪ sᴇᴍᴇɴ ɪɴ ᴏs ᴍɪsᴇʀɪᴛ] *deest* IL   **2** Si]
deest L   **2** os] hos L   **2** ɪɪɪɪ] quattuor LM   **2** peniteat] paeniteat M   **3** CCXCI]
CCLXXXVIII M   **3** Dᴇ ɢᴜsᴛᴀɴᴅᴏ sᴀɴɢᴜɪɴɪs] *deest* IL   **4** quae] qui LM   **4** ue]
uel L *deest* M   **5** dies] *deest* M   **6** CCXCII] CCLXXXVIIII M   **6** Dᴇ ᴀʙsᴛɪɴᴇɴᴛɪᴀ ᴀɴᴛᴇ ᴘᴀsᴄʜᴀ] *deest* IL   **7** abstineat] absteneat L   **7–8** ut in apostolo: Ut uacetis orationi] *deest* L   **7** in] *superscriptum* I   **9** CCXCIII] CXC M   **9** Dᴇsᴘᴏɴsᴀᴛᴀ
ᴘᴜᴇʟʟᴀ] *deest* IL   **10** Disponsatam puellam] Disponsata puella L   **10** altero] alteri M
11 monasterium] masterium L   **12** CCXCIIII] CCXCI M   **12** sᴀɴᴄᴛᴀᴍᴏɴɪᴀʟᴇ] sᴀɴᴄ-
ᴛᴀᴇᴍᴏɴɪᴀʟᴇ ꜰᴏʀɴɪᴄᴀʀɪᴀ LM   **13** Sanctaemoniales] Sanctaemonialis L   **13** cum missa]
commissa L   **13** consecrari] conserare L   **14** CCXCV] CCXCII M   **14** Dᴇ ꜰᴏʀɴɪᴄᴀʀɪᴀ ᴄᴜᴍ ɪʟʟᴀ] *deest* IL Dᴇ ꜰᴏʀɴɪᴄᴀᴛɪᴏɴᴇ ᴄᴜᴍ ɪʟʟᴀ M   **15** sanctamoniale] sanctaemoniale L
15 consecrata] consecrate L   **16** sententia] sententiae L   **16** peniteat] paeniteat M

Collectio CCCC capitulorum

CCXCVI De illa penitentia

Ipsa uirgo sacra fornicans, vii annos peniteat.

CCXCVII De escis inmundis

Qui manducat carnem inmundam aut a uulpis laceratam, xl dies peniteat.

CCXCVIII Qui a bestiis lacerantur

Animalia, quae a lupis, seu a canibus lacerantur, non sunt comedenda, nisi porcis et canibus, nec ceruus, nec capra, si mortui inuenti fuerint.

CCXCVIIII De morticinis

Greci autem carnem non dant morticinorum porcis suis, pelles eorum ad calciamenta liceant, et lana et cornua accipere licet, tamen non in sanctum aliquod.

CCC De porcis

Si casu porci comedent carnem morticinorum aut sanguinem hominis, non abiciendos credimus, nec gallinas.

CCCI De porcis manducantibus cadauera

Porci ergo, qui sanguinem hominis gustantes tetigerunt manducantur. Sed qui cadauera mortuorum lacerantes manducauerint, carnem eorum manducari non licet, usque dum macerentur post annum.

---

2 cf. *Iud. Theod. U* I.8.6; *D* 87   **4** cf. *Iud. Theod. U* I.7.6   **6–7** cf. *Iud. Theod. U* II.11.1   **9–11** *Iud. Theod. U* II.8.7   **13–14** *Iud. Theod. U* II.11.7   **16–18** cf. *Iud. Theod. U* II.11.7-8

---

1 CCXCVI⟧ CCXCIII M   **1** De illa penitentia⟧ *deest* L   **1** penitentia⟧ paenitentia M
2 vii⟧ septem M   **2** peniteat⟧ paeniteat M   **3** CCXCVII⟧ CCXCIIII M   **3** De escis⟧
De scis L   **3** inmundis⟧ mundum L   **4** peniteat⟧ paeniteat M   **5** CCXCVIII⟧ CCXCV
M   **5** Qui a bestiis lacerantur⟧ *deest* IL   **6** quae a⟧ que ea L   **6** lupis, seu a canibus⟧
canibus seu a lupus L   **7** canibus⟧ dentur *superscriptum* M   **8** CCXCVIIII⟧ CCXCVI M
8 De morticinis⟧ *deest* IL   **9** Greci⟧ Grecis L   **9** carnem non dant⟧ non dant carnem
L   **9** ad⟧ a L   **10** liceant⟧ licent M   **12** CCC⟧ CCXCVII M   **12** De porcis⟧ De
porcis bibentibus sanguinem M   **13** hominis⟧ homines L   **14** abiciendos⟧ abiciendas* I
abicientes* L   **14** gallinas⟧ gallibus L gallinus M   **15** CCCI⟧ CCXCVIII M   **15** De
porcis manducantibus cadauera⟧ *deest* IL   **17** qui⟧ quia L   **18** macerentur⟧ macerantur
L   **18** annum⟧ annum paeniteat M

102   Collectio CCCC capitulorum

CCCII   De piscibus et auibus
Pisces autem licet comedere, quia alterius naturae sunt.   *L 113v*

Aues uero et animalia cetera, si in retibus strangulantur, non sunt comedenda.

CCCIII   Si accipiter obpresserit
5 Nec si accipiter oppresserit, si mortui inueniuntur, quia iiii capitulo Actus apostolorum ita precipiunt, abstinere a fornicatione, et sanguine et suffocato et
idolatria.

CCCIIII   De equum manducandum
Equum non prohibent, consuetudo non est comedere. Leporem licet comedere
10 et bonus est pro desinterio et fel eius cum pipero pro dolore.   *I 184v*

CCCV   De animale gustato a bestiis
Animal uulneratum a bestiis et gustatum licitum est manducare, si homo prius
illud animal uiuum occiderit. Si uero mortuum prius fuerit, deiciatur caro eius.

CCCVI   Si apes occident
15 Si apes occidunt hominem, occidi debent festinanter, mel tamen manducetur.

CCCVII   De libertate
Puella xvi annorum sui corporis potestatem habet.

_____

2   *Iud. Theod. U* II.11.3   3   cf. *Iud. Theod. U* II.11.2   5–7   *Iud. Theod. U* II.11.2   9–10
Iud. Theod. U II.11.4-5   15   *Iud. Theod. U* II.11.6   17   *Iud. Theod. U* II.12.36

_____

1 CCCII] CCXCVIIII M   1 De piscibus et auibus] *deest* IL   2 comedere] commede-
re L   2 naturae] natura L   3 cetera] et cetera M   3 strangulantur] stragulantus* I
4 CCCIII] CCC M   4 Si accipiter obpresserit] *deest* IL   5 si] sic L   5 oppresserit]
obpresserit L   5 si mortui…capitulo] *deest* L   5 iiii] iiiior M   5 capitulo] capitula M
5–6 apostolorum] apostulorum* M   8 CCCIIII] CCCI M   8 De equum manducandum]
deest IL   9 Equum] Aequum I   9 consuetudo] sed tamen consuetudo M   10 desinterio]
dysinterio M   10 cum] miscendum est cum L   10 dolore] dolore an munda I dolore ani-
moda L dolore an muda M   11 CCCV] CCCII M   11 De animale gustato a bestiis]
deest IL De animale gustato a besteis M   12 bestiis] besteis LM   13 uiuum] uum* L
13 prius] *deest* L   13 caro] corro L   14 CCCVI] CCCIII M   14 Si apes occident]
deest IL Si apes occident *corr.* Si apes occidunt M   16 CCCVII] CCCIIII M   16 De
libertate] De puella xvi annorum M   17 xvi] xvii IL

Collectio CCCC capitulorum

103

CCCVIII De puero xv annorum

M 201r   Puer usque ad xv annos sit in potestate patris sui.

CCCVIIII De ordinatione pueri

Puerum monasterii ante xxv annos non licet ordinare.

CCCX De monachato pueri

Puer xv annorum per se ipsum potest se monachum facere; puella xvi uel xvii, quia ante in potestate parentum sunt.

CCCXI De seruitute filii

Pater filium suum necessitate coactus potestatem habet tradere in seruitium

I 185r   vii annos; deinde sine uoluntate filii tradendi licentiam non habet.

CCCXII De seruitio semetipsius

Homo post xiiii annos se ipsum seruum facere.

CCCXIII De testimonio

Duodecim debent in testimonium uenire.

CCCXIIII De pregnante

Si pregnantem mulierem prius liberam conparat aliquis, liber est ex ea generatus.

CCCXV De ancilla pregnante

Qui ancillam pregnantem liberat, quem generat seruus est.

---

2 cf. *Iud. Theod. U* II.12.37   4 *Iud. Theod. U* I.9.9   **6–7** cf. *Iud. Theod. U* II.12.37   **9–10** *Iud. Theod. U* II.13.1   **12** *Iud. Theod. U* II.13.2   **16–17** *Iud. Theod. U* II.13.6   **19** *Iud. Theod. U* II.13.7

---

1 CCCVIII⌉ CCCV M   **1** De puero xv annorum⌉ *deest* IL   **2** ad⌉ *deest* M   **2** xv⌉ quindecimum M   **2** annos⌉ anum M   **3** CCCVIIII⌉ CCCVI M   **3** De ordinatione pueri⌉ *deest* IL   **5** CCCX⌉ CCCVII M   **5** De monachato pueri⌉ *deest* IL De monacho pueri M   **6** xvii⌉ x et vii I   **7** quia⌉ qui L   **8** CCCXI⌉ CCCVIII M   **8** De seruitute filii⌉ *deest* IL De filio M   **11** CCCXII⌉ CCCVIIII M   **11** De seruitio semetipsius⌉ *deest* IL   **12** annos⌉ annis L   **12** facere⌉ facere potest M   **13** CCCXIII⌉ CCCX M   **13** De testimonio⌉ *deest* IL   **14** testimonium⌉ testimonio L   **15** CCCXIIII⌉ CCCXI M   **15** De pregnante⌉ *deest* IL   **16** pregnantem⌉ prignantem L   **16** liberam⌉ libera M   **16** conparat⌉ conparet L   **18** CCCXV⌉ CCCXII M   **18** De ancilla pregnante⌉ *deest* IL   **19** pregnantem⌉ prignantem L

104 Collectio CCCC capitulorum

CCCXVI DE LIBERTATE MONASTERII   *L 114r*
Lauandi pedes laicorum, nisi in caena Domini non cogunt.

CCCXVII DE PUGNATIONE SERUORUM DEI
Seruo Dei nullatenus licet pugnare, nisi multorum licet sit consilio seruorum
Dei.

CCCXVIII DE INFIRMANTIUM ESU
Infirmis licet omni hora cibum et potum sumere, quantumcumque desiderant,
si oportune non possunt manducare.

CCCXVIIII DE DIE DOMINICO
Qui operantur die dominico, eos Greci prima uice arguunt, secunda tollunt   *M 201v*
aliquid ab eis, tertia uice tertiam partem de rebus aut uapulant uel VII diebus   *I 185v*
peniteant.

CCCXX DE COMMUNIONE DIE DOMINICO
Greci omni dominico communicant clerici et laici; et qui tribus dominicis non
communicauerint, excommunicantur sicut canones habent. Romani similiter
communicant qui uolunt; qui autem nolunt, non excommunicantur.

CCCXXI DE ABSTINENTIA MARITORUM
Greci et Romani tribus diebus abstinent se a mulieribus ante panes propositionis, sicut in lege scriptum est.

---

2 *Iud. Theod. U* II.6.15   **4–5** *Iud. Theod. U* II.14.4   **7–8** cf. *Iud. Theod. U* II.14.14
10–12 cf. *Iud. Theod. U* I.11.1   **14–16** *Iud. Theod. U* I.12.1-2   **18–19** *Iud. Theod. U*
I.12.3

---

1 CCCXVI] *deest* L CCCXIII M   **1** DE LIBERTATE MONASTERII] DE PURGATIONE SERUO-
RUM DEI M   **2** caena] cena LM   **2** cogunt] coguntur L cogantur M   **3** CCCXVII]
deest M   **3** DE PUGNATIONE SERUORUM DEI] *deest* IL   **4** multorum] in multorum L
6 CCCXVIII] CCCXIIII M   **6** DE INFIRMANTIUM ESU] *deest* IL DE INFIRMO M   **7** Infirmis]
Infirmus L   **7** omni hora] omnino ora L   **7** cibum et potum] potum et cybum L
7 quantumcumque] quandocumque LM   **7** desiderant] desiderat L   **9** CCCXVIIII] CC-
CXV M   **10** operantur] operatur IL   **10** eos] *deest* L   **10** Greci] Grec L   **10** arguunt]
argunt L argunt* M   **10** secunda] seconda L   **11** tertia] tertiam L   **11** diebus] dies LM
12 peniteant] paeniteant M   **13** CCCXX] CCCXVI M   **13** DE COMMUNIONE DIE DOMINI-
CO] QUI OPERANTUR DIE DOMINICO M   **13** COMMUNIONE] COMMUNICATIONE L   **14** dominico]
die dominico M   **14** laici] laci M   **15** communicauerint] communicauerit L   **15** canones]
canon L   **17** CCCXXI] CCCXVII M   **17** MARITORUM] MATRIMONIO L   **18** a] a a I

Collectio CCCC capitulorum   105

CCXXII De disperatione
Si homo uexatus est a diabolo et nescit aliquid nisi discurrere ubique et contigit ut occidat semetipsum, quacumque causa potest, ut oretur pro eo, si ante
religiosus erat.

CCCXXIII De disperatione
Si pro disperatione aut pro timore aliquo aut pro causis incognitis, Deo reli-
quemus hoc iuditium et non ausi sumus orare pro illo.

CCCXXIIII De iuramento
I 186r Periurium qui fecerit in ecclesia, xi annos peniteat.

CCCXXV Necesse in manus
Qui uero per necessitatem coactus, iii quadragesimas.

M 202r Si uero iurauerit in manu episcopi uel presbiteri seu in altari siue in cruce
consecrata et mentitus est, iii annos peniteat. Si in cruce non consecrata, i
annum peniteat.

Si quis iurauerit in manu hominis, nihil est apud Grecos.

L 114v Nos secundum Christum: Ex uerbis tuis iustificaueris.

2–4 *Iud. Theod. U* II.10.1   **6–7** *Iud. Theod. U* II.10.2   **9** *Iud. Theod. U* I.6.1   **11** *Iud.*
Theod. U I.6.2   **12–14** *Iud. Theod. U* I.6.4   **15** *Iud. Theod. U* I.6.3   **16** Mt 12:37

---

1 CCXXII⌉ CCCXVIII M   1 De disperatione⌉ De uexatione diabolica M   2 diabolo⌉
diabulo M   2 discurrere⌉ discurere L   2 et⌉ et si M   2–3 contigit⌉ contingit
L   3 causa⌉ causae M   4 religiosus⌉ relegiosus LM   5 CCCXXIII⌉ CCCXVIIII
M   5 De disperatione⌉ *deest* IL   6 timore⌉ mortem L   6–7 reliquemus⌉ relinqui-
mur I   7 iuditium⌉ iudicium LM   7 ausi sumus⌉ ausimus L   8 CCCXXIIII⌉ CCXC M
9 peniteat⌉ paeniteat M   10 CCCXXV⌉ CCXCI M   10 Necesse in manus⌉ Necesse I
Si iurauerit in manu episcopi M   11 Qui uero...quadragesimas⌉ *cum cap.* CCCXXIIII LM
11 coactus⌉ actus* I   11 iii⌉ tres M   11 quadragesimas⌉ quadragisimas M   12 altari⌉
altare LM   13 iii annos⌉ annos iii L   13 peniteat⌉ paeniteat M   13–14 i annum⌉ annum i L   13 i⌉ unum M   14 annum⌉ annos I   14 peniteat⌉ paeniteat M   15 Grecos⌉
Crecos L   16 iustificaueris⌉ iustificaueris et ex uerbis tuis condempnaueris L iustificaueris
et ex uerbis tuis condemnaueris M

106 Collectio CCCC capitulorum

CCCXXVI Interrogatio romanorum
De iuramento: Non iurare omnino: hoc consequentia lectionis docet non adiu-
randum esse per creaturam aliam, sed per Creatorem, ut mos est prophetis:
Uiuit Dominus, cui adsisto hodie.

5 **CCCXXVII** De contradictione
Finis autem contradictionis adiuramentum est, sed Domino: Omne enim quod
dominatur hoc et adiurat. Alii periures iii annis peniteat.

De contradictione duorum absque testibus: Statuunt ut per sancta iiii euan-   *I 186v*
gelia antequam communicant testantur, qui adprobantur et deinde sub iudice
10 flamma relinquantur.

CCCXXVIII De paenitentia iuramenti
Si quis periurauerit, vi annis peniteat, iii integros, ut et iuret numquam postea.
Si quis coactus pro qualibet necessitate aut nesciens periurauerit, tribus annis
peniteat, i integrum.

15 **CCCXXVIIII** De furtu
Si quis furtum capitale commiserit, id est quadrupedia uel casas efregerit, aut
quolibet meliorem presidium furauerit, v annos peniteat, iii integros.   *M 202v*

2–4 *Syn. II Patr.*, 23 (fragment) **6–7** *Syn. II Patr.*, 23 (fragment) **8–10** *Syn. II Patr.*,
24 **12–14** cf. *P. Burg.* §§5–6; *P. Bobb.* §§6–7; *P. Slet.* §§5–6; *P. Flor.* §§5–6 **16–17** cf. *P.
Burg.* §7; *P. Slet.* §7; *P. Flor.* §7

---

1 CCCXXVI⌉ CCXCII M   1 Interrogatio romanorum⌉ In interrogatione romanorum:
De confirmatione iuramenti M   2 consequentia⌉ sequentia L   2 docet⌉ de est ILM
2–3 adiurandum⌉ iurandum LM   3 per⌉ pro L   3 aliam⌉ aliquam M   3 ut⌉ aut
L   4 Uiuit⌉ uiui L   4 Dominus⌉ Dominus et uiuit anima mea et uiuit Dominus LM
4 adsisto⌉ ad isto L adsto M   4 hodie⌉ hodiae L   5 CCCXXVII⌉ CCXCIII M   5 De
contradictione⌉ De contradictione iuramenti M   6 Omne⌉ Omnae L   7 dominatur⌉
dominator M   7 et adiurat⌉ adiuratur L   7 periures⌉ per uires M   7 peniteat⌉ paenitat
M   8 testibus⌉ testis L   8 iiii⌉ quattuor M   9 iudice⌉ iudicet I   10 relinquantur⌉
reliquantur* I   11 CCCXXVIII⌉ CCXCIIII   11 De paenitentia iuramenti⌉ *deest* IL De
paenitentia iuranti M   12 vi⌉ vii M   12 peniteat⌉ paeniteat M   12 iii⌉ tres LM
12 iuret⌉ iurat L   12 postea⌉ pretereat L   13 necessitate⌉ necessitatem L   13 tribus⌉
iii L   14 peniteat⌉ paeniteat M   14 i⌉ unum LM   15 CCCXXVIIII⌉ CCXV M   15 De
furtu⌉ De furtu et penitentia furi M   16 capitale⌉ capitalem LM   16 quadrupedia⌉
quatrupedia L   16 casas⌉ casa L   16 efregerit⌉ effrigerit L effringerit M   17 v⌉ quinque
LM   17 peniteat⌉ paeniteat M   17 iii⌉ tres L

Collectio CCCC capitulorum

107

Qui saepe furtum fecerit, vii annos penitentia eius, aut quomodo iudicauerit sacerdos.

CCCXXX De homicidiis

Si quis uero homicidium casu fecerit, v annos peniteat, iii integros. Qui ad homicidium faciendum consenserit et factum fuerit, vi annos, iii integros. Si autem uoluerit et non poterit, iii annos.

CCCXXXI Si clericus homicidium facit

I 187r Clericus qui homicidium fecerit, et proximum suum occiderit, x annos exul peniteat. Post hos recipiatur in patriam, si paenitentia conprobatur episcopo ut et satisfaciat parentibus eius, quem occidit, uicem filii reddet. Si autem non satisfaciat parentibus illius, numquam recipiatur in patriam, sed more Cain fugus et uagus super terram.

CCCXXXII De occisione

L 115r Qui occiderit hominem, xl diebus abstineat se ab ecclesia, et vii annos seu iii per consilium peniteat.

CCCXXXIII Si pro ultione occiditur

Si quis pro ultione proximi hominem occiderit, peniteat sicut homicida, iii uel vii annos. Si tamen reddere uult propinquis pecuniam aestimationis, leuior erit penitentia id est dimidio spatio.

1–2 *Iud. Theod. U* I.3.3; *G* 94   4–6 cf. *P. Burg.* §§2-3; *P. Flor.* §§2-3   8–12 cf. *P. Burg.* §§1; *P. Merseb. a* §1   14–15 cf. *Iud. Theod. U* I.4.2   17–19 cf. *Iud. Theod. U* I.4.1

1 penitentia] paenitentia M   2 sacerdos] sacerdus M   3 CCCXXX] CCXCVI M
4 peniteat] paeniteat M   4 iii integros] *deest* L   5 faciendum] *deest* L   5 consenserit]
conserserit* M   5 et factum fuerit] *deest* L   5 vi] vii L   5 iii] tres M   6 poterit]
poterint L   6 annos] annus L   7 CCCXXXI] CCXCVII M   7 Si clericus homicidium
facit] *deest* IL   8 qui] *deest* L   8 fecerit] *deest* L   8 suum] tuum* I   9 peniteat]
paeniteat M   9 paenitentia] penitentiam L   10 quem] quemque L   10 reddet] reddat
L   12 uagus] fagus IL uagus sit M   13 CCCXXXII] CCXCVIII M   13 De occisione]
deest L Qui occiderit hominem M   14 abstineat] absteneat L   15 peniteat] paeniteat M
16 CCCXXXIII] CCXCVIIII M   16 Si pro ultione occiditur] *deest* IL   17 peniteat]
paeneteat L paeniteat M   18 aestimationis] stimationis L   19 penitentia id est dimidio
spatio] *deest* M   19 dimidio] demonio L

108   Collectio CCCC capitulorum

CCCXXXIIII   Qui in publico bello occidit
Similiter, qui occiderit hominem publico bello uel per iussionem domini sui,   *M 203r*
peniteat.

CCCXXXV   Qui non conposuit furtum aut homicidium
5 Qui homicidium uel furtum commiserit et non conposuit illis quibus nocuit,
quando confessus fuerit episcopo uel presbitero peccata sua, debet illis aut pro-   *I 187v*
pria reddere uel conponere. Si uero non habuerit substantiam unde conponere
potest uel nescierit quibus nocuerit, plus augeat penitentia.

CCCXXXVI   Si aliter percusserit
10 Si quis alium aliter percusserit et sanguinem effuderit, xl diebus peniteat, et
uulnus restituat.

CCCXXXVII   Si quis beneficium faciat
Si quis malefitio suo aliquem perdiderit vi annos peniteat, iii integros.

CCCXXXVIII   Qui monachum occidit
15 Qui occiderit monachum uel clericum, arma relinquat et Deo seruiat uel vii
annos peniteat.

CCCXXXVIIII   Qui episcopum aut presbiterum occidit
Qui autem episcopum aut presbiterum occiderit, regi dimittendus est.

2–3 cf. *Iud. Theod. U* 1.4.6   **5–8** *Iud. Theod. D* 88   **10–11** cf. *Exc. Cumm.* VI.18   **13**
Exc. Cumm. VII.1   **15–16** *Iud. Theod. U* I.4.5   **18** *Iud. Theod. U* I.4.5

---

1 CCCXXXIIII] CCC M   **1** Qui in publico bello occidit] *deest* IL   **2** publico] in publico
M   **2** iussionem] iussione L   **3** peniteat] paeniteat M   **4** CCCXXXV] CCCI M   **4** Qui
non conposuit furtum aut homicidium] *deest* IL   **6** episcopo] episcopus L   **6** peccata sua]
peccato suo L   **7** Si uero...conponere] *deest* L   **8** nescierit] nescerit L   **8** penitentia] paenitentia LM   **9** CCCXXXVI] CCCII M   **9** Si aliter percusserit] *deest* IL   **10** peniteat]
paeniteat M   **12** CCCXXXVII] CCCIII M   **12** Si quis beneficium faciat] *deest* IL Si
quis ueneficium facit M   **13** malefitio] maleficio LM   **13** vi] vii LM   **13** iii] tres
M   **14** CCCXXXVIII] CCCIIII M   **14** Qui monachum occidit] *deest* IL   **15** relinquat]
relinquatur L   **16** peniteat] paeniteat M   **17** CCCXXXVIIII] CCCV M   **17** Qui episcopum aut presbiterum occidit] *deest* IL   **18** autem] aut L   **18** episcopum aut presbiterum
occiderit] occiderit episcopum aut presbiterum M   **18** regi] rei L   **18** dimittendus est]
iudicandum est L dimittendum est iudicium M

Collectio CCCC capitulorum 109

CCCXL Sɪ ʟᴀɪᴄᴜs ʟᴀɪᴄᴜᴍ
Si laicus alterum occidit odii meditatione, peniteat vɪɪ annos sine carne et uino,
si per iram ɪɪɪ, si casu ɪ.

CCCXLI Dᴇ ᴘᴀᴇɴɪᴛᴇɴᴛɪᴀ ᴀᴅᴜʟᴛᴇʀɪɪ
Qui adulterium conmiserit, id est, cum uxore aliena uel sponsa uel uirginem
corruperit, si clericus ɪɪɪ annos peniteat, unum integrum.

CCCXLII Dᴇ ᴅɪᴀᴄᴏɴᴏ ᴇᴛ ᴘʀᴇsʙɪᴛᴇʀᴏ ᴅᴀᴛᴜᴍ
I 188r Si diaconus v annos, ɪɪ integros; et monachus si presbiter vɪɪ, omnia autem ut
supra.

CCCXLIII Sɪ ᴘʀᴇsʙɪᴛᴇʀᴏ ᴄᴏɴᴍᴇɴᴅᴀᴛᴜs ɪɴғᴀɴs ɪɴғɪʀᴍᴜs
M 203v;
L 115v Infirmus infans et paganus conmendatus presbitero, si fuerit mortuus depo-
natur.

CCCXLIIII Dᴇ ɴᴇɢʟᴇɢᴇɴᴛɪᴀ ᴘᴀʀᴇɴᴛᴜᴍ
Si neglegentia parentum erit, uno annum peniteat.

CCCXLV Dᴇ ᴘᴏʟʟᴜᴛɪᴏɴᴇ sᴀᴄᴇʀᴅᴏᴛᴜᴍ
Sacerdos si tangendo aut osculando mulierem coinquinatur, xʟ diebus peniteat.

2–3 *Iud. Theod. U* I.4.4 **5–6** cf. *P. Burg.* §8 **8–9** cf. *P. Burg.* §8 **11–12** cf. *Iud.*
Theod. U II.14.28 **14** *Iud. Theod. U* II.14.29 **16–17** *Iud. Theod. U* I.8.1

---

1 CCCXL⟧ CCCVI M **1** Sɪ ʟᴀɪᴄᴜs ʟᴀɪᴄᴜᴍ⟧ *deest* IL **2** occidit⟧ occiderit L
2 meditatione⟧ meditati relinquere L meditatione relinquere M **2** peniteat⟧ paeniteat M
3 ɪɪɪ⟧ ɪɪɪ annos L tres M **3** ɪ⟧ uno M **4** CCCXLI⟧ CCCVII M **4** ᴘᴀᴇɴɪᴛᴇɴᴛɪᴀ⟧
ᴘᴇɴɪᴛᴇɴᴛɪᴀ L **4** ᴀᴅᴜʟᴛᴇʀɪɪ⟧ ᴀᴅᴜʟᴛᴇʀɪ L ᴀᴅᴜʟᴛᴇʀɪᴏʀᴜᴍ M **5** adulterium⟧ adulterum L
5 conmiserit⟧ commiserit M **5** uxore⟧ muliere L **6** corruperit⟧ corrumperit* I corrup-
serit L corrumperit M **7** CCCXLII⟧ CCCVIII M **7** Dᴇ ᴅɪᴀᴄᴏɴᴏ ᴇᴛ ᴘʀᴇsʙɪᴛᴇʀᴏ ᴅᴀᴛᴜᴍ⟧
deest IL **8** ɪɪ⟧ duos M **8** si⟧ et L **8** vɪɪ⟧ vɪɪ annus L vɪɪ annos M **8** ut⟧ *deest*
IL **10** CCCXLIII⟧ CCCVIIII M **10** Sɪ ᴘʀᴇsʙɪᴛᴇʀᴏ ᴄᴏɴᴍᴇɴᴅᴀᴛᴜs ɪɴғᴀɴs ɪɴғɪʀᴍᴜs⟧ *deest*
IL **11** conmendatus⟧ commendatus LM **13** CCCXLIIII⟧ *deest* M **13** Dᴇ ɴᴇɢʟᴇɢᴇɴᴛɪᴀ
ᴘᴀʀᴇɴᴛᴜᴍ⟧ *deest* IL **14** annum⟧ anno LM **14** peniteat⟧ paeniteat LM **15** CCCXLV⟧
CCCXL M **15** Dᴇ ᴘᴏʟʟᴜᴛɪᴏɴᴇ sᴀᴄᴇʀᴅᴏᴛᴜᴍ⟧ *deest* IL **16** Sacerdos⟧ Sacerdus LM **16** si⟧
deest L **16** aut⟧ *deest* L **16** coinquinatur⟧ quoinquinat L **16–17** peniteat⟧ paeniteat
M

110   Collectio CCCC capitulorum

CCCXLVI   De osculi pollutione

Si osculatus presbiter feminam per desiderium, xx dies, si semen per osculum fuderit, xl peniteat.

CCCXLVII   De cogitationis pollutione

5 Si per cogitationem fuderit semen, ebdomada ieiunet. Si tangit manu cum manu, iii ebdomadas.

De his Apostolus Iacobus melior intimabat: Confitemini, inquid, alter utrum peccata uestra et orate pro inuicem ut saluemini.

CCCXLVIII   De gradu perdito

10 De maioribus gradu perdito penitentia mortua est, anima uiuet.

CCCXLVIIII   De uiolentia cogitationis

Si quis sepe per uiolentiam cogitationis semen funderit, xx diebus.

CCCL   De ebrietatis uomitu

Si presbiter aut diaconus per aebrietate uomitat, xl dies peniteat. Si monachus   *I 188v*
15 xxx dies peniteat, si laicus fidelis xv dies peniteat.

2–3   *Iud. Theod. G* 118; *C* 30–31   5–6   *Iud. Theod. G* 118; *C* 25–6; cf. *U* I.8.3–4   7–8   Iac 5:16   10   cf. *Iud. Theod. U* I.9.1b; *G* 167; *B* 97   12   *Iud. Theod. G* 119; cf. *U* I.8.7   14–15 *Iud. Theod. G* 121; *U* I.1.3, I.1.2, I.1.5

---

1 CCCXLVI] CCCXLI M   1 De osculi pollutione] *deest* IL   2 osculatus] osculatur M   2 xx] xxx M   3 xl] xl dies LM   3 peniteat] paeniteat M   4 CCCXLVII] CC-CXLII M   4 De cogitationis pollutione] *deest* ILM   5 cogitationem] cogitationibus L 5 ebdomada] ebdomata M   5 tangit] tangendo L   5 manu] manum M   6 iii] tres M 7 Apostolus Iacobus] Iacobus Apostolus M   7 melior] melius M   7 inquid] inquit M 8 saluemini] saluimini LM   9 CCCXLVIII] CCCXLIII M   9 De gradu perdito] *deest* IL   10 penitentia] paenitentia LM   11 CCCXLVIIII] CCCXLIII M   11 De uiolentia cogitationis] *deest* IL   12 sepe] saepe M   12 uiolentiam] uoluntate L   12 cogitationis] cogitationes L   12 funderit] fuderit L   12 xx] xxx M   12 diebus] dies L diebus paeniteat M   13 CCCL] CCCXLV M   13 De ebrietatis uomitu] *deest* IL   14 Si] Si quis L *deest* M   14 per] pro I pro L   14 aebrietate] hebrietate L ebrietatem M   14 uomitat] uomit M   14 peniteat] paeniteat M   14–15 Si monachus...peniteat] si laicus fideles xv dies peniteat, si monachus xxx L   15 peniteat] *deest* M   15 peniteat] paeniteat M

Collectio CCCC capitulorum

111

CCCLI De ebrietate sacerdotum
Si quis episcopus aut aliquis ordinatus in consuetudine uitium habet aebrietatis, aut desinat aut deponatur.

CCCLII Presbiter non prodendum peccata
Presbitero non licet peccatum episcopi prodere, quia super eum est.

CCCLIII De pollutione puerorum
Pueros qui fornicationem faciunt inter semetipsos, iudicauit ut uapulentur.

Si semen excitauerit, primus xx dies, si altero xl dies, si plus addantur ieiunia.

CCCLIIII Si monachus fornicat
Monachus fornicationem faciens vii annos peniteat.

CCCLV De uoto pueri
Puero non licet iam nubere prelato monachi uoto.

CCCLVI De commutatione
Infans pro infante potest dari ad monasterium Deo, quamuis alium uouisset, tamen melius est uotum implere. Similiter pecora aequali pretio possunt mutari, si necesse sit.

CCCLVII De terra rapta a rege
Rex, si alterius regis terram habuerit, potest dare pro anima sua.

2–3 *Iud. Theod. G* 40; *U* I.1.1   **5** *Iud. Theod. U* II.2.9   **7** *Iud. Theod. G* 99; *U* I.2.11; *C* 160   **8** *Iud. Theod. G* 119; *U* I.8.9; *C* 28   **10** cf. *Iud. Theod. U* I.8.6   **12** *Iud. Theod. U* II.6.11   **14–16** *Iud. Theod. U* II.14.5-6   **18** *Iud. Theod. U* II.14.7

---

1 CCCLI] CCCXLVI M   **1** De ebrietate sacerdotum] *deest* IL   **2** habet] habuerit M   **2–3** aebrietatis] hebrietatis L ebrietatis M   **4** CCCLII] CCCXLVII M   **4** Presbiter non prodendum peccata] *deest* IL   **5** Presbitero] Presbiter L   **5** episcopi] episcopo M   **6** CCCLIII] CCCXLVIII M   **7** Pueros] Pueri M   **7** uapulentur] uapulent I uapulant L   **8** excitauerit] excitauerint M   **8** primus] *deest* L primo M   **9** CCCLIIII] CCCXLVIIII M   **9** Si monachus fornicat] *deest* IL Si mochus fornicationem facit M   **10** peniteat] paeniteat M   **11** CCCLV] CCCL M   **11** De uoto pueri] *deest* IL   **13** CCCLVI] CCCLI M   **13** commutatione] commotatione IM   **14** dari] dare LM   **14** monasterium] monesterium L   **14–15** uouisset] nouisset L   **15** aequali] equali LM   **17** CCCLVII] CCCLII M   **17** De terra rapta a rege] *deest* IL De terra reptu a rege M   **18** terram] terra M

112   Collectio CCCC capitulorum

CCCLVIII DE INUENTIONE IN UIA
Inuentio in uia tollenda est; si inuentus fuerit possessor, reddatur ei.

CCCLVIIII DE TRIBUTU AECCLESIAE
Tributum aecclesiae sit sicut consuetudo prouintiae est, tantum ne pauperes   *L 116r*
5 in decimis aut in aliquibus rebus uim patientur.

CCCLX NON TOLLENDUM A SERUO PECUNIA
Non licet homini a seruo suo tollere pecuniam sine uoluntate eius, quoniam
ille de labore suo adquesierit.

CCCLXI DE FALSITATE COMMISSA
10 Si quis falsitatem commisit, VII annos peniteat. Qui autem consentit, V annos
peniteat.

CCCLXII DE IEIUNIIS LEGITIMIS
Ieiunia legitima tria: XL ante pascha, et XL post pentecosten, et XL ante natiui-   *M 204v*
tatem Domini.

15 **CCCLXIII** UTRUMQUE IN BAPTISMUM ACCIPIAT
Uiro licet in baptismo suscipere feminam similiter feminae uirum.

---

2 *Iud. Theod. U* II.14.9   **4–5** *Iud. Theod. U* II.14.10   **7–8** *Iud. Theod. U* II.13.3   **10–11**
cf. *Exc. Cumm.* V.10   **13–14** *Iud. Theod. G* 61; *U* II.14.1   **16** *Iud. Theod. G* 180; *U* II.4.10

---

1 CCCLVIII⏌ CCCLIII M   1 DE INUENTIONE IN UIA⏌ *deest* IL   2 possessor⏌ possessi-
sor L   2 ei⏌ *deest* L   3 CCCLVIIII⏌ CCCLIIII M   3 DE TRIBUTU AECCLESIAE⏌ *deest* IL
DE TRIBUTO ECCLESIAE M   4 aecclesiae⏌ ecclesiae LM   4 sicut⏌ *deest* L   4 prouintiae⏌
prouincie L prouinciae M   5 patientur⏌ pacientur L patienter M   6 CCCLX⏌ CCCLV M
6 NON TOLLENDUM A SERUO PECUNIA⏌ *deest* IL   7 homini a⏌ homnia L   7 sine uoluntate
eius⏌ *deest* L   7 quoniam⏌ quam M   8 adquesierit⏌ adquisierit L   9 CCCLXI⏌ CCCLVI
M   9 DE FALSITATE COMMISSA⏌ *deest* IL   10 commisit⏌ commiserit LM   10 consentit⏌
consensit L   11 peniteat⏌ *deest* M   12 CCCLXII⏌ CCCLVII M   12 DE IEIUNIIS LEGITI-
MIS⏌ *deest* IL   13 tria⏌ trias I   13 XL⏌ et quadraginta dies M   13 XL⏌ quadraginta M
13 XL⏌ quadraginta M   13–14 natiuitatem⏌ natale LM   15 CCCLXIII⏌ CCCLVIII M
15 UTRUMQUE IN BAPTISMUM ACCIPIAT⏌ *deest* IL   16 suscipere⏌ suscipe* M   16 feminam⏌
feminam feminam L   16 feminae⏌ *deest* L

Collectio CCCC capitulorum 113

CCCLXIIII De reuerentia ecclesiae
Ligna ecclesiae non debent ad aliud opus iungi, nisi ad ecclesiam aliam, si necesse est, uel igne conburenda uel ad profectum in monasterio fratribus. In laicata tamen opera non debent procedere, et in loco altaris crux ponatur.

I 189v

CCCLXV De mutata ecclesia
Ecclesiam licet ponere in alium locum si necesse sit et non debet iterum sanctificari, nisi tantum presbiter aquam aspargere debet.

CCCLXVI In uno altare duas missas
In uno altare duas missas facere conceditur in uno die.

CCCLXVII Post pentecostam reuerentia septimana
Pro reuerentia regenerationis: in albas post pentecosten, una septimana stando orandum est, ut ante in quinquagesima.

CCCLXVIII De furata ecclesiae pecunia
Pecunia ecclesiastica furata siue rapta reddatur quadruplum, popularia dupliciter.

CCCLXVIIII De missa offerenda
Dionisius Aropagita dicit: Blasphemias Deo facere, qui missas offerat pro homine malo.

2–4 *Iud. Theod. G* 134; *U* II.1.3   **6–7** *Iud. Theod. G* 135; cf. *U* II.1.1   **9** *Iud. Theod. U* II.1.2   **11–12** cf. *Iud. Theod. U* II.14.12   **14–15** *Iud. Theod. G* 166; *U* I.3.2   **17–114.2** *Iud. Theod. U* II.5.8-9

---

1 CCCLXIIII] CCCLVIIII M   **1** ecclesiae] ecclesia LM   **2** ecclesiae] ecclesie L   **2** debent] debet M   **2** aliud opus] aliam L   **2** ecclesiam aliam] aliam ecclesiam L   **3** conburenda] conburende L conburendam M   **3** profectum] perfectum I profecte *corr.* profectum L   **3** monasterio] monasterium L   **4** opera] opere L   **5** CCCLXV] CCCLX M   **5** De mutata ecclesia] *deest* IL   **5** mutata] motata M   **6** alium locum] alio loco L   **6–7** sanctificari] sanctaficari I   **7** aquam] aqua LM   **7** aspargere] spargere L   **8** CCCLXVI] CCCLXI M   **8** In uno altare duas missas] *deest* IL   **9** die] diae L   **10** CCCLXVII] CCCLXII M   **10** Post pentecostam reuerentia septimana] *deest* IL Post pentecosten reuerentia septimana M   **11** Pro] Pre L   **11** post] potest L   **12** quinquagesima] quinquagisima fuit M   **13** CCCLXVIII] CCCLXIII M   **13** De furata ecclesiae pecunia] *deest* IL   **14** ecclesiastica] ecclesiestica L   **16** CCCLXVIIII] CCCLXIIII M   **16** De missa offerenda] *deest* IL   **17** Aropagita] Ariopagita LM   **17** Blasphemias] Blaspemias L

114 Collectio CCCC capitulorum

Augustinus dicit: Pro omnibus Christianis esse faciendum, quia uel eis proficit,
aut offerentibus aut petentibus consulationem prestat. *M 205r*

CCCLXX Missas pro infantibus
Pro infantibus licet missas facere cui uult ante vii annos.

5 **CCCLXXI** De baptismo clericorum in infirmitate
Si clericus peruenerit ad infirmum paganum, melior est baptizare eum cum *I 189a-*
aqua signata in nomine sanctae trinitatis.

CCCLXXII De indicto ieiunio
Si quis indictum ieiunium contemserit in ecclesia, xl dies peniteat. *L 116v*

10 **CCCLXXIII** Si in quadragisima
Si in xl paschae, annum peniteat.

CCLXXIIII De fugientibus reis ad aecclesiam
Synodus Aurelianense: De homicidis, adulteris et furibus, ad ecclesia confu-
gientibus, ecclesiastici canones et lex romana decreuit: ut ab ecclesiae atriis
15 et a domo episcopi abstrahi omnino non liceat; sed nec alteri consignari, ante
omni periculo sint securi, ita ut eis, quibus rei sunt, satisfaciant.

---

4 cf. *Iud. Theod. U* II.5.7 **6–7** cf. *Iud. Theod. G* 30 **9** cf. *Iud. Theod. G* 60; *U* I.11.4
11 cf. *Iud. Theod. G* 60; *U* I.11.4 **13–16** cf. *Aurel.* §1

---

1 Pro⌉ *deest* L **2** aut⌉ aut *corr.* sium I autem M **2** petentibus⌉ paentibus I
2 consulationem prestat⌉ consolatur LM **2** consulationem⌉ consulatur* I **2** prestat⌉
superscriptum I **3** CCCLXX⌉ CCCLXV M **3** Missas pro infantibus⌉ *deest* IL Missa
pro infantibus M **4** cui⌉ qui M **5** CCCLXXI⌉ CCCLXVI M **5** De baptismo clericorum in infirmitate⌉ *deest* IL **6** melior⌉ melius L **8** CCCLXXII⌉ CCCLXVII M
8 De indicto ieiunio⌉ *deest* IL **9** contemserit⌉ contemnerit* I contempnerit L contempserit M **9** peniteat⌉ paeniteat M **10** CCCLXXIII⌉ CCCLXVIII M **10** Si in quadra-
gisima⌉ *deest* IL **11** Si⌉ *deest* L **11** xl⌉ xl^{ma} M **11** paschae⌉ pascha L paschale
M **11** peniteat⌉ paeniteat M **12** CCLXXIIII⌉ CCCLXVIIII M **12** De fugientibus
reis ad aecclesiam⌉ *deest* IL De fugientibus reis ad ecclesiam M **13** Synodus⌉ Sinodus
L **13** Aurelianense⌉ Aurianensis I Aurelianensis L Aurelianensis dicit M **13** homicidis⌉
homicidiis LM **13** furibus⌉ fratribus L **13–14** ad ecclesia confugientibus⌉ *deest* L
13 ecclesia⌉ ecclesiam M **14** ecclesiae⌉ ecclesie L **15** abstrahi⌉ abstrai L **15** liceat⌉
licet M **15** nec⌉ sic M **15** ante⌉ antequam M

Collectio CCCC capitulorum   115

CCCLXXV De raptoribus et incensoribus
Si quis uirginem aut uiduam raptus fuerit, iii annos peniteat.

CCCLXXVI De captiuantibus homines
Si quis seruum aut quemcumque hominem quodlibet ingenio in captiuitatem
duxerit aut transmiserit iii annos peniteat.

CCCLXXVII De incensoribus domus
Si quis domum uel aream cuiuscumque uoluntate igne cremauerit, superiori
sententia subiaceat.

CCCLXXVIII De percussione in rixu
Qui occiderit hominem per rixam, x annos peniteat, in iuditio episcopi est.

CCCLXXVIIII De gustu sanguinis
Sanguinem inscius sorbens cum saliua non est magnum peccatum.

CCCLXXX De raptore fugiente ad aecclesiam
Cum raptor ad ecclesiam cum rapta confugerit, statim femina de potestate
raptoris liberetur et ipse mortis uel penarum inpunitate concessa ad seruiendi
conditionem subiectus sit aut redimat et pretium suum patri raptae reddat.

---

2 cf. *Paen. Hubertense, Paen. Bobbiense, Paen. Parisiense, Paen. Merseb. a, Paen. Merseb. b, Aurel.*
§2 **4–5** cf. *Paen. Hubertense, Paen. Bobbiense, Paen. Parisiense, Paen. Merseb. a, Paen. Merseb. b,
Aurel.* §3 **7–8** cf. *Hubertense, Paen. Bobbiense, Paen. Parisiense, Paen. Merseb. a, Paen. Merseb.
b* **10** *Iud. Theod. G* 111; cf. *U* I.4.7 **12** cf. *Iud. Theod. U* I.7.11 **14–16** cf. *Aurel.* §2

---

1 CCCLXXV] CCCLXX M **1** et incensoribus] *deest* M **2** iii] tres M **2** peniteat]
paeniteat M **3** CCCLXXVI] CCCLXXI M **3** De captiuantibus homines] *deest* IL
4 quemcumque] quecumque LM **4** quodlibet] quolibet LM **5** peniteat] paeniteat M
6 CCCLXXVII] CCCLXXII M **6** De incensoribus domus] *deest* IL **7** aream] ariam
L **7** superiori] superiore L **8** subiaceat] subiaciat* I **9** CCCLXXVIII] CCCLXXIII
M **9** De percussione in rixu] *deest* IL **10** peniteat] paeniteat M **10** iuditio] iudicio M
11 CCCLXXVIIII] CCCLXXIIII M **11** De gustu sanguinis] *deest* IL **12** inscius] in-
sciens M **12** saliua] salibo* I saliba L salibo M **13** CCCLXXX] CCCLXXV M **13** De
raptore fugiente ad aecclesiam] *deest* IL De raptore fugiente ad ecclesiam M **14** rapta]
rapta est L **14** confugerit] fugerit LM **15** mortis] mortes L **15** penarum] paena-
rum L poenarum M **15** concessa] concensa L **16** aut redimat] *deest* L **16** redimat]
redemat* I se redimat M **16** raptae] raptor L

116 Collectio CCCC capitulorum

CCCLXXXI Seruus fugiens ad ecclesiam

Seruus ecclesiae pro qualibet culpa confugiens, datis a domino suo de inpunitate eis sacramentis, statim ad seruitium redire cogatur.

CCCLXXXII De culpa abbatis

5 Si peccauerit abbas, nec episcopo licet tollere possessionem monasterii, quamuis peccauerit abbas, sed mittat eum in aliud monasterium in potestatem alterius abbatis.

CCCLXXXIII Non uertendum terram aecclesiae

Nec licet abbate neque episcopo terram ecclesiae uertere ad aliam, quamuis   *L 117r*
10 ambae in potestate eius sint.

CCCLXXXIIII Cum consensu mutat terram

Si mutare uult terram ecclesiae, cum consensu amborum faciat.   *I 190r*

CCCLXXXV Monasterii commutatio

Si quis uult monasterium suum in alium locum ponere, faciat cum consilio epi-
15 scopi et fratrum suorum et dimittat in priori loco presbiterum ad ministerium   *M 208r*
ecclesiae.

2–3 cf. *Aurel.* §3   **5–7** *Iud. Theod. G* 76; *Iud. Theod. U* II.6.5   **9–10** cf. *Iud. Theod. G* 77; *Iud. Theod. U* II.6.6   **12** cf. *Iud. Theod. G* 77; *Iud. Theod. U* II.6.6   **14–16** *Iud. Theod. U* II.6.7

---

1 CCCLXXXI⌉ CCCLXXVI M   1 Seruus fugiens ad ecclesiam⌉ *deest* IL   2 ecclesiae⌉ ecclesie L   2 culpa⌉ culpae L   2–3 inpunitate⌉ inpuniate L   3 eis⌉ ei M   3 sacramentis⌉ sacramentum L   4 CCCLXXXII⌉ CCCLXXVII   4 De culpa abbatis⌉ De abbatis confirmandas I   5 episcopo⌉ episcopus L   6 potestatem⌉ potestate M   8 CCCLXXXIII⌉ CCCLXXVIII M   8 Non uertendum terram aecclesiae⌉ *deest* IL   8 uertendum⌉ reuertendum M   9 Nec⌉ Non M   9 abbate⌉ abbato* I   10 ambae⌉ ambiae L   10 sint⌉ sunt LM   11 CCCLXXXIIII⌉ CCCLXXVIIII M   11 Cum consensu mutat terram⌉ *deest* IL   11 mutat⌉ mota *corr.* mutare M   12 mutare⌉ motare* M   13 CCCLXXXV⌉ CCCLXXX M   13 Monasterii commutatio⌉ *deest* IL Monasterio commotatio M   14 suum⌉ *deest* L   14 cum⌉ com* L   14 consilio⌉ consensu L consili* M   15 priori⌉ priore L   15 presbiterum⌉ presbiter L   16 ecclesiae⌉ ecclesie L

Collectio CCCC capitulorum

117

CCCLXXXVI Non cogendum abbatem ad synodum

Episcopus non debet abbatem cogere ad synodum ire, nisi etiam aliqua rationabilis causa sit.

CCCLXXXVII De electione alterius abbatis

Abbas pro humiliatione cum permissione episcopi locum suum derelinquere, tamen fratres elegant sibi abbatem de ipsis, si habent, sin autem, de extraneis.

CCCLXXXVIII De non retinendo abbato in loco suo

Nec episcopus debet uiolenter retinere abbatem in loco suo esse.

CCCLXXXVIIII De congregationis electione abbatis

Congregatio debet elegere sibi abbatem post mortem eius aut eo uiuente si ipse discesserit uel peccauerit. Ipse non potest aliquem ordinare de suis propinquis neque alienis neque alio abbate sine uoluntate fratrum.

CCCXC De monacho digno episcopatus

I 190v Abbas si habuerit monachum dignum episcopatum, debet dare si necesse est.

CCCXCI De ordinatis non adunatis

Qui ordinati sunt ab episcopis, qui in pascha et tonsura adunati non sunt catholicae ecclesiae, iterum ab episcopo catholico manus inpositione confirmentur.

2–3 *Iud. Theod. U* II.2.3   **5–6** *Iud. Theod. U* II.6.1   **8** *Iud. Theod. U* II.6.2   **10–12** *Iud. Theod. U* II.6.3-4   **14** *Iud. Theod. U* II.6.10   **16–17** cf. *Iud. Theod. U* II.9.1; cf. *Iud. Theod. G* 116

---

1 CCCLXXXVI] CCCLXXXI M   **1** Non cogendum abbatem ad synodum] *deest* IL Non agendum abbatem ad synodum M   **2** abbatem] abbate L   **2** synodum] sinodum L   **4** CCCLXXXVII] CCCLXXXII M   **4** De electione alterius abbatis] *deest* IL **5** humiliatione] humiliationem L   **5** permissione] permissionem M   **5** derelinquere] derelinquere potest M   **6** elegant] elongant L   **6** sibi] si L *deest* M   **7** CCCLXXXVIII] CCCLXXXIII M   **7** De non retinendo abbato in loco suo] *deest* IL   **9** CCCLXXXVIIII] CCCLXXXIIII M   **9** De congregationis electione abbatis] *deest* IL   **10** sibi] si L **12** abbate] abbate abbate L   **13** CCCXC] CCCLXXXV M   **13** De monacho digno episcopatus] *deest* IL   **14** episcopatum] episcopatu M   **15** CCCXCI] CCCLXXVI M   **15** De ordinatis non adunatis] *deest* IL   **16** episcopis] episcopo L   **16** tonsura] tunsura L **16–17** catholicae] catholice L   **17** confirmentur] confirmetur I

118 Collectio CCCC capitulorum

CCCXCII De confirmatione aecclesiae
Similiter et ecclesiae quae ab ipsis episcopis ordinentur, aqua exorcizata aspargantur et aliqua collectione confirmentur.

M 206v

CCCXCIII De non dando chrisma non adunatiss
5 Licentiam quoque non habemus, eis poscentibus chrismam uel eucharistiam dare, nisi ante confessi fierint, uelle se nobiscum esse in unitate ecclesiae.

CCCXCIIII De inmundo liquore
Si sorex uel mus ceciderit in liquorem, tollatur inde et aspargatur aqua sancta et sumatur, si uiuens. Si uero mortua, omnis liquor proicitatur foras et
10 mundatur uas.

L 117v

CCCXCV De non confirmatis ab episcopo
Nullum perfectum credimus in baptismo sine confirmatione episcopi, non disperamus tamen.

CCCXCVI De consecratione abbatis
15 In abbatis uero ordinationem episcopus debet missam celebrare et eum benedicere inclinato capite cum duobus uel tribus testibus de fratribus suis, et dat ei precepta uitae aeternae custodia.

I 191r

2–3 *Iud. Theod. U* II.9.2 **5–6** cf. *Iud. Theod. U* II.9.3 **8–10** *Iud. Theod. U* I.7.8 **12–13** *Iud. Theod. U* II.4.5 **15–17** *Iud. Theod. U* II.3.5

---

1 CCCXCII⟧ CCCLXXXXVII M   1 De confirmatione aecclesiae⟧ *deest* IL De confirmatione ecclesiae M   2 et⟧ *deest* L   2 quae⟧ que L   2 ordinentur⟧ ordinantur L   2 exorcizata⟧ exorcizata L   2–3 aspargantur⟧ spargantur L aspergantur M   3 collectione⟧ collectionem L   3 confirmentur⟧ confirmantur L   4 CCCXCIII⟧ CCCLXXXVIII M   4 De non dando chrisma non adunatiss⟧ *deest* IL De non dando chrisma non adunatis M   5 chrismam⟧ crismam LM   6 fierint⟧ fuerint M   6 uelle se⟧ uelles est L   6 nobiscum⟧ uobiscum L   7 CCCXCIIII⟧ CCCLXXXVIIII M   7 De inmundo liquore⟧ *deest* IL   8 sorex⟧ sarex* I surrex L surex M   8 aspargatur⟧ spargatur* L aspergatur M   9 uiuens⟧ uiuens sit M   9 proicitatur⟧ proitiatur I   10 mundatur⟧ mundetur M   11 CCCXCV⟧ CCCXC M   11 De non confirmatis ab episcopo⟧ Nectio qui sita IL   12 perfectum⟧ profectum M   12 sine⟧ si non I   12–13 non disperamus tamen⟧ tamen non disperamus M   14 CCCXCVI⟧ CCCXCI M   14 abbatis⟧ abbatis et abbatissa IL   15 ordinationem⟧ ordinatione LM   15 celebrare⟧ caelebrare L   16 dat⟧ data M   17 aeternae⟧ aeterne L aeterna M

Collectio CCCC capitulorum

119

CCCXCVII De consecratione abbatissae
Presbiter potest abbatissam consecrare cum missae celebratione.

CCCXCVIII Bigamus
Digamus peniteat uno anno, iiii et vi feria et in tribus quadragesimis abstineat
se a carnibus. Non dimittat tamen uxorem.

CCCXCVIIII <Et trigami>
Trigamus et supra, id est in iiii aut quinto uel plus, vii annos, iiii feria et vi et
in tribus xlmis abstineat se a carnibus. Non separantur tamen. Basilius hoc
iudicauit in canone autem iiii annos.

CCCC De baptismo hereticorum
Si quis baptizatus est ab heretico qui recte trinitatem non crediderit iterum
debet baptizari.

M 207r **CCCCI** De Simone et Saulo
Si necessitas extrema cogerit, catholicum ut alium non inueniat et per aliquem
extra unitatem catholicam positum acciperit, quae olim erat in ipsa catholicae
I 191v unitate accepturus, eum baptizatum et moriturum catholicum deputamus.

Aliud sit sacramentum, quod habere potuit Simon Magus, aliud operatio spiritus, qui in malis etiam hominibus fieri solet, sicut Saul habuit prophetiam;

---

2 *Iud. Theod.* U II.3.4   **4–5** *Iud. Theod.* U I.14.2; *Exc. Cumm.* III.19   **7–9** *Iud. Theod.*
U I.14.3; *Exc. Cumm.* III.20   **11–12** cf. *Iud. Theod.* G 27; U I.5.6   **14–16** cf. Aug., *De
baptismo* I.2   **17–120.4** cf. Aug., *De baptismo* III.16

---

1 CCCXCVII] CCCXCII M   **1** De consecratione abbatissae] *deest* IL   **2** missae] missa L   **2** celebratione] celebrationae L   **3** CCCXCVIII] CCCXCIII M   **3** Bigamus] De
bigamus L De bigamis M   **4** Digamus] Bicamus L   **4** peniteat] paniteat L paeniteat M
4 iiii] iii feria L   **4** feria] ferias I   **4** quadragesimis] xl^{mis} LM   **5** carnibus] carnalibus
L   **5–8** dimittat tamen…Non] *deest* M   **6** <Et trigami>] *deest* IL   **7** iiii] iiiia feria L
7 aut] et L   **7** quinto] vi L   **7** feria] ferias I   **8** tribus] tres L   **8** separantur] seperen-
tur L separentur M   **9** autem] aut IM   **9** iiii] iiiior M   **9** annos] annus L   **10** CCCC]
CCCXCIIII M   **10** De baptismo hereticorum] *deest* IL   **11** non crediderit] crediderit I
12 baptizari] baptizare L baptizare *corr.* baptizari M   **13** CCCCI] CCCXCV M   **13** De
Simone et Saulo] *deest* IL De Symone et Saule M   **14** extrema] extra M   **14** cogerit] coierit L   **15** acciperit] accipere L   **15** quae] que L quia M   **15** erat] erant M   **15** ipsa]
ipsam M   **15** catholicae] cotholica I catholica L catholicam M   **18** prophetiam] prophetam
L

120 Collectio CCCC capitulorum

aliud operatio eiusdem spiritus, quam nisi boni habere non possunt, sicut est finis precepti caritas de corde puro et conscientia bona et fide non ficta, quod heretici non habent, quia caritas proprium donum est catholicae unitatis et pacis.

5 CCCCII De aqua ecclesiae
Aqua quippe ecclesiae fidelis et salutaris et sancta est bene utentibus. Ea uero bene uti extra ecclesiam nemo potest. Ergo ecclesia paradiso conparata: *L 118r*
nam et flumina de fonte paradisi foras largiter per terras fluant extra paradisum. Constituta sunt, omnibus notum est. Nec tamen in Mesopotamia, uel
10 in Aegypto, quo illa flumina peruenerunt, est felicitas uitae, quod in paradiso commemoratur. Ita sit, ut, cum paradisi aqua sit extra paradisum, beatitudo tamen non sit nisi intra paradisum. Sic ergo baptismum ecclesie potest esse   *I 192r;*
extra ecclesiam, munus autem beatae uitae non nisi intra ecclesiam repperitur,   *M 207v*
quae super petram etiam fundata est, quae ligandi et soluendi accipit claues.
15 Haec est una quae habet et possidet omnem sponsi sui et Domini potestatem.

CCCCIII De libertate a rege terreno
Et tu si uis nihil debere terreno regi, relinque omnia quae tua sunt, et sequere Christum.

Reddite ergo quae sunt Caesaris Caesari, id est, tributum et pecuniam, Et quae

---

1–2 1 Tim 1:5   **6–7** Aug., *De baptismo* IV.2   **7–15** cf. Aug., *De baptismo*, IV.1   **17–18** cf. Mt 19:27; *Hibernensis* 24.10 (p. 152, ln. 21-2)   **1–4** cf. *Anonymi in Matthaeum*, 22.21; Beda, *In Lucae euangelium* V.20; Beda, *In Marci euangelium*, III.12

---

1 operatio] *deest* L   1 est] *deest* L   2 precepti] precepta L   2 caritas] caritatis* I
3 habent] habes L   3 donum] domum L   3 catholicae] catholice L   5 CCCCII] CC-
CXCVI M   5 De aqua ecclesiae] *deest* IL   6 quippe] *deest* M   6 ecclesiae] ecclesie L
6 salutaris] saluatoris L   7 uti] utentibus L   7 ecclesiam] ecclesia M   7 nemo] ne L
7 paradiso] paradyso M   8 paradisi] paradysi LM   8 fluant] flant L   8–9 paradisum]
paradysum LM   10 Aegypto] Egypto L   10 in] *superscriptum* I   10 paradiso] paradyso
LM   11 commemoratur] commeratur L   11 paradisi] paradysi LM   11 paradisum]
paradysum LM   12 tamen] autem L   12 intra] in M   12 paradisum] paradysum
LM   12 Sic] Si L   12 baptismum] baptismus L baptismi M   12 ecclesie] ecclesiae
L   13 munus] minus M   13 beatae] beate L   14 quae] que L   14 petram] petram
corr. petrum I   14 etiam] aetiam L   14 quae] que L   14 accipit] accepit L   15 Haec]
Hec L   15 quae] que L   15 Domini] Deum M   16 CCCCIII] CCCXCVII M   16 De
libertate a rege terreno] *deest* IL   17 quae] que L   1 quae] que L   1 Caesaris]
Cesaris LM   1 Caesari] Cesari LM   1 quae] que L

Collectio CCCC capitulorum

121

Dei sunt Deo, decimas et primitias, oblationes ac uictimas sentiamus, quomodo et ipse reddidit tributa pro se et pro Petro et reddit Deo quae sunt Patris
faciens eius uoluntatem.

CCCCIIII DE TERMINIS ANTIQUIS
Ne transgredieris terminos antiquos qui a patribus constituti sunt.

Aurelius episcopus dixit: Auaritiae cupiditatem quam uero omnium malorum
matrem esse, nemo quis dubitet. Proinde inhibendum est ut ne quis alienum
finem usurpet aut per premium terminos patrum statutos transcendat.

I 192v Uae qui coniungitis domum ad domum et agrum agro copulatis, usque ad
terminum loci: numquid uos soli habitatis in medio terrae?

Si contempsi subire iuditium cum seruo meo, et ancillae meae cum disceptarent
aduersum me.

L 118v Denique non presumat quis respuere, non iudicari cum monacho.

Quae acciperis, reddenda sunt, cum fenore fortisque dilatio usuram parturiit.

---

5 Prov 22:28   **6–8** *Can. in causa Apiarii A* §5   **9–10** Isa 5:8   **11–12** Iob 31:13   **14**
Hibernensis 32.11 (p. 236, ln. 12-13)

---

1 Dei sunt] sunt Dei M   **1** et] *deest* LM   **1** primitias] primicias L   **1** ac] aut
M   **1** uictimas] uictimen L   **2** reddidit] reddidet* I reddet LM   **2** pro Petro] Petro M   **2** quae] que L   **2** sunt] Dei sunt M   **2** Patris] Patri M   **3** eius] ^{I} *deest* LM
4 CCCCIIII] CCCXCVIII M   **4** DE TERMINIS ANTIQUIS] *deest* IL   **5** transgredieris] tra-
sgredieris* L   **5** qui] que L quae M   **5** constituti sunt] constitum L constitutum est M
6 Auaritiae] Auariciae L   **7** est] *deest* M   **7** alienum] alienus L alienis M   **8** finem]
fines M   **8** transcendat] transcendas* L   **9** agro] ad agro L ad agrum M   **10** terminum]
termium M   **10** terrae] terre L   **11** iuditium] iudicium LM   **11** ancillae] ancille
L   **12** me] mae L   **13–14** Denique...parturiit] *lacuna* M   **13** iudicari] iudicare L
14 Quae] Que L   **14** acciperis] acceperis L   **14** parturiit] parturit L

Appendix 1

Index titulorum Paris 2316, fols. 34V–35V

	HAEC SUNT PRECEPTA QUOD DOMINUS PRECEPIT MOYSI CAPITULA XXXVIII
	Moyses turpitudinis multiplicius consanguinitatis quam legis Theodosi et romanorum CAPITULA VII
	DE SEPTEM AETATIS PARENTORUM XL
	DE PROPINQUI DE MATRIMONIO
LXVIII	Interrogacio Augustinus si debeant duo germani fratres singulas sorores accipere qui sunt ab illis longa progenia generati
LXVIII	De propinquitate
LXXXVIII	Interrogacio Augustinus cum unu sit fides
LXXXVIIII	Haec noua testamenti canones subsequentes apostolorum Clemens [canones]
	DE GRADU ECCLESIE CAPITULA L
CLII	LEONIS PAPE respondit ad Posicium episcopi Narbonensis
CLIII	De monachis qui aut militare coperint aut uxores acciperint
CLIIII	De puellis non consecratis si post nupserint
CLV	De his qui parentibus paruoli derelicti sunt seu ab ostibus capti et utrum baptizati sunt non potest inueniri annus debeant baptizari
CLVI	Si nesciunt in qua secta sunt baptizati
CLVII	De paruolis baptizatis agentibus capti et gentiliter uiuere
CLVIII	Horum causa dei iudiciore seruanda est
CLVIIII	Sergii papae
CLX	
CLX	Sinodus quirinensium

123

CLXII	
CLXIII	Et in alia
CLXIIII	Anquirinensium
CLXV	
CLXVI	Et in alia
CLXVII	
CLXVIII	
CLXVIIII	Anquirinensium
CLXXVI	Anquirinensium
	canones cesarum CLXXVII
	Gangrensium [canones] CLXXXI
	Sinodus calcidonensium CXCV
	canones constancii episcopo CCI
	Canones sardicenses CCVII
	Statuta Acionemsium CCVII
	SINODUS SILUESTRI IN ROMA CUM CCLXXXIIII EPISCOPIS ET CONSTANTINO ET HELENA CCXII
CCXVIII	Caelestinus papa
CCXXI	Caelestinus papa de ultima penitencia
CCXXII	Leonis non inponendis manibus penitencia
CCXXIII	diaconus uel prebiteris
	STATUTA ECCLESIA UNICA INCIPIUNT
CCXXVIII	De paenitencia
CCXXVIIII	Innocencius papae
CCXLVI	Aratensis DC episcoporum
CCL	Sinodus aralatensis
CCLI	Sinodus agatensis
CCLV	Sinodus auilianensis
CCLVII	In capitulum cononis
CCLX	Interrogande romanis
CCLXI	De paenitentibus propter uinus
CCLXV	De confitentibus
CCLXVII	De adultera
CCLXXI	Ab ostibus capta
CCLXXVI	De uoto mulieris
CCLXXVIII	De paenitentia intima
CCXCIIII	De sanctaemoniale fornicaria

PRIMARY SOURCES

Augustinus Hipponensis, *De baptismo libri septem*, ed. M. Petschenig, *Sancti Aureli Augustini Scripta contra Donatistas*, CSEL 51 (Vienna/Leipzig, 1908), 143–376.

Augustinus Hipponensis, *Sermones 1–50*, ed. C. Lambot, CCSL 41 (Turnhout, 1961).

Beda Uenerabilis, *In Lucae evangelium exposition*, ed. D. Hurst, *Beda Venerabilis: Opera exegetica*, CCSL 120 (Turnhout, 1960, repr. 2001), 1–425.

Beda Uenerabilis, *In Marci evangelium expositio*, ed. D. Hurst, *Beda Venerabilis: Opera exegetica*, CCSL 120 (Turnhout, 1960, repr. 2001), 427–648.

Bonifatius, *Epistolae*, ed. Michael Tangl, MGH, Epp. sel. 1 (Berlin, 1916).

Breviarium Pauli, ed. Gustavus Hänel, *Lex Romana Visigothorum* (Leipzig, 1849), 338–445.

Caelestinus I, *Epistola 4*, *PL* 50, cols. 429–36.

Caelestinus I, *Epistula 5*, *PL* 50, cols. 436–38.

Canones Apostolorum, ed. A. Strewe, *Die Canonessammlung des Dionysius Exiguus in der ersten Redaktion* (Berlin, 1931), 1–10; and in: *EOMIA*, 1:32a–32ii.

Canones in causa Apiarii ed. C. Munier, *Concilia Africae A. 345–A. 525*, CCSL 149 (Turnhout, 1974), 95–165.

Capitularia Benedicti Levitae, *PL* 97, cols. 699–912; ed. Pertz, MGH LL II.2, 39–158.

Collectio canonum Hibernensis, ed. Roy Flechner, *The Hibernensis. Book 1: A Study and Edition*, Studies in Medieval and Early Modern Canon Law (Washington DC, 2019); ed. Hermann Wasserschleben, *Die irische Kanonensammlung*, 2nd edition (Leipzig, 1885, repr: Aalen, 1966).

Columbanus, *Paenitentiale*, ed. Ludwig Bieler, *The Irish Penitentials*, Scriptores Latini Hiberniae 5 (Dublin, 1963), 96–107.

Concilium Agathense (Agde, 506), ed. Charles Munier, *Concilia Galliae A. 314-A. 506*, CCSL 148 (Turnhout, 1963), 189–228.

Concilium Ancyrense (Ancyra, 314), in: *EOMIA* II, 54–115.

Concilium Antiochense, (Antioch, 341), in: *EOMIA* II.2, 216–320.

126   Collectio CCCC capitulorum

Concilium Arausicanum (Orange, 441), ed. Charles Munier, *Concilia Galliae A. 314-A. 506,* CCSL 148 (Turnhout, 1963), 76–93.

Concilium Arelatense (Arles, 314), ed. Charles Munier, *Concilia Galliae A. 314-A. 506,* CCSL 148 (Turnhout, 1963), 3–25.

Concilium Arelatense secundum (Arles, 442–506), ed. Charles Munier, *Concilia Galliae A. 314-A. 506,* CCSL 148 (Turnhout, 1963), 111–30.

Concilium Aurelianense (Orléans, 511), ed. Charles Munier, *Concilia Galliae A. 511-A. 695,* CCSL 148A (Turnhout, 1963), 3–19.

Concilium Carthaginense (Carthage, 390), ed. Charles Munier, *Concilia Africae A. 345-A. 525,* CCSL 149 (Turnhout, 1974), 11–19.

Concilium Carthaginense (Carthage, 419), ed. Charles Munier, *Concilia Africae A. 345-A. 525,* CCSL 149 (Turnhout, 1974), 89–94.

Concilium Chalcedonense (Chalcedon, 451), ed. E. Mühlenberg, in: Giuseppe Alberigo *et. al., The oecumenical councils, volume 1: From Nicaea I to Nicaea II (325–787),* Conciliorum Oecumenicorum Generaliumque Decreta, Corpus Christianorum (Turnhout, 2006), 119–51.

Concilium Constantinopolitanum (Constantinople, 381), ed. A.M. Ritter, in: Giuseppe Alberigo *et. al., The oecumenical councils, volume 1: From Nicaea I to Nicaea II (325–787),* Conciliorum Oecumenicorum Generaliumque Decreta, Corpus Christianorum (Turnhout, 2006), 35–70.

Concilium Gangrense (Gangra, *ca.* 340), in: *EOMIA* II, 147–214.

Concilium Neocaesariense (Neocaesarea, 315), ed. A. Strewe, *Die Canones-sammlung des Dionysius Exiguus in der ersten Redaktion* (Berlin, 1931), 38–40; and in: *EOMIA* II, 12–14, 116–41.

Concilium Nicaenum I (Nicaea, 325), ed. Giuseppe Alberigo, in: Giuseppe Alberigo *et. al., The oecumenical councils, volume 1: From Nicaea I to Nicaea II (325–787),* Conciliorum Oecumenicorum Generaliumque Decreta, Corpus Christianorum (Turnhout, 2006), 1–34.

Concilium Regense A. (Riez, 439), ed. Charles Munier, *Concilia Galliae A. 314-A. 506,* CCSL 148 (Turnhout, 1963), 61–75.

Concilium Sardicense (Sardica, 342–3), *PL* 56, cols. 773–84; and in: *EOMIA* I, 452–544.

Concilium Ualentinum (Valence, 374), ed. Charles Munier, *Concilia Galliae A. 314-A. 506,* CCSL 148 (Turnhout, 1963), 35–45.

Constitutum Sylvestri, ed. Eckhard Wirbelauer, *Zwei Päpste in Rom: Der Konflikt zwischen Laurentius und Symmachus (498–514). Studien und Texte,* Quellen und Forschungen zur antiken Welt (Munich, 1993), 227–47.

Epitome Gai, ed. J. Baviera, *Fontes iuris Romani antejustiniani* (Florence, 1968), II: 229–57.

Primary Sources 127

Gregorius I, *Libellus responsionum*, ed. L.M. Hartmann, *Gregorii I Registrum*, MGH Epp. 2 (Berlin, 1899), pp. 332–43 (no. 11.56) and ed. Valeria Mattaloni, *Rescriptum beati Gregorii papae ad Augustinum episcopum quem saxoniam in praedicatione direxerat, seu Libellus responsionum* (Florence 2017), pp. 505–53.

Gregorius I, *Regula Pastoralis*, ed. B. Judic, F. Rommel, and C. Morel, *Règle pastorale*, Sources chrétiennes 381–82 (Paris, 1992).

Hermas Pastor, ed. Christian Tornau and Paolo Cecconi (eds.), *The Shepherd of Hermas in Latin: Critical edition of the oldest translation Vulgata*, Texte und Untersuchungen zur Geschichte der altchristlichen Literatur 173 (Berlin/Boston, 2014) ('Vulgate' version); ed. A. Vezzoni, *Il Pastore di Erma* (Florence 1994) 48–230 ('Palatine version')

Hieronymus, *Commentarii in euangelius Mattheaei, PL* 26, cols. 15–218.

Hieronymus, *Commentarii in iu epistulas Paulinas*, ed. G. Raspanti, CCSL 77C (Turnhout, 2006).

Hieronymus, *Epistulae*, ed. I. Hilberg, CSEL 54–6 (Vienna, 1910–1918).

Innocent I, *ep. 2, ad Victricium*, ed. P. Coustant, *Epistolae Romanorum Pontificum ... ab anno Christi 67 ad annum 440* (Paris, 1721), 746–58.

Innocent I, *ep. 6, ad Exsuperium*, ed. P. Coustant, *Epistolae Romanorum Pontificum ... ab anno Christi 67 ad annum 440* (Paris, 1721), 789–96.

Iudicia Theodori, ed. Paul Willem Finsterwalder, *Die Canones Theodori Cantuariensis und ihre* Überlieferungsformen, Untersuchungen zu den Bußbüchern des 7., 8. und 9. Jahrhunderts 1 (Weimar, 1929); see also the online edition by Michael Elliot, http://individual. utoronto.ca/michaelelliot/manuscripts/texts/iudicia_theodori. html (accessed December 2022)

Iudicia Theodori, Canones Cottoniani (C), 271–84

Iudicia Theodori, Capitula Dacheriana (D), 239–52

Iudicia Theodori, Canones Gregorii (G), 253–70

Iudicia Theodori, Discipulus Umbrensium (U), 285–334

Iudicia Theodori, Canones Basilienses (Ba), ed. Franz Bernd Asbach, 'Das Poenitentiale Remense und der sogen. Excarpsus Cummeani' (Unpubl. Ph.D thesis, University of Regensburg, 1975), supplement: 79–89.

Leo I, *Epistula 159, ad Nicetam, PL* 54, cols. 1135B–1140A.

Leo I, *Epistula 167, ad Rusticum, PL* 54, cols. 1197A–1209B.

Paenitentiale Bobbiense, ed. Raymund Kottje, *Paenitentialia Franciae et Italiae saeculi VIII-IX*, CCSL 156 (Turnhout, 1994), 66–71.

128   Collectio CCCC capitulorum

Paenitentiale Burgundense, ed. Raymund Kottje, *Paenitentialia Franciae et Italiae saeculi VIII-IX*, CCSL 156 (Turnhout, 1994), 61–65.

Paenitentiale Columbani, ed. Ludwig Bieler, *The Irish Penitentials*, Scriptores Latini Hiberniae 5 (Dublin, 1963), 96–107

Paenitentiale Cummeani, ed. Ludwig Bieler, *The Irish Penitentials*, Scriptores Latini Hiberniae 5 (Dublin, 1963), 108–35

Paenitentiale Ecgberhti, ed. H.J. Schmitz, *Die Bussbücher und das kanonische Bussverfahren, nach handschriftlichen Quellen dargestellt* (Düsseldorf, 1898; repr. Graz, 1958), 661–74.

Paenitentiale Excarpsus Cummeani, ed. H.J. Schmitz, *Die Bussbücher und das kanonische Bussverfahren: Nach handschriftlichen Quellen dargestellt* (Düsseldorf, 1898; repr. Graz, 1958), 597–644.

Paenitentiale Floriacense, ed. Raymund Kottje, *Paenitentialia Franciae et Italiae saeculi VIII-IX*, CCSL 156 (Turnhout, 1994), 95–103

Paenitentiale Hubertense, ed. Raymund Kottje, *Paenitentialia Franciae et Italiae saeculi VIII-IX*, CCSL 156 (Turnhout, 1994), 105–15.

Paenitentiale Merseburgense A, ed. Raymund Kottje, *Paenitentialia Franciae et Italiae saeculi VIII-IX*, CCSL 156 (Turnhout, 1994). 123–69.

Paenitentiale Merseburgense B, ed. Raymund Kottje, *Paenitentialia Franciae et Italiae saeculi VIII-IX*, CCSL 156 (Turnhout, 1994). 173–77.

Paenitentiale Sletstatense, ed. Raymund Kottje, *Paenitentialia Franciae et Italiae saeculi VIII-IX*, CCSL 156 (Turnhout, 1994), 81–85

Statuta Bonifatii, ed. R. Pokorny, MGH Capit. episc. 3 (Hannover, 1995), 354–56.

Statuta Ecclesiae Antiqua, ed. Charles Munier, *Les Statuta Ecclesiae Antiqua* (Paris, 1960).

Sylloge canonum Africanorum Collectionis Laureshamensis, ed. Charles Munier, *Concilia Africae A. 345–A. 525*, CCSL 149 (Turnhout, 1974), 320–22.

Symmachus, *Epistula 15, ad Caesarium Arelatensem*, ed. Andreas Thiel, *Epistolae Romanorum pontificum... a S. Hilaro usque ad Pelagium II* (Braunsberg, 1868), 723–28.

Synodus II S. Patricii (Second Synod of Patrick), ed. Ludwig Bieler, *The Irish Penitentials*, Scriptores Latini Hiberniae 5 (Dublin, 1963), 184–97; and ed. Aidan Breen, 'The Date, Provenance and Authorship of the Pseudo-Patrician Canonical Materials', *Zeitschrift der Savigny-Stiftung für Rechtsgeschichte, Kanonistische Abteilung*, 112:125 (1995), 83–129, at 112–21.

SECONDARY LITERATURE

Archi, Gian Gualberto, *'L'Epitome Gai'*, *Studio sul tardo diritto romano in occidente* (Milan, 1937; repr. Naples, 1991).

Bieler, Ludwig, *The Irish Penitentials*, Scriptores Latini Hiberniae (Dublin, 1963).

Bischoff, Bernhard, 'An Hiberno-Latin introduction to the Gospels', *Thought: a Review of Culture and Idea* 54 (1979), 233–37.

——, *Die südostdeutschen Schreibschulen und Bibliotheken in der Karolingerzeit*, 2 vols. (Wiesbaden, 1974–80).

——, *Katalog der festländischen Handschriften des neunten Jahrhunderts (mit Ausnahme der wisigotischen)*, 3 vols. (Wiesbaden, 1998–2014).

Breen, Aidan, 'The date, provenance and authorship of the pseudo-Patrician canonical materials', *Zeitschrift der Savigny-Stiftung für Rechtsgeschichte, Kanonistische Abteilung* 112:125 (1995), 83–129.

Charles-Edwards, Thomas, 'The penitential of Theodore and the Iudicia Theodori', in: Michael Lapidge (ed.), *Archbishop Theodore. Commemorative Studies on his Life and Influence* (Cambridge 1995), 141–74.

Conrat (Cohn), Max, *Breviarium Alaricianum* (Leipzig, 1903).

——, *Geschichte der Quellen und Literatur des römischen Rechts im frühen Mittelalter* (Aalen, 1891).

Davies, Luned Mair, 'Statuta ecclesiae antiqua and the Gallic councils in the Hibernensis', *Peritia* 14 (2000), 85–110.

Elliot, Michael D., 'Canon law collections in England ca 600–1066: The manuscript evidence' (Unpubl. PhD thesis, University of Toronto, 2013).

Elsakkers, Marianne, 'The Early Medieval Latin and Vernacular Vocabulary of Abortion and Embryology', in: Michèle Goyens, Pieter de Leemans, An Smets (eds), *Science Translated: Latin and Vernacular Translations of Scientific Treatises in Medieval Europe* (Louvain, 2008), 377–414.

Finsterwalder, Paul Willem, *Die Canones Theodori Cantuariensis und ihre Überlieferungsformen*, Untersuchungen Zu Den Bußbüchern Des 7., 8. Und 9. Jahrhunderts (Weimar, 1929).

130   Collectio CCCC capitulorum

Flechner, Roy, 'An insular tradition of ecclesiastical law: fifth to eighth century', in: James Graham-Campbell and Michael Ryan (eds.), *Anglo-Saxon/Irish relations before the Vikings*, Proceedings of the British Academy (Oxford, 2009), 23–46.

——, 'The problem of originality in early medieval canon law: legislating by means of contradictions in the Collectio Hibernensis', *Viator* 43:2 (2012), 29–47.

——, *The Hibernensis*, Studies in Medieval and Early Modern Canon Law, 2 vols. (Washington DC, 2019).

Fournier, Paul, 'De l'influence de la collection irlandaise sur la formation des collections canoniques', *Nouvelle revue historique de droit français et étranger* 23 (1899), 27–78.

——, 'Le Liber ex lege Moysi et les tendances bibliques du droit canonique Irlandais', *Revue Celtique* 30 (1909), 221–34.

Fournier, Paul and Gabriel Le Bras, *Histoire des collections canoniques en occident dépuis les Fausses Décrétales jusqu'au Décret de Gratien* (Paris, 1931).

Fransen, Irénée, 'Trente-quatre questions sur Saint-Paul passés sous le nom de Saint Grégoire', *Revue Bénédictine* 73 (1963), 244–76.

Gaudemet, Jean, 'Survivances romaines dans le droit de la monarchie francque du Ve au Xe siècle', *Tijdschrift voor Rechtsgeschiedenis* 23 (1955), 149–206.

Glauche, Günter, *Katalog der lateinischen Handschriften der Bayerischen Staatsbibliothek München: Die Pergamenthandschriften aus Benediktbeuern: Clm 4501–4663* (Wiesbaden, 1994).

Haggenmüller, Reinhold, 'Zur Rezeption der Beda und Egbert zugeschriebenen Bußbücher', in Hubert Mordek (ed.), *Aus Archiven und Bibliotheken. Festschrift für Raymund Kottje zum 65. Geburtstag*, Freiburger Beiträge zur mittelalterlichen Geschichte, Studien und Texte 3 (Frankfurt am Main, 1992), 149–59.

Hartmann, Wilfried, *Kirche und Kirchenrecht um 900. Die Bedeutung der spätkarolingischen Zeit für Tradition und Innovation im kirchlichen Recht*, MGH Schriften 58 (Hannover, 2008).

Hauswald, E., 'Pirmins Scarapsus. Einleitung und Edition', unpubl. PhD diss. University of Konstanz, 2006).

Hoffmann, Hartmut and Rudolf Pokorny, *Das Dekret des Bischofs Burchard von Worms. Textstufen–Frühe Verbreitung–Vorlagen*, MGH Hilfsmittel 12 (Munich, 1991).

Secondary Literature 131

Hörmann, Walther von, 'Bußbücherstudien I', *Zeitschrift der Savigny-Stiftung für Rechtsgeschichte, Kanonistische Abteilung* 1 (1911), 195–250.

——, 'Bußbücherstudien II', *Zeitschrift der Savigny-Stiftung für Rechtsgeschichte, Kanonistische Abteilung* 2 (1912), 11–181.

——, 'Bußbücherstudien III', *Zeitschrift der Savigny-Stiftung für Rechtsgeschichte, Kanonistische Abteilung* 3 (1913), 413–92.

——, 'Bußbücherstudien IV', *Zeitschrift der Savigny-Stiftung für Rechtsgeschichte, Kanonistische Abteilung* 4 (1914), 358–483.

Kéry, Lotte, *Canonical collections of the early Middle Ages (ca. 400–1140): a bibliographical guide to the manuscripts and literature*, History of Medieval Canon Law (Washington, DC, 1999).

Körntgen, Ludger, 'Der Excarpsus Cummeani, ein Bußbuch aus Corbie', in: O. Münsch and T. Zotz, *Scientia Veritatis: Festschrift für Hubert Mordek zum 65. Geburtstag* (Ostfildern, 2004), 59–75.

Kottje, Raymund, *Die Bussbücher Halitgars von Cambrai und des Hrabanus Maurus: Ihre Überlieferung und ihre Quellen* (Berlin/New York, 1980).

——, 'Paenitentiale Theodori', in: *Handwörterbuch zur deutschen Rechtsgeschichte* 3 (Berlin 1984), cols. 1413–16.

Lapidge, Michael and Richard Sharpe, *A Bibliography of Celtic-Latin Literature 400–1200* (Dublin, 1985).

Maassen, Friedrich, *Geschichte der Quellen und der Literatur des canonischen Rechts im Abendlande bis zum Ausgang des Mittelalters* (Graz, 1870).

Mahadevan, Letha, 'Überlieferung und Verbreitung des Bußbuchs "Capitula Iudiciorum"', *Zeitschrift der Savigny-Stiftung für Rechtsgeschichte, Kanonistische Abteilung* 72 (1986), 17–75

Mair Davies, Luned, 'Statuta ecclesiae antiqua and the Gallic councils in the Hibernensis', *Peritia* 14 (2000), 85–110.

Masson, A. *Manuscrits des Bibliothèques sinistrées de 1940 à 1944*, Catalogue général des manuscrits des bibliothèques publiques de France 53 (Paris, 1962).

Mazal, O., 'Die Salzburger Dom- und Klosterbibliothek in karolingischer Zeit', *Codices Manuscripti* 3 (1977), 44–61.

McKitterick, Rosamond, 'Knowledge of canon law in the Frankish kingdoms before 789: the manuscript evidence', *Journal of Theological Studies* 36 (1985), 97–117.

132   Collectio CCCC capitulorum

Meeder, Sven, 'Biblical past and canonical present: the case of the Collectio 400 Capitulorum', in: Clemens Gantner, Rosamond McKitterick, and Sven Meeder (eds.), *The Resources of the Past in Early Medieval Europe* (Cambridge, 2015), 103–17.

——, 'Text and identities in the Synodus II S. Patricii', *Zeitschrift der Savigny-Stiftung für Rechtsgeschichte, Kanonistische Abteilung* 98 (2012), 19–45.

——, 'The Liber ex lege Moysi: notes and text', *Journal of Medieval Latin* 19 (2009), 173–218.

Meens, Rob, *Het tripartite boeteboek. Overlevering en betekenis van vroeg-middeleeuwse biechtvoorschriften (met editie en vertaling van vier tripartita)*, Middeleeuwse Studies en Bronnen (Hilversum, 1994).

——, *Penance in Medieval Europe, 600–1200* (Cambridge, 2014).

Mistry, Zubin, *Abortion in the Early Middle Ages, C. 500–900* (York, 2015).

Mordek, Hubert, *Kirchenrecht und Reform im Frankenreich: die Collectio Vetus Gallica, die älteste systematische Kanonessammlung des Fränkischen Gallien*, Beiträge Zur Geschichte Und Quellenkunde Des Mittelalters (Berlin, 1975).

Munier, Charles, *Les statuta ecclesiae antiqua*. Édition, *études critiques*, Bibliothèque de l'Institut de Droit Canonique de l'Université de Strasbourg 5 (Paris, 1960).

Naz, Raoul, 'Quatre cents chapitres (Collection en)', in: Raoul Naz and Antoine Villien (eds.), *Dictionnaire de droit canonique, contenant tous les termes du droit canonique, avec un sommaire de l'histoire et des institutions et de l'état actuel de la discipline*, 7 vols. (Paris, 1935–1965), VII: col. 425.

Nürnberger, August J, 'Über die Würzburger Handschrift der irischen Canonensammlung', *Archiv für Katholisches Kirchenrecht* 60 (1888), 1–84.

Ó Corráin, Donnchadh, 'Synodus II Patricii and vernacular law', *Peritia* 16 (2002), 335–343.

Reynolds, Roger E., 'Canon law collections in early ninth-century Salzburg', in: S. G. Kuttner and K. Pennington (eds.), *Proceedings of the fifth international congress of medieval canon law, Salamanca 21–25 September 1976* (Vatican City, 1980), 15–34.

——, 'Unity and diversity in Carolingian canon law collections: the case of the Collectio Hibernensis and its derivatives', in: U.-R. Blumenthal (ed.), *Carolingian essays: Andrew W. Mellon lectures in early Christian Studies* (Washington, DC, 1983), 99–135.

Secondary Literature 133

Schiller, A. Arthur, *Roman Law: Mechanisms of Development* (The Hague/ New York, 1978).

Seckel, Emil, 'Benedictus Levita decurtatus et excerptus: eine Studie zu den Handschriften der falschen Kapitularien', in: *Festschrift für Heinrich Brunner zum fünfzigjährigen Doktorjubiläum* (Munich/ Leipzig, 1914), 377–464.

Vogel, Cyrille, *Les 'libri paenitentiales'*, Typologie des Sources du Moyen Âge Occidental 27 (Turnhout, 1978).

Wirbelauer, Eckhard, 'Zum Umgang mit kanonistischer Tradition im frühen Mittelalter: Drei Wirkungen der Symmachianischen Documenta', in: Ursula Schaefer (ed.), *Schriftlichkeit im frühen Mittelalter*, ScriptOralia (Tübingen, 1993), 207–28.

———, *Zwei Päpste in Rom: Der Konflikt zwischen Laurentius und Symmachus (498–514). Studien und Texte*, Quellen Und Forschungen Zur Antiken Welt (Munich, 1993).

Wurm, Hubert, *Studien und Texte zur Decretalensammlung des Dionysius Exiguus* (Rome, 1939).

INDEX FONTIUM

SCRIPTURA

Ex	4.11	8.b
	20.3	18.a
	20.4–5	18.b
	20.7	11.a
	20.12	17.a
	20.13–14	10.a
	21.2–4	26
	21.7–11	27
	21.18–19	31
	21.20–21	30
	21.22–23	32
	21.24	13.a
	21.26–27	29
	21.28–30	34
	21.31–32	35
	21.33–34	38
	21.35	36
	21.36	37
	22.1, 3–4	42
	22.2–3	43
	22.5	49
	22.6	50
	22.7	44
	22.8–9	45
	22.10–11	46
	22.16	28
	22.17	28

	22.25	51.a
	22.26–27	52
	22.29	24
	22.31	21.a
	23.1	9.f
	23.2	54.c
	23.4–5	51.d
	23.6–7	54.a
	23.7	10.c
	23.8	19.a
	23.9	20.a
Lev	2.11	10.b
	7.24	21.c
	18.19	62.a
	18.22	78
	18.23	79.a
	19.11	9.a
	19.14	8.a
	19.15	3.a
	19.16	6.a
	19.17	4.a
	19.18	5.a; 12.a; 14.a
	19.26	22.a
	19.33–34	20.b
	19.35–36	51.d
	20.10	10.d
	20.15	79.a
	20.16	80.e
	20.18	62.a

136 Collectio CCCC capitulorum

	20.27	23	Iob	29.16	54.b	
	24.20	13.a		31.13	404.d	
	24.22	51.d	Ps	14.5	51.d	
	25.37	51.c	Prov	6.19	6.c	
	27.32–33	24		18.21	9.a	
Deut	1.16–17	3.e		19.9	54.c	
	5.17–18	10.a		22.28	404.a	
	5.20–21	2.b	Sap	1.11	9.e	
	6.5	1		13.17	58.b	
	6.6–8	*praefatio*		14.21–24	7.b	
	17.6	53.a	Ecclus	28.15	6.b	
	17.7	53.b	Isa	10.2	86.a	
	18.10	22.b		5.8	404.c	
	18.11	23	Dan	5.17	19.b	
	19.16–19	54.a				
	19.21	13.a	Mt	5.21–24	10.f	
	20.14	82		5.25–26	14.c	
	22.28–29	28		5.27–28	10.e	
	23.10–11	57.a		5.31	15.a	
	23.21–22	58.a		5.33–37	11.b	
	23.24	25.b		5.39–41	13.b	
	23.25	25.a		5.42	51.b	
	24.16	84		5.43	12.a	
	25.1–3	56.a		5.44–48	12.b	
	25.11	33		6.14–15	5.b	
	27.18	8.c		7.1–2	3.b	
Num	27.8–11	73		12.36	6.d	
	30.3	58.a		12.37	9.b; 325.d	
	30.4	58.c		15.20	9.d	
	30.5	58.c		18.15–17	4.b	
	30.10–12	58.c		19.3	15.b	
	30.14	58.c		19.6	15.b	
	35.20	54.a		19.9	15.b	
	35.22–25	55.a		19.18	9.d	
1 Sam	30.24–25	83		19.19	2.a	
2 Reg	14.6	84		19.27	403.a	
Tob.	4.15	7.a		22.37–39	1	

Index fontium 137

	22.39	2.a
	22.40	2.c
Mc	7.10	17.c
	10.19	17.c
	12.40	96.b
Lc	10.37	2.a
	17.3–4	14.b
	18.20	17.c
	20.47	96.c
	21.34	109.b
Act	10.34	3.c
	8.20	19.d
	21.25	21.b
Rom	13.13	109.c
1 Cor	6:10	9.c; 109.d
	7.4	15.c
	7.10–11	15.d
	7.5	15.d
	7.12	16.a
	7.14	16.b
	7.15	16.c
2 Cor	3.6	*praefatio*
Gal	5.14	2.a
Eph	6.1	17.b
Phil.	4.12	99.c
1 Tim	3.6	89.b
	3.15	89.d
Iac	2.8	2.a
	2.9–10	3.d
	2.12–13	55.b
	2.13	56.b
	5.4	7.c
	5.12	11.c
	5.16	347.b
Mal	3.5	86.a

CONCILIA

Agathense, *Agde* (506)
§7   257
§41   109.e
§18   251
§27   252–54

Arausicanum, *Orange* (441)
§9   131
§12 (13)   248
§13, 15 (14, 16)249

Arelatense, *Arles* (314)
§17   93.b
§1   246

Arelatense secundum, *Arles*
(442–506)
§§37 (38)   248
§§39–40
(38–39)   249
§50   250

Ancyrensis, *Ancyra* (314)
§20   161
§21   162
§22   164–65
§24   169.a
§25   176

Antiochense, *Antioch* (341)
§15   210
§22   136

Aurelianensis, *Orléans* (511)
§1   374
§2   380

138

§3 381
§6 132
§19 256
§25 255

Canones in causa Apiarii, recensio A (*ca.* 420)
§16 182
§16 183
§23 184
§33 185

Carthaginense, *Carthage* (390)
§2 181

Chalcedonense, *Chalcedon* (451)
§9 195, 196
§13 197
§18 198
§22 199
§24 200

Constantinopolitanum, *Constantinople* (381)
§3 201–6

Gangrense, *Gangra* (c. 343)
§18 190.a
§19 190.b

Synodum Neocaesariense, *Neocaesarea* (315)
§2 177
§8 178
§9 179

Collectio CCCC capitulorum

Nicaenum I, *Nicaea* (325)
§2 89.b
§3 151
§4 90.b, 103.b
§5 107.b
§8 247
§10 147
§11 148–49
§17 96.d
§20 (Rufin.) 150

Regense, *Riez* (439)
§5–6 130

Sardicense, *Sardica* (342–43)
§4 207
§14 209
§18 208
§23 211

Ualentinum, *Valence* (374)
§4 129

Index fontium 139

PAENITENTIALIA

Columbanus, *Paenitentiale*

§3	80.b

Iudicia Theodori, Canones Basilienses (Ba)

32	71
97	348

Iudicia Theodori, Canones Cottoniani (C)

25–26	347.a
30–31	346
79–80	71
81	69.b
104	168
123	81
133	85
145	169.b
147	163
148	169.c
160	353.a, 353.b
199–200	60.b
201–2	59

Iudicia Theodori, Capitula Dacheriana (D)

29–30	70
54	81
82	173–74
87	296
88	335
110	69.b
167	60.b

Iudicia Theodori, Canones Gregorii (G)

27	400
30	371
38b–39	265
40	351
44	60.b
60	372–73
61	362
71	69.b
76	382
77	383–84
80–81	68
92	80.d
94	329.b
96	289
97	175
99	353.a
100	290
102	166
103	167
104	168
106	168, 284
107	170
111	378
116	391
117	169.c
118	346, 347.a
119	349, 353.a
121	350
134	364
135	365
139	81
154	85
166	368
167	348
180	363

Collectio CCCC capitulorum

Iudicia Theodori, Discipulus Umbrensium (U)

I.1.1	351
I.1.2	350
I.1.3	350
I.1.5	350
I.2.1	173, 174
I.2.2	80.a
I.2.3	80.a, 80.f
I.2.6	80.c
I.2.11	353.a
I.2.12	171
I.2.13	175
I.2.14	279
I.2.15	290
I.2.16	288.b
I.2.17	288.a
I.2.18	80.d, 289
I.3.2	368
I.3.3	329.b
I.4.1	333
I.4.2	332
I.4.4	340
I.4.5	338–39
I.4.6	334
I.4.7	378
I.5.6	400
I.6.1	324
I.6.2	325.a
I.6.3	325.c
I.6.4	325.b
I.7.2	85
I.7.3	80.c
I.7.6	297
I.7.8	394
I.7.11	279
I.8.3–4	347.a

I.8.6	296, 354
I.8.7	349
I.8.9	353.b
I.8.12	266
I.9.1	345
I.9.1b	348
I.9.2	61
I.9.9	309
I.11.1	319
I.11.4	372, 373
I.12.1–2	320
I.12.3	321
I.12.4	278
I.14.2	398
I.14.3	399
I.14.4	169.b, 267
I.14.5	276.a
I.14.7	276.b
I.14.8	285
I.14.15	171, 172
I.14.16	291
I.14.21–22	170, 287
I.14.23	286
I.14.24	163
I.14.25	166, 280
I.14.26	167, 281
I.14.27	284
I.14.29	282
I.14.30	168, 283
I.15.2	169.c
I.15.4	169.a
II.1.1	365
II.1.2	366
II.1.3	364
II.1.5	78, 79.b
II.2.3	386
II.2.9	352

Index fontium

II.3.4	397	II.12.14–15	273
II.3.5	396	II.12.19	275
II.3.6	294	II.12.21	272
II.4.5	395	II.12.24–25	271
II.4.10	363	II.12.26–27	70
II.5.7	370	II.12.29	69.b
II.5.8–9	369	II.12.30	268
II.6.1	387	II.12.31	276.c
II.6.2	388	II.12.33	270
II.6.3–4	389	II.12.34	293
II.6.5	382	II.12.36	307
II.6.6	383–84	II.12.37	308, 310
II.6.7	385	II.13.1	311
II.6.9	60.b	II.13.2	312
II.6.10	390	II.13.3	360
II.6.11	355	II.13.6	314
II.6.15	316	II.13.7	315
II.8.7	299	II.14.1	362
II.9.1	391	II.14.4	317
II.9.2	392	II.14.5–6	356
II.9.3	393	II.14.7	357
II.10.1	322	II.14.9	358
II.10.2	323	II.14.10	359
II.11.1	298	II.14.12	367
II.11.2	302.b, 303	II.14.14	318
II.11.3	302.a	II.14.28	343
II.11.4–5	304	II.14.29	344
II.11.6	306		
II.11.7	300	*Paenitentiale Bobbiense*	
II.11.7–8	301	§§6–7	328
II.11.9	81	§12	295
II.12.2	292		
II.12.3–4	68	*Paenitentiale Burgundense*	
II.12.7–8	71	§1	331
II.12.10	274	§§2–3	330
II.12.11	269	§5–6	328
II.12.12	277	§7	329.a
		§8	341, 342

142 Collectio CCCC capitulorum

Paenitentiale Excarpsus Cummeani

III.19	398
III.20	399
V.10	361
VI.18	336
VII.1	337

Paenitentiale Floriacense

§§2–3	330
§§5–6	328
§7	329.a

Paenitentiale Merseburgense A

§13	295
§1	331

Paenitentiale Sletstatense

§5–6	328
§73	329.a

Synodus II S. Patricii

§1	260.a
§3	261
§4	260.b
§5	262
§10	263
§18	264
§23	326
§23–24	327

CAETERA

Anonymi in Matthaeum

22.21	403.b

Augustinus, *De baptismo*

I.2	401.a
III.16	401.b
IV.2	402.a

Augustinus, *Sermones*

sermo 9	96.e

Beda Uenerabilis, *In Lucae euangelium*

V.20	403.b

Beda Uenerabilis, *In Marci euangelium*

III.12	403.b

Bonifatius, *Epistulae*

ep. 68, *a Zacharias Papa*	245

Breviarium Pauli

IV.10	39

Caelestinus I, *Epistula 4* (J³ 821; JK 369)

§5	125.a, 125.b, 218–19
§2	221

Caelestinus I, *Epistula 5* (J³ 823; JK 371)

§1	128
§3	241

Index fontium

Canones Apostolorum

§1	90.a
§2	91
§7	99.a
§8	92
§9	104
§11	138
§12	139
§13	140–41
§14	93.a
§§15–16	134
§17	89.a
§18	89.c
§21	89.c
§22	89.c, 143
§23	144
§24	145
§§25–26	114
§28	105
§29	106
§30	100
§31	101
§32	137
§33	135
§34	108
§35	103.a
§36	102
§37	133
§38	107.a
§39	97
§40	113, 142
§41	94.a, 95
§§42–43	109.a
§44	96.a
§45	110
§46	111
§47	112
§48	146

Collectio canonum Hibernensis
(Wasserschleben edition in brackets)

17.9 (17.9)	60.a
38.14 (39.14)	242
24.10 (25.10)	403.a
32.11 (33.11)	404.f

Constitutum Sylvestri

ll. 105–11	212
ll. 111–16	213.a
ll. 187–39	213.b
ll. 190–94	214
ll. 195–98	215
ll. 201–4	216
ll. 205–7	217

Epitome Gai

I.4	40

Gregorius I, *Libellus responsionum*

1	94.b
4	48, 69.a
6	41, 88, 90.d
7	93.c
8	62.b, 63–67, 72
9	57.b

Gregorius I, *Regula Pastoralis*

III.27	77

Hermas Pastor

mandatum 4.1	15.d

Hieronymus, *Commentarii in iu epistulas Paulinas: Ad Titum*

II.9–10	47

144   Collectio CCCC capitulorum

Hieronymus, *Epistula 120, ad*
Hebidiam
  § 1   86.b, 87

Hieronymus, *Commentarii in*
euangelius Mattheaei
  1.10   19.c

Innocentius, *Epistula 2, ad*
Victricium (J³ 665; JK 286)
  §2   220
  §6   127

Innocentius, *Epistula 6, ad*
Exsuperium (J³ 675; JK 293)
  §2   229

Leo I, *Epistula 167, ad Rusticum*
(J³ 1098; JK 544)
  §2   152, 222
  §4   74
  §§5–6   76
  §6   75
  §8   158
  §14   153
  §15   154
  §16   155
  §18   156
  §19   157

Leo I, *Epistula 159, ad Nicetam* (J³
1086; JK 536)
  §7   245

Statuta Bonifatii
  §10   126
  §35   71

Statuta Ecclesiae Antiqua
  Prologus   89.a, 89.d
  §1   224
  §2   223
  §3–4   99.b
  §5   225
  §7   98
  §8   226
  §9   227
  §10   115
  §11   116
  §12   117
  §14   118
  §15   119
  §16   120
  §20   228
  §26   231
  §29   232
  §31   230
  §36   238
  §43   239
  §44   240
  §47   121
  §48   122
  §53   124
  §54   123
  §66   236
  §70   237
  §75   235
  §79   233
  §88   234
  §93   188
  §94   189
  §95   190
  §96   191
  §97   192
  §98   193

Index fontium

§99	187
§101	186
§102	194

Symmachus, *Epistula 15, ad Caesarium Arelatensem* (J³ 1460; JK 764)

§5	243–44

Monumenta Iuris Canonici, Series A, Corpus Glossatorum

1. Summa 'Elegantius in iure diuino' seu Coloniensis, tom. I-IV, edd. Gérard Fransen, adlaborante Stephano Kuttner. Città del Vaticano 1969, 1978, 1986, 1990.

2. Constitutiones Concilii quarti Lateranensis una cum Commentariis glossatorum, ed. Antonio García y García. Città del Vaticano1981.

3. Johannis Teutonici Apparatus glossarum in Compilationem tertiam, tom. I, ed. Kenneth Pennington. Città del Vaticano 1981.

4. Distinctiones 'Si mulier eadem hora' seu Monacenses, ed. Rosalba Sorice, Città del Vaticano 2002.

5. Magistri Honorii Summa 'De Iure Canonico Tractaturus', tom. I-III, edd. Rudolf Weigand†, Peter Landau, Waltraud Kozur; adlaborantibus Stephan Haering, Karin Miethaner-Vent, Martin Petzolt. Città del Vaticano 2004, 2010, 2010.

6. Huguccio Pisanus, Summa Decretorum, tom. I, ed. Oldřich Přerovský, adlaborante Istituto Storico della Facultà di Diritto Canonico della Pontificia Università Salesiana. Città del Vaticano 2006.

7. Summa 'Omnis qui iuste iudicat' sive Lipsiensis, tom. I-V, edd. Rudolf Weigand†, Peter Landau, Waltraud Kozur; adlaborantibus Stephan Haering, Karin Miethaner-Vent, Martin Petzolt, Ioannis K. Grossmann. Città del Vaticano 2007, 2012, 2014, 2018, 2018.

8. Summa in Decretum Simonis Bisinianensis, ed. Petrus V. Aimone Braida, Citta del Vaticano 2014.

9. Summa 'Reverentia sacrorum canonum', ed. John C. Wei. Città del Vaticano, 2018.

Monumenta Iuris Canonici, Series B, Corpus Collectionum

1. Diuersorum patrum sententiae siue Collectio in LXXIV titulos digesta, ed. John T. Gilchrist. Città del Vaticano 1973

2. Collectio canonum Remedio Curiensi episcopo perperam ascripta, ed. Herwig John. Città del Vaticano 1976.

3. Studies in the Collections of Twelfth Century Decretals from the Papers of the Late Walther Holzmann, edd. Christopher R. Cheney, Mary G. Cheney. Città del Vaticano 1979.

4. Decretales ineditae saeculi XII from the Papers of the late Walther Holzmann, edd. Stanley Chodorow, Charles Duggan. Città del Vaticano 1982.

5. Collectio canonum Registro Farfensi inserta, ed. Theodor Kölzer. Città del Vaticano 1982.

6. Extrauagantes Iohannis XXII, ed. Jacqueline Tarrant. Città del Vaticano 1983.

7. Liber canonum diuersorum sanctorum patrum siue Collectio in CLXXXIII titulos digesta, ed. Joseph Motta. Città del Vaticano 1988.

8. Collectio trium librorum, tom. I-II, ed. Joseph Motta. Città del Vaticano 2005, 2008.

9. Die Collectio Francofurtana: eine französische Dekretalensammlung; Analyse beruhend auf den Vorarbeiten von Walther Holtzmann(✝), edd. Peter Landau, Gisela Drossbach. Città del Vaticano 2007.

10. Die Collectio Cheltenhamensis: eine englische Dekretalensammlung; Analyse beruhend auf den Vorarbeiten von Walther Holtzmann(✝), ed. Gisela Drossbach. Città del Vaticano 2014.

11. Collectio CCCC capitulorum, ed. Sven Meeder. Washington, D.C., 2024.

Monumenta Iuris Canonici, Series C, Subsidia

1. Proceedings of the Second International Congress of Medieval Canon Law, Boston College, 12–16 August 1963, edd. Stephan Kuttner, J. Joseph Ryan. Città del Vaticano 1965.

2. Bibliographia synodorum particularium, ed. Jakob Sawicki. Città del Vaticano 1967.

3. Codices Pseudo-Isidoriani: A Paleographico-Historical Study, ed. Schafer Williams. Città del Vaticano 1971.

4. Proceedings of the Third International Congress of Medieval Canon Law, Strasbourg, 3–6 September 1968, ed. Stephan Kuttner. Città del Vaticano 1971.

5. Proceedings of the Fourth International Congress of Medieval Canon Law, Toronto, 21–25 August 1972, ed. Stephan Kuttner. Città del Vaticano 1976.

6. Proceedings of the Fifth International Congress of Medieval Canon Law, Salamanca, 21–25 September 1976, edd. Stephan Kuttner, Kenneth Pennington. Città del Vaticano 1980.

7. Proceedings of the Sixth International Congress of Medieval Canon Law, Berkeley, California, 28 July–2 August 1980, edd. Stephan Kuttner, Kenneth Pennington. Città del Vaticano 1985.

8. Proceedings of the Seventh International Congress of Medieval Canon Law, Cambridge, 23–27 July 1984, ed. Peter Linehan. Città del Vaticano 1988.

9. Proceedings of the Eighth International Congress of Medieval Canon Law, San Diego, University of California at La Jolla, 21–27 August 1988, ed. Stanley Chodorow. Città del Vaticano 1992.

10. Proceedings of the Ninth International Congress of Medieval Canon Law, Munich, 13–18 July 1992, edd. Peter Landau, Jörg Müller. Città del Vaticano 1997.

11. Proceedings of the Tenth International Congress of Medieval Canon Law, Syracuse, New York, 13–18 August 1996, edd. Kenneth Pennington, Stanley Chodorow, Keith Kendall. Città del Vaticano 2001.

12. Proceedings of the Eleventh International Congress of Medieval Canon Law, Catania 30 July–6 August 2000, edd. Manlio Bellomo, Orazio Condorelli. Città del Vaticano 2006.

13. Proceedings of the Twelfth International Congress of Medieval Canon Law, Washington D.C. 1–7 August 2004, edd. Uta-Renate Blumenthal, Kenneth Pennington, Atria A. Larson. Città del Vaticano 2008.

14. Proceedings of the Thirteenth International Congress of Medieval Canon Law, Esztergom, 3–8 August 2008, edd. Peter Erdő, Szabolcs Anzelm Szuromi. Città del Vaticano 2010.

15. Proceedings of the Fourteenth International Congress of Medieval Canon Law, Toronto, 5–11 August 2012, edd. Joseph Goering, Stephan Dusil, Andreas Thier. Città del Vaticano 2016.

16. Proceedings of the Fifteenth International Congress of Medieval Canon Law, Paris, 17–23 July 2016, edd. Florence Demoulin-Auzary, Nicolas Laurent-Bonne, Franck Roumy, adlaborante Anna Claire Montealegre. Città del Vaticano, 2022.